D1176434

travels
with
my
trombone

travels with my trombone

a caribbean journey

henry shukman

Crown Publishers, Inc.
New York

This Book Is Dedicated to All Calypsonians

Published by Crown Publishers, Inc., 201 East 50th Street, New York, New York 10022. Member of the Crown Publishing Group.

Random House, Inc. New York, Toronto, London, Sydney, Auckland

Originally published in Great Britain by HarperCollins Publishers in 1992.

CROWN is a trademark of Crown Publishers, Inc.

Manufactured in the United States of America

LIBRARY OF CONGRESS CATALOGING-IN-PUBLICATION DATA

Shukman, Henry.
    Travels with my trombone : a Caribbean journey / Henry Shukman.—1st ed.
        p.   cm.
    Originally published: Hammersmith, London : HarperCollins Publishers, 1992.
    Includes index.
    1. Shukman, Henry—Journeys—Caribbean Area   2. Trombonists—Biography.   3. Caribbean Area—Description and travel—1981–4. Popular music—Caribbean Area—History and criticism.   I. Title. ML419.S56A3   1993
788.9'3'09729—dc20   92-40765
                                                             CIP
                                                             MN

ISBN 0-517-59360-2

10 9 8 7 6 5 4 3 2 1

FIRST AMERICAN EDITION

CONTENTS

ACKNOWLEDGEMENTS

The list of people who have helped bring this book into being is long, and a long list hardly makes a good start to a book. But I am so deeply indebted to them that I cannot forgo this opportunity to record my gratitude.

All the musicians I played with in the Caribbean helped open my eyes to the wealth of the area's culture and history. In particular I would like to thank the following: Bobby Quan and Bunny Raymond of the Blue Ventures, who put aside their time to teach me brass lines at short notice and imparted much of their feel for Trinidad music; David Rudder, whose passion for, faith in, and knowledge of calypso were deeply inspiring; Tony Wyke of Roots, Stems and Branches, who coached me through my first bars of zouk; the members of the Police Band of Grenada, who generously shared their rehearsal time and wonderful old instruments with me; Carlos Rodriguez of Bemtu, who showed me the many faces of Colombian music; and Viviano Torres of Anne Zwing, who introduced me to the world of West African Bantu music in South America.

Closer to home, I would like to thank above all Richard Wheaton of HarperCollins, whose reading and editing were both painstaking and inspired and have done more than anything else to help solidify and clarify my vague meanderings, and Michael Fishwick for his faithful and indispensable support from the beginning; Malcolm Deas, director of the Latin American Centre at Oxford University, for his expert advice, and for giving generously of his time to make corrections and suggestions; also Lucy Duran of the National Sound Archive, for her invaluable guidance; and Len Homer of the London-based steel band Homer's Odyssey, who put the idea into my head in the first place.

PART I

Carnival

ONE

It was midnight when I made it through the crush at the door, where my name was down under 'entertainers'. I didn't dare go near the band. They were flanked by two fat columns of speakers twenty feet high and my chest began to shake to each beat while I was still fifty yards away from the stage. Every thump of the bass drum knocked a little breath out of me.

The crowd was dancing two ways, jumping and wining. Whenever the singer screamed out 'Everybody jump, jump, jump', they would start leaping into the air without thought for what or whom they landed on. It was a real Trinidad jump-up. I made for the safety of the sound desk, the only solid immobile thing in sight. But most of the time the crowd was wining, and it sent my innocent eyes leaping out on stalks.

Wining, the basic soca or calypso move, happens below the belt. The hips of the crowd had taken on a life of their own, swinging, rolling, jerking, pumping, grinding at one another, going through an encyclopaedia of lovemaking motions. Hands meanwhile were playing the part of roamers, finding out everything they could about each partner without actually undressing them.

The concert was a big fete, or party, and it was being thrown for the workers of the Metal Box factory inside the 'compound', the factory car park, at Tunapuna out east from Port of Spain. The street outside was as crowded as the venue, lined with vendors of drinks and 'boil corn' (corn on the cob). Two high stages had been set up inside, topped with yellow marquees, one for each of the two bands that took turns playing the event. At one end were Shandileer, whose energetic vocalist, Ronnie MacIntosh, always wore a raincoat and trilby on stage. At the opposite end were the Blue Ventures, the band that particularly interested me.

Their leader, Bobby Quan, had heard that I could play the trombone. He was toying with the idea of having me join and had given me a tape of their songs, the year's soca hits, to practise to. I had spent an afternoon playing through the parts with the leader of the horn section, and the final step in Bobby's formula for preparing me was to have me watch his band perform.

Blue Ventures, amid flashing blue and orange lights, the three vocalists leaping about with unflagging energy, were now going through the numbers I had been practising, but at double speed. The six percussionists were putting out an irresistible rhythm which didn't stop between numbers – in fact in every break they cranked it up another notch. The songs were already fast dance music. The audience, well into the thousands, rocked in time. Now and then a singer called on them to raise a hand; a forest of hands appeared. Then to wave a hand, and the whole mass of arms swayed. Sometimes they said wave something, anything, in the air. White rags appeared, not here and there but densely.

There was no encore. After the last song the roar for more was swiftly silenced by the DJ. The record he immediately put on sounded insipid after the live band, but the crowd got moving to it. Meanwhile I still clung to the sound desk, my islet of terra firma. Soon the tide turned and began a brisk flow up to the other end of the compound, for Shandileer's next set. It would ebb back and forth like a swimming pool on a cruise ship, from band to band, till dawn.

When the crowd looked thin enough to press through I made my way to the stage. Bunny, the leader of the horn section, had his sax on its stand. His feet were at my eye level. He was wearing white trousers and a short-sleeved shirt with blue splashes – everyone was, except the girl singer who was in a black mini-dress. He squatted down, one knee dropped, and shook my hand. 'How do you like it?' he yelled into my ear over the din of Shandileer's music.

Bunny had a long, friendly face and a small moustache. He had his eyebrows raised at me now, and was smiling.

'Brilliant,' I shouted back.

'Eh, Michael,' he called up to the other trombonist, who was very tall. Michael pulled an earplug from his ear and stooped down to shake my hand.

'He say it was brilliant,' Bunny screamed at him.

Michael's face broke into an oversized smile. 'So when are you going to play with us? Bunny says you're all set.'

'It's up to Bobby Quan,' I shouted.

Bunny invited me up onto the stage. On his mike stand hung a pair of airport ground-staff headphones. Just then Bobby Quan came over. He was a small Chinese man with a long, thin moustache and an eye that wouldn't stop blinking. He leaned his face close to mine so I could hear, blinked at me, and hollered into my ear, 'Hilton poolside six o'clock.'

'OK,' I shouted back, a few inches from his face. It was the location and time of the next show he wanted me to watch.

The Hilton occupies one corner of the Savannah, the park in the centre of Port of Spain, and is backed against a hill. You drive up behind it to reach the reception on the top floor. The pool has a view over the city and the Savannah.

It was warm dusk when I arrived. Nigel, one of the singers, was sitting on a low wall in the car park explaining something emphatically to his girlfriend. He was a young man with strings of long black braids in his hair and a fine chiselled face. He beckoned me over, asked my name, shook my hand.

'This my first carnival with Blue Ventures,' he told me. 'I play carnival before but not with these guys.' He glanced up at me. 'You gonna have some good time.'

'If Bobby wants me,' I said.

'Bobby want you. Otherwise why would Bobby tell you come here?'

But I wasn't convinced: Bobby was still checking me out. Nigel asked me where I was staying, how I liked Trinidad.

'I not from Port of Spain, man,' he told me. 'I from Toco.' Toco was up beyond the Northern Range, the big heap of jungle-covered volcanoes behind Port of Spain, on the north-east corner of Trinidad. I had read that it was still a remote unspoilt place.

'You have to check out Toco,' he said. 'I did sing with a band up there. Toco is the best place it have on the island. Toco is relax.'

The crowd at the Hilton was smart. The women wore elaborate wraps and the men tropical shirts. Ranked fountains of water catching submerged blue lights fell into the swimming pool. The sky over the Savannah was a dusty orange, while the park itself smoked.

Again there were two bands. The second was Atlantik, another big soca band formed a year ago from disaffected members of other bands. They had stages next to each other, facing a large food stall serving pelau and rotis (a mix of rice and lentils, and stuffed Indian pancakes). Blue Ventures' stage was beside an alcove into which Bunny invited me. I stood there partially hidden from the audience, just behind the brass, while they played.

The sound system at the Hilton was as loud as it had been the night before. Everybody was wining. One slim Chinese girl stood on a low wall in white tights and singlet dancing with herself intently and erotically. Grey-haired and bald men were demonstrating their intimate loin skills with abandon. I saw a tall man in Hawaiian shirt, grey beard and steel-rim glasses laugh heartily and inaudibly. A younger woman was pressing against him, backwards. He had his arms raised high, as if to feel her better. There was a hint of wonder in his face. He shouted along to the music. A breath of the Saturnalia blew through the crowd, but without menace of later regret. There was nothing to regret. Everyone would be doing it tomorrow too.

A scuffle broke out at the front. A woman clambered up onto the stage losing her balance and falling against Nigel. The band stopped. One of the ironmen ran out from behind the guitars to the front and took her by the arm.

'I don't care who wife and who husband,' Nigel shouted into his mike. 'Please no fights here.'

The ironman led her off the stage. She was crying. Bunny told me later that it was a foreign woman not used to Trinidad ways. Some guy coming on hot.

The last Blue Ventures show that I was planning to watch from the audience was at Soca Village, an area of tarmac the size of a football field enclosed by a tall, iron fence. It has four stages, two at either end, and a long bar down either side. For the two months before carnival it fills with teenagers every night from eleven till dawn.

The first problem was how to get a drink. By the time the bottle was in my hand, after a battle that required a saint's patience and an all-in wrestler's power, Blue Ventures were into their third number.

I wanted to get behind the speaker stack, where my ears would be safer. This was a dangerous plan because there was no way to get there other than by passing directly in front of them. I would have to get to within a few feet of the source of the seismic explosions that tore through the flesh twice a breath.

I did it anyway. Right in front of the lethal cavern mouths there was a gathering of people who didn't dance consistently and energetically, people who stood about gently shaking their hips and drinking and tapping their feet. They might have been chatting with one another and the atmosphere was that of a party late at night when most people have left. The scene had a dreamlike quality. It was the calm at the eye of the storm. These people had made it to the centre and survived. Two men in sullen mood stood with their backs up against the gaping mouths and actually shelved their drinks within the speakers' jaws.

Something enticed me to stay. My ears no longer felt the onslaught so harshly. The music even seemed quiet. This was a sirenland that bewitched the ears. But I stood firm by what I knew to be the reality of the situation, that every minute here cost a day of intracranial singing, and made for the haven behind the stack.

Here too there was an odd air of suspension. For example, of the ten or twelve people hanging around, looking up at the band or sitting on old boards at the foot of the fence, none were wining. They looked at one another guiltily, silently. Just a few feet away thousands of people were grinding one another into a collective frenzy. Here one man leant against the back of the speakers tapping a foot, hands in pockets, hips gently, just perceptibly, pulsing back and forth. Two others made private jokes to each other in signs, and laughed. It was like a silent movie. Three girls came in in a chain wining more with drunken heartiness than sensuality. They broke up and gradually wound down, one by one, to a standstill. There was a thin, tall young man in a blue cap resting against the stage whom the girls seemed to know. He smiled at one of them, the slimmest, in loose blue trousers and top, pretty, her hair on her shoulders. Suddenly she was leaning back arms in the air, loins thrust forwards grinding at him. He was up at once, almost touching her, one leg between hers. They interlocked comfortably. They moved as one. She turned round, stepped her feet further apart, pressed back against him, reached out and down with her long arms until her hands touched the ground. Then she rested her hands on her knees. Her movements were beautiful, elegant, masterfully erotic. She had grace and vitality. The dance was her medium. The music seemed to grant her motion. She smiled calmly.

At the end of the set Bunny called me up onto the stage. Beside him hands were plunging into the icy water of the band's cool-box, groping among the cans of Sprite for bottles of Carib beer. The lights of a stage at the opposite end of the football field were already flashing and the crowd was thinning at this end.

Bobby wanted to talk to me. He was sitting on a ledge in front of the drum kit. 'I call you tomorrow.' That was all he said.

Dread suddenly overcame me. Here I was all alone in Trinidad chasing a dream. Would he or would he not have me? I imagined the worst. Bobby Quan was going to call and say, I'm sorry, I'd like to help out, but you're really not up to it. I would have to pick up the phone and call around the other contacts I had, trying to convince them at least to meet me. There were scarcely two weeks left till carnival and Blue Ventures hadn't even tried me yet. I had been playing along to their tape every day on my own and I was sure that I knew all the songs by heart. After the session I had had with Bunny in his sitting room he had pronounced me ready. Watching these concerts was supposed to be the next step, the last step. Would Bobby string me along like this only to ditch me once I had fulfilled his requirements?

He didn't call the next day, which was ominous.

TWO

My obsession with being elsewhere began in childhood. My father used to say, 'You always think the grass is greener, Boychick.' He told me about the Indian brave who did everything backwards. He washed his hands in the sand and dried them in the water and rode his horse back to front. I was like him. While I did one thing I would be thinking about doing another. There was always something better. My father was right. But I was right too. There was greener grass.

I first heard about it when I was seven. It was on a summer day on the lawn outside my mother's house, where my brother and I spent the whole afternoon listening to a man who had come for lunch. He was a priest, but he was unlike any other priest I had ever seen. He had long hair and a long, black beard. He wore jeans and a loose shirt. He was from Colombia.

He talked for hours about his country. Colombia had everything. It had glaciers, high mountains, volcanoes that erupted, miles and miles of hot, steaming jungle, huge rivers, deserts, farms and forests and snow-white beaches and mangrove swamps. There were Indians in the jungle who wore feathers and went hunting with bows and arrows. There were cowboys. There were divers who went diving for giant shells and sponges who could hold their breath for five minutes and swim down two hundred feet.

He asked me if I knew those medieval paintings that were crammed full of details – a man feeding his horse, women milking the cows, a market-place, oxen crossing a bridge. I didn't, but

I could picture vividly what he was describing and said I did. Colombia was like that, he said.

In Colombia children were little adults. They could do what adults did, if they were strong enough. There were children who drove taxis in Colombia. There were even offices and radio stations and telephone services run by children. And if children were doing what adults did, adults were doing amazing things. There were Indian men in Colombia who could make themselves die. They could die and then come back to life again. The priest told us that when he had lived enough he would lie down and make himself die, starting in his feet. He could already make his body go without air for a long time. He showed us. He took some deep breaths and then rested his chin on his chest, sitting cross-legged, and stayed like that for five minutes. We used my brother's watch to time him. We looked closely to check he wasn't breathing.

In Colombia you could live in whatever climate you liked. There was the seaside, the jungle, and everything all the way up the mountains to the cold, dry climate of the highest plains. You could take your pick. Colombia was obviously a better place to live than England. That afternoon I realized not only that home was not the best place on earth, but that I actually knew where a better place was.

I finally stepped over onto the greener side of the hill when I was eighteen. I went to the Andes for six months. I travelled and wrote a book and thought that I had finally satisfied my yearning to see that land.

But when I came home to go to university I found that I wanted to be in South America more than ever. As soon as I left it I missed it. I missed the simplicity of my life there – sleeping in my tent, in cheap, run-down hotels, building camp fires, living off rice and eggs and learning to find a whole spectrum of flavours in the occasional treat like an *empanada*, a meat-filled pastry, or a Chinese meal in a big city. I missed the overwhelming natural beauty of the mountains and coastlines and deserts, and the exceptional freedom I had enjoyed as a young traveller to explore them, and above all I missed being in a place that perfectly matched, because it was so foreign, my growing curiosity about the world and its peoples.

To leave there for home, and for an academic institution where I would have to go back to studying, which was all I had been doing for as long as I could remember, seemed as bad a move as I could make. But I did return, and as soon as I reached England again and saw my parents and old friends I realized that I was re-entering a life I had outgrown. It could offer me little of the fulfilment and pleasure I had discovered in the Andes. I either had to stay and accept it, or else find a way of leaving again.

I did stay, though without ever coming to terms with it. In the back of my mind I was always preparing to get away again. I became incurably restless. I could settle down to nothing for very long. But eight long years were to go by before I finally took off again.

THREE

I had played trombone since my early teens and although I had always had a love–hate relationship with the instrument, music was to become my way of continuing my journey up the Andes. My first South American journey had taken me as far north as Ecuador, which is the southern edge of salsa country. Salsa came blaring out of every bar and shop and bus and I found that I loved it. My heart sank when barmen turned off the radio, and jumped when a builder turned up his cassette deck on the street. The rhythms fascinated me. I tried to untangle the strands of the various percussion instruments. My ear homed in on the brass lines, my fingers twitched involuntarily to imagined trombone slide positions. I decided I wanted to play in a salsa band.

When I got back to England there were no salsa bands, but my love of Latin music endured. I bought records and went to any salsa concerts I could find. Eventually, three years after my return, I heard of a Latin band that needed a trombonist. They were called El Tropical and rehearsed every Sunday night in a garage in Bromley and had a show two times a month in a wine bar. They had a trumpet and saxophone but no trombone. I quickly brushed up my playing, learned my parts and they took me on.

Through their conga-player, who was also a DJ and had a large collection of records, I got to know the classics of Latin music and other Caribbean styles. 'Man centipede bad bad,' sang the calypsonian on a scratchy old recording, 'but woman centipede more than bad.' He played me many old calypsos and I fell in love with them too.

A year later I began performing weekly in London's first calypso tent, which was doomed also to be its last. I played in the brass section of the band and was allowed a stint as a calypsonian. The calypsonians each sang a song with the band, their entry for the year's Notting Hill Carnival contest, having been introduced, with a crescendo of praise that was utterly unintelligible over the PA, by the MC, a bald man with four buck teeth whose job it was to fill the gaps between singers with booming bravado talk. He dubbed me the Mighty English. He had granted me this honour ever since one night when I had chatted to him after the show. I told him I knew a few calypsos myself and strummed through one on a guitar. A man got up from the one table of guests who hadn't yet left and came over to listen.

'Uh-huh, uh-huh,' he said at the end of each verse, nodding vigorously, and as soon as I finished he declared, 'You sing good. That good. But you ain't got the rhythm.'

He introduced himself as Len Homer, leader of the steel band Homer's Odyssey. He took the guitar off me and showed me the right rhythm to strum and then tapped along with me until I had the feel of it. 'Now sing again,' he told me.

At the end of every line he stopped me and sang it himself with a different emphasis and pronunciation. Finally, an hour later, I put it all together and the MC declared, 'We got to get you a name, boy, so you can sing here. You're on that stage next week.'

'Good,' Len Homer affirmed. 'I believe he could go far. They'll like that over in Trini. A white boy playing calypso.' He chuckled.

All week his words went round my head: 'They'll like that in Trini.' What a thing to do: to go and play calypso *in situ*. And why not salsa too? I could not imagine a more fulfilling and exciting way to travel.

But next week when I appeared on stage with a guitar round my neck as Mighty English things didn't go so well. The crowd certainly numbered more than twenty that night, which made it a good night, but I had had no chance to rehearse with the band. They were convinced they knew my song, a Trinidad classic called 'The Big Bamboo', about what a woman really wants from her man. As I walked on in my Hawaiian shirt, whose scarlet and yellow swirls suddenly appeared bland after the Golden Cockerel's golden suit and Mighty Tiger's skin-tight black satin cat suit that had preceded me, the keyboard player asked me, 'What key?'

'E minor.' But the key wasn't the problem. The problem was firstly that they knew a different version of the song to mine, and secondly that they themselves were not unanimous over which version to play. But I was up at the front with an audience to address so all I could do was plough through it my way and hope they followed, which they didn't. The mixer turned the mike up high so that at least the words of the song would rise clear of the cacophony, until they got tangled up in screeches and whines of feedback. At the end the crowd looked and sounded happy, but I couldn't tell whether the laughter was inspired by comedy or relief.

The tent closed after carnival and was never to reopen. But I kept thinking about Trinidad and going there to join in the music scene. Meanwhile the salsa band, which I had continued to play with, lost their spot in the pub. They played less and less. There were personality clashes. The bassist wanted to play funk. The lead singer wanted to croon romantic Latin melodies.

Suddenly I found myself caught high and dry, with no Caribbean music to play in at all. I would have given up the trombone then and there, with few regrets, had I not suddenly been turned into a full-time professional by a friend who persuaded me to join London's first world music orchestra, which he had recently founded. I would have to play not only trombone, but also mandolin and Macedonian shepherd's pipes, he told me.

I had been playing with them for a year when we went on tour to Barcelona. One afternoon I was sitting alone in a bar, a small place lost among the alleyways down by the port. It was tiled all over like a lavatory, as if prepared for unimaginably savage night-time debauches. A middle-aged hooker was sitting three stools along from me. She kept looking at me. She might have taken me for a sailor on shore leave. I was resolutely avoiding her eye, and drinking a San Miguel, enjoying a rare day off. I had been playing hard for the last few months, performing most nights. Now I wanted a change. I was thinking about what to do with my life. It seemed mad when everything was going so well, but I still thought about Trinidad and I still longed to go back to South America. I had never reached Colombia or the Caribbean on my first trip, and they lay there glittering in the sunshine just a few thousand miles away.

The hooker sidled over to the jukebox. She smiled at me and punched the numbers. The speakers were turned up loud. A guitar came in, and beneath it a mellow acoustic bass. A drum skipped in, and after it a pair of congas. I felt my stomach rise in anticipation. It was salsa. The trumpets came in: unmistakably Matancera. And then there it was, Celia Cruz's voice of honey and steel singing, 'Caramelo, caramelo, caramelo.' The whole room rang with her voice. A smile rose uncontrollably to my face.

FOUR

Finally I am flying away from England again, looking down on rocky mountains that glide by below with their blue shadows flung across the Arctic wastes. The wind has strewn the snow with fine hieroglyphics. I wonder why it has taken me so long to make this simple step.

'Greenland?' a German woman says in my ear. She goes to ask the steward and comes back to tell me, with a nervous fastidiousness, 'He says he doesn't know. He only works the aisle.'

Greenland, Labrador, the Arctic Ocean, I'm flying over them all, down away from the upper reaches of the globe to its belt, its middle, where the shadows are short. With me I bring a bag of books that I will probably never read, a change of clothes, a spirit somewhat corroded by years of London rain, a trombone and a few vague doubts attached to the contents of the trombone case.

I did love the music, but here I was launching myself back into the continent that had done so much for me, returning to end years of yearning, and I wondered if it wouldn't be better to come free and empty-handed. I wanted to be the wanderer at large again, fired by a quest or a mission, not burdened with a trombone. It wasn't just the bathos of it, but the instrument itself. Even now I still suffered the same mix of love and hate for it.

The trombone is the oldest instrument in the orchestra, with a noble history going back five centuries. It is also the simplest and the hardest to master: it offers no mechanical assistance to the player at all. The violin at least has four strings and a bow, the oboe holes and keys, the horn valves. The trombone is simply a tube whose length you can adjust. Everything is down to your arms and lips. As you play you feel you are harnessing the physics of sound with your bare hands. When you hit a note right in the middle the tiny vibrations of your lips set up a deep, rich resonance the same way a tiny aircraft high in the sky can set the whole blue vault droning.

Yet it is the most neglected instrument in the orchestra, after the timpani. A good trombonist is above all a good counter, able to sit for five hundred bars' rest and drop a note here and there.

And it is a difficult instrument to look after. A trombone slide is highly delicate. Merely holding it at the wrong angle can be enough to tweak it out of true. The righting of trombone slides is so fine an art that a few years ago all the professionals of London took their horns over to the Hague to have them done: no one in the British Isles was reliable enough.

Quite apart from the instrument itself and my feelings towards it there was the whole question of what I was setting out to do. Would bands have me? Would I be good enough? Would they like me? Would I get lonely?

I had spoken to Len Homer at his home in Willesden before leaving and he had given me various names of musicians in Port of Spain, but I had no idea if his name would carry any weight. I didn't know whether carnival, which was starting soon, would be strictly and professionally run, or whether it would be a relaxed free-for-all.

I sat mulling these things over to myself for the next six hours of my flight. We left the Arctic behind and made a stop in New York. Then as we climbed southwards above the Jersey shore I found myself thinking about John, the first brass player I got to know well. It was because of him that I had taken the trombone seriously.

John was a trumpeter and he rode a motorbike. He had all the gear – leathers, boots, silk underhelmet, panniers – and serviced his V-twin Honda himself twice as often as necessary. He obeyed traffic regulations scrupulously. I knew because I rode pillion often, between him and his trumpets. But off the bike he hid his law-abiding self behind a fiendish grin. 'It's a corker at the top end,' he used to boast. 'If you really give it some welly you can't half shift . . . '

This was how he talked about his trumpets too. He came out of the Midlands brass-band tradition where stamina and agility were prized. He could play very high and fast, as he would demonstrate after each rehearsal with the youth orchestra in which I met him. But the playing was always the property of the instrument: 'Look what it can do,' he'd say. 'If you slam it at the top end it doesn't half sizzle . . .'

John would enthusiastically suggest trips to the pub. I was only a young-looking fourteen-year-old at the time, so when I couldn't get in to the local pub we went to the off-licence. I was already used to slugging neat spirits but John would buy us small cans of beer and make his last half an hour. He puffed uncomfortably at cigarettes, often throwing them away half smoked.

Conductors and music teachers liked John. He was polite and he could play whatever they wanted. When he left school he could have gone to any music college in the country. But he sang in his school choir and the choirmaster suggested that he try for a choral scholarship to Cambridge, which he won. He felt some doubt over not going to music college, but pride at having gained a place at the famous university won through.

It was the turning-point in his precocious career. At eighteen he was the best young trumpeter in Britain; at twenty-two he was mediocre, barely up to professional standard. I heard him years later at a party. He was drunk and blasting out Baroque concerti. He had a nerves problem, he told me. Give him a drink and he could play fine. But he only did it now and then. He had been working in a computer company for six years.

But had it not been for John I would never have kept playing the trombone. Trombonists were fat men who wore corks in their ears to protect themselves from their own raspberries and glissandos. It was a circus instrument, an embodiment of the Victorian grotesque.

My teacher, Mr Pokes, was a short, fat Yorkshireman with huge red cheeks. His father had been a coalminer who had decided that his son would not follow him down the pit. From the age of six he locked the boy in a room all day with a trombone. By the age of thirteen my teacher was principal of the Black Dyke Mills

Colliery Band. Thomas Beecham heard him playing a solo with
the band on the radio and was astounded to hear the virtuoso's
age at the end of the performance. He at once invited him to join
the BBC Symphony Orchestra.

He played in the old lyrical style, with a reedy legato. His
trombones were of gleaming salmon-pink brass. He used to
take me through his own hand-written scrapbook of orchestral
passages, and tell me about the different conductors he had played
them under. I practised daily because it hurt him when I didn't.
But it was only when I met John that I could see a future for
brass and me.

John's life was exciting. He rode his motorbike all over the
country, he was friends with famous brass men, he never went
more than a night or two between girlfriends. He was my only
independent access to a world where people did real things like
earn money and drive cars. So I took my diploma from the Royal
College of Music, bought a dinner jacket from a thrift store, and
even ended up riding a scooter. I never thought about actually
becoming a trombonist, I just wanted to be the kind of person
who aspired to it.

But now here I was flying across the Atlantic ocean some ten
years later with a trombone in the baggage locker above me. It
looked like I had become a pro after all.

A few hours later, at midnight local time, I found myself
standing in the queue at Trinidad Immigration. It was a long
queue of Venezuelan families and Brooklyn West Indians which
moved one pace forward per hour. My clothes were wet – the
exertion of walking down the plane steps, into the Turkish bath
of a Trinidad night, had been enough to drench them. The strap
of my travelling trombone case felt hot on my shoulder. The air
smelt like a greenhouse. It was late, I was exhausted, but my heart
rose. I was in the Caribbean.

FIVE

Trinidad has two long arms that reach towards Venezuela and almost touch the continent. They embrace the Gulf of Paria, a hot murky stretch of sea beside the delta of the Orinoco river. From Point Cumana and Icacos Point, on the end of each arm, you can look out over the graphite water and see a thin green line along the horizon.

It is a low-lying island. Wide plains of sugar cane thicken its air with their malty scent. After the sugar harvest the air is dusty like England in late August, and heavy and fragrant above the swamps where scarlet ibises live. Out of the low mote-thick atmosphere rises the Northern Range, a wild forested range along the north coast inhabited by bandits and boars. These mountains were what Columbus first saw when he called at Trinidad on his third voyage. He sailed down from the north. When he first sighted land he could see three of the Range's peaks resting on the horizon. He called them the Trinity.

Port of Spain, hemmed in by the Northern Range, spreads all around the pit of Trinidad's northern arm. Residential developments, shopping malls and plazas, factories, grids of luxury bungalows sprouting enormous satellite dishes, all strung along the main highway which runs east–west, link the capital and Arima, the next big town. Half of Trinidad's one million people live in Port of Spain's relay of developments.

There are shanty towns up on the hills behind the city, and rows of uniform shacks along the highway, new welfare housing to ease the overcrowding in the shanties. Old Port of Spain, the original port city down by the sea known as downtown, is a strict grid of streets. The houses are a mix of rusting, crumbling turn-of-the-century British and Creole, and bland modern concrete.

Downtown is the heart of Trinidad, and throbs with noise and music. Every other shop and bar has a sound system stacked in the door blaring calypso. Pick-up trucks piled high with coconuts, okra, yams, green oranges and lemons line the streets on either pavement, while their owners cry out their prices over the sound systems.

Independence Square, the main square of Port of Spain, is a short boulevard of modern office buildings, their ground-floor windows covered with cascades of tee-shirts hung there by clothes vendors. In the road maxi taxis, white and yellow minibuses, try to attract passengers with displays of the wattage of their inboard hi-fis.

A few blocks up lies the Queen's Park Savannah, a wide field of dry grass, a great park in the heart of Port of Spain. It stretches from downtown across to the suburbs in the foothills of the Northern Range. For two centuries it has been the centre of Trinidad social life: a race track and a grandstand where today all the contests of carnival take place.

On one side of the Savannah stands the Port of Spain museum, and on the lawn in front lies an old iron anchor with a placard claiming, 'Columbus's anchor'. In the middle of the nineteenth century a Corsican farmer who had emigrated to Trinidad, François Agostini, was digging a new drainage ditch on his farm at Icacos Point when he found an old anchor. He knew at once that it was very old because it was buried several feet deep and because it had a wooden shank. For at least a century anchors had been made entirely of iron. He cleaned it and propped it on his porch.

It was his son who read Columbus's diaries and found that on his third voyage Columbus had moored in the Serpent's Mouth, the southerly entrance into the Gulf of Paria, by Icacos Point. There Columbus first deduced from the force of water flowing out of the Orinoco river that he had discovered a large continent. A storm hit and the ships had had to weigh anchor fast. Columbus's anchor had been snared, and not liking the look of the seas he gave the order to cut it free.

As soon as the second Agostini realized whose anchor he had on his porch he carted it up to Port of Spain, at the other end of the island, and loaned it to the museum. For a hundred years the museum had it displayed on the lawn, until 1956 when they sent it up to Montreal for an exhibition. When it came back it had become the iron anchor which still sits on the lawn today with the same old placard, while the planter's great-grandson still maintains a one-way correspondence with the Montreal museum.

SIX

I arrived in Trinidad three weeks before carnival. It was by far the busiest time of year in the music scene, and my chances of playing were at their highest. The prospect of actually being part of carnival, seeing it from the inside, was now tantalizingly close.

Len Homer had given me the phone number of Ellis Chow Linon, the manager of Charlies Roots, a big calypso band. He had many friends in the calypso scene and might know of a band that needed a trombonist. I also hoped to meet David Rudder, who sang with Charlies Roots.

I called him on my first morning when I was still feeling dazed by jetlag and hardly knew where I was. He told me to come right over.

I found the right yard, after some searching, a dusty space off a road through one of Port of Spain's many suburbs. There were seven modern houses built around it, homes and offices – a Peugeot parts dealership, a paint store – and one of them was the band room. A man in shades sitting against a wall under the eaves and listening to a Walkman nodded me to the door.

Inside there was no furniture apart from an enormous desk, at which sat a large, middle-aged Chinese man. He was on the telephone. He waved me in.

'You came late,' he told me, putting down the phone. 'Ellis Chow.' He reached out his hand without a smile. His cheeks sagged a little and his eyes were dull. When he left later on I noticed that he unplugged the telephone and took it with him. He was a serious businessman, which was why Charlies Roots had become the most successful Trinidad band.

I got lost on the way, I explained.

'No, no,' he said. 'I mean you come Trinidad late. Only three weeks to carnival.' He leaned back in his chair, revealing the big belly of a successful manager. 'So you a friend of old Len Homer. He still in London? I don't reckon Len's coming back to T and T now after all these years.'

He said he would call around for me and stretched back to knock on a door behind him.

The door opened and a tall thin man walked in. He had an attractive face fringed with short dreadlocks. I warmed to him at once. I felt myself finally waking up.

'This is the man you wanted to meet,' said Ellis Chow. 'David Rudder.'

David Rudder is the only young calypsonian to have found an international audience. He used to work as an accountant in Customs and Excise and sang on the side. But in 1986, his *annus mirabilis*, he was winner of all the carnival contests, the Young Kings, the Calypso King contest, and the Road March prize. He has a keen knowledge of Caribbean history and politics and many of his songs are topical, such as 'I Got to Go to Panama', a song about a group of government ministers and their recent escape to Panama with profits from illicit dealings on behalf of BWIA, the national airline. According to the song, they used to live in Trinidad like lords, but moved to Panama to live like kings.

Rudder's widest-known song, used by radio stations all around the islands as the signature tune for their cricket commentary, is 'Rally Round the West Indies'. It begins as a call for greater support of the cricket team, and becomes a plea for Caribbean unity. The islands were once so influential, in the days of slavery and King Sugar, the seventeenth and eighteenth centuries, and they can be again, declares the song.

He is now one of the very few calypsonians who live entirely by their singing. 'Calypso helps keep our society on an even keel,' he says. 'The songs become our violent acts.

We kill each other with songs. And we heal ourselves through our music.'

David Rudder smiled, shook my hand, invited me to hang out in the studio next door while they jammed. The studio was a small room stacked full of speakers. There were two other musicians, and together the three of them were the core of Charlies Roots, and three of Trinidad's best musicians. Pelham Goddard, a small man with a long face at the keyboards and drum machine – he had arranged thousands of calypsos and soca hits and steel band numbers – Julian, the Charlies Roots lead guitarist, and Rudder himself, who sat on the floor with his long legs stretched out in front of him, singing into a mike. On top of a speaker beside him he had a stack of loose papers scribbled all over with new song lyrics. They were working out songs for an album and show about South Africa.

Goddard pulled a rainbow of expressions over his face as he played. Eyebrows soared to his hairline, then plummeted like hawks to his lashes. Julian sat with legs crossed, hunched over his guitar rocking and smiling to himself. Everything about Rudder was magnetic: voice, physique, looks. He was wearing a new white tee-shirt and blue trousers. Between numbers he offered me a beer from an ice box and said, 'You can just chill out and enjoy the music.'

I listened for a while, enjoying the rare insight into the birth of song, and then went outside. My wakefulness was already waning and my ears were beginning to ache mildly from the high volume. My head was reeling gently from the beer and jetlag. Immediately, right in front of me, I saw the Northern Range. I let my eyes stroll along its ragged silhouette, and feel the swelling contours of the nearer ridges that rose bearded with foliage. They were smoky blue, and big.

Ellis Chow Linon had no luck with bands for me.

That afternoon, when I had been in Trinidad only twenty hours, I made contact with the Blue Ventures. My one friend on the island had a friend who had a friend. He took me to their band room. Everything was open and easy in these small tropical countries, I thought to myself. The Blue Ventures were a hard core soca band, one of the best on the island.

The leader, Bobby Quan, came out to shake my hand. He already knew that I wanted to play in his band and right away he said he'd like to help me out, there was no problem. The onliest thing was, I had to speak with the head of the horns, play through the parts with him and he would be honest with me as to whether or not I could get around this kind of music quick enough. And Bobby wanted me to see the Blue Ventures perform.

Bunny, the leader of the horns, played the alto sax. He was tall and slim, and came sauntering down the steps from the band room asking, 'Which one of you is the trumpeter?'

'Me. Trombone.'

We shook hands. He reiterated what Bobby had said. We arranged to meet, and he invited my friend and me inside.

The band was learning a new number, 'You Keep Me Pumping Until the Morning'. The bassist in the corner played it over and over again on a cassette deck, and the band jammed along. After half an hour they tried launching out on their own, without the tape. My friend, who had no professional interest in a repetitive rehearsal of a repetitive song, grew restless. And he knew that on the other side of town a pan yard was swinging: Phase Two Pan Groove.

Boogsie Sharpe was the man. He wore a small round leather cap to which Port of Spain had given his name: a Boogsie hat. He led Phase Two from the heart of the band, the engine room. Phase Two was a big band, over a hundred pan beaters, and their rehearsals drew a crowd. There were stalls selling cold beer and fish sandwiches and bananas and oranges. Behind the band two men were welding frames to hold the drums. A banner said, 'Phase Two – D'Hardest Hard.'

The drums were all made of brightly polished stainless steel and fitted to wheeled frames so they could be pushed through the streets. A steel band is a ship: in the prow the bass drums, the foremost set up at an angle like a row of cannons. Then tenor, cello and guitar pans, and in the middle the engine room, the rhythm section up on its raised deck overlooking the rest: a drum kit, congas and plenty of iron men, who beat old brake drums and wheel hubs.

It was approaching midnight. The moon was close to overhead, small and sharp in the silky sky. The band had been swinging through a number. Boogsie brought it to a halt by rapping on a metal frame. A few more taps in his Morse and they were repeating the last phrase at half speed. He and his righthand men dispersed among the tenor pans showing the beaters exactly how it went. There was a timing problem. Some people were lagging behind the beat.

Then after more Morse they were under way again at full speed. I had had a lingering flu virus for a couple of months. Now I felt good inside. The music, so richly harmonious, was good for the psyche, and the rhythm was good for the nervous system. I began to feel healthy again, and my body became warm and fluent. And I was feeling confident about the Blue Ventures.

SEVEN

I was staying in St Ann's, a suburb near the Savannah. My host was Doctor Chow, a member of Trinidad's intelligentsia who spoke very softly. He wore glasses and had smooth, pale cheeks. He had left general practice and was now in charge of the island's AIDS programme. He gave lectures on the history of sexuality and the pernicious Christian dogma that attacked homosexuality. His enemies were the Catholic and Fundamentalist churches, against whom he had to fight for the practice of safe sex.

He was a good cook, though his techniques, primarily Chinese, were exotic. He laid aubergines naked and raw directly on the burning gas ring until they peeled themselves. He pickled his own vegetables and ginger. The fridge was full of little pots of different roots chopped and steeping for months in particular oils, peanut, coconut, soya.

'Fortunately there's nothing in there that Shona recognizes as food,' he said of his maid. 'Otherwise it would all be gone.'

Shona was a Barbadian who came two mornings a week. She had been living in Trinidad for over two decades. She had enormous round cheeks and a wispy beard and just fitted snugly through the doors.

One morning we got into a conversation about music. She broke up all her phrases with nods and uh-huhs so deep and long that sometimes you could even miss them, thinking she had finished and was just exhaling and adjusting her posture. She had a way of flicking her eyes up at the ceiling, like someone clucking conventional disapproval, when she was nodding her agreement.

She urged me to go to the final of the women's calypso contest, which was being held soon. The promoters called it Woman Rising. Shona told me it was in the 'Jimpy Complex'. She explained at length that the Jimpy Complex was the stadium, for I had never heard of it, until it finally dawned on me that she was describing the Jean Pierre Complex.

I said, 'Ah.'

To which much nodding.

I told her I hoped to play with the Blue Ventures. She said she saw me a few years from now with my own soca band, which, she predicted, a girlfriend of mine would manage.

But I have no girlfriend here, I objected. Mind you, I joked, some of these girls here—

'If you loves music,' Shona broke in, nodding heavily and knowingly, 'and I believe you does love music, it don't matter where or how, you will get your own band. And some of them Trini girls does love a bandleader.' She slowed down on the final words as if more confident of her grammar there. But it wasn't that, it was just for emphasis.

I knew this because I had recently read a newspaper article on local grammar: 'Vernacular, dialect, we kinda talk, call it what you wish, but doh get tie up, dis is we ting. Ever stop to think about the way we does talk? . . . We does really talk wrong side out.'

My second morning I caught a taxi at the end of the road from Doctor Chow's house and went downtown. Taxis in Trinidad, large old Japanese saloons, are identifiable only by their registration numbers, which begin with the letter H for hackney. They drive along certain routes only. To catch one you have to stand on the route, and unless you pay extra they will only drop you on the route. They are called route taxis. The drivers, usually male, hold a fat wad of red one-dollar bills in the hand, worth an American quarter each, ready to give change. People pay at any point in their journey, and drivers hand back change regardless of the demands of the road. I once saw a driver leave off steering round a bend to extract notes from his bundle. He stopped when a third wheel climbed off the road.

Port of Spain shops were better stocked than the shops of London. I wanted to buy vitamins. The drug stores had a range of ranges, from laboratorially chemical, in thick glass with plain scientific labels, to earthily, almost dirtily, herbal, with straw-coloured and rainbowed labels that you expected to smell of hay.

I also needed earplugs. My ears were still ringing from the Blue Ventures rehearsal. The continual noise in my head made me feel frail like a convalescent. On Frederick Street, the main street of downtown, running from the Savannah to the port and forming one side of Woodford Square on the way, was the only music shop. It was the ground floor of a modern building, its windows covered with large stickers of instrument and amplifier manufacturers.

Someone was trying out an electric guitar, unamplified. The owner, half Chinese with long frizzy hair, was talking to him without pause in rising and falling cadences. He kept up his rap regardless of whether or not anyone listened to him. He never waited for a response. The guitarist made it as clear as he could, ear tilted to the strings, frown on the forehead, that he was paying attention to something else.

The store owner's subject was carnival. He was sure it was rigged. The contests, Panorama, Calypso Monarch, Kings and Queens of the Bands, were all fixed. It was all a media conspiracy. They had just held the first round of Panorama, for example, to select the bands for the semi-final. Phase Two was all over the front pages of the papers and on TV. Phase Two came third. You didn't hear nothing about Amoco Renegades or Desperadoes who both did better than Phase Two. Renegades were twenty points clear of Phase Two. But all you heard was Boogsie, Boogsie. Why? Phase Two were a Woodbrook band, the Renegades came from Laventille, the hill of Laventille (a rough area).

'Yes, yes,' he said to me as if I had been talking. 'What happen?'

'Do you have any earplugs?'

'Music too loud for you?' He moved behind a glass counter. 'All sold out.' He resumed his monologue on the social inequalities ingrained in carnival's contests.

On an electric organ in the window was a printed score of Lord Kitchener's hit this year, 'The Iron Man'. It tells the story of a Yankee girl who comes to Trinidad from Michigan to learn to play the steel drum. She loves all the pans but eventually falls for the Iron Man whose iron instrument puts her in a 'zeal'. There was something tender and touching about seeing that sheet music on the organ in the window. Otherwise the display was bare. It was so thoughtful a touch, suggesting, 'You might like to play this.'

In another drug store I found earplugs for swimmers which the store supervisor assured me were effective against noise too. I discovered later that they were only effective when pushed so deep in the ear that they could not be extracted digitally. They had little tabs for purposes of removal, but even these would be sunk irretrievably in the channel. They induced a mild panic in me, even before I had tried to get them out. I felt cut off from the world, isolated in the world of inner sounds. The effect was of suffocating. Breathing seemed unquestionably harder. And when I tried playing the trombone the sound I heard was a thin metallic gurgle.

A few days later I found some others, American, made of the latest silicon technology. They were if anything too good. They were so airtight that by some unfathomable law of acoustics they sent every sound a semitone sharp.

After my shopping foray I sat on a bench in Woodford Square. There was plenty of shade beneath the big trees densely hung with blossom. The square was one block of railinged garden with a bandstand and benches. Clusters of people were listening to soap-box ranters who stood on the benches, a replica of speakers' corner. The speaker nearest me was complaining about the politicians. He had drawn a small excited crowd of office workers taking lunch. One man kept heckling him.

The Shouters were there too, in white dresses that reached to the ground and turbans of primary colours, each colour representing the particular saint to whom the wearer had dedicated their head. They had drawn a thin listless crowd. The Shouters are the most African of the Christian sects on the island and use chanting to invoke the saints, who 'mount' them the same way the voodoo deities mount their devotees. Once in the saddle the gods not only shout, but also dance and jump and quiver and fall unconscious. The Shouters suffered a long ban under the colonial authorities earlier this century, which greatly increased their standing in the community. They became known as healers and seers. However, since their beliefs became legal some thirty years ago, after Independence, their appeal has tailed off. They have been eclipsed by the more overtly African cult of Shango, Trinidad's voodoo.

They were all holding bibles. One woman kept up a monologue of preaching interspersed with prayer, until they broke into a lugubrious hymn, a tune that barely moved, and heaved to a halt at every cadence. They swayed wearily as they sang.

A man wearing sawn-off jeans and a frilled pink blouse too small to button up had attached himself to them. He did exercises at the side of their semi-circle. He pumped his arms back and forth like someone imitating a steam engine for a child, raised and dropped his knees, and pulled a range of exaggerated expressions over his face. At first I wasn't sure whether he was one of them or not. He certainly seemed like he might be possessed. Maybe he was a sudden new convert. Or else simply one of the Woodford Square habitués.

One of the trees in the square had lost all its yellow blossoms overnight and each bloom was the size of a large rose. They lay as thick on the ground as the hair around a barber's chair.

 EIGHT

Saint Joseph is the oldest town in Trinidad. It was founded in 1590 by a giant Extremaduran soldier, Domingo de Vera y Ibargoen, on behalf of the man he served, Antonio de Berrio, who was away at the time on an expedition. He called it San José de Oruna.

After the Conquests of the Aztecs and Incas rumours of a third and greater civilization in the north of the Andes had grown stronger and stronger as the different explorers passed stories back and forth. El Dorado, in the land where the world's richest gold sources were to be found, was a city largely built of gold. It was said to be located behind some mountains, on a plateau, right on the Equator. Its equatorial location was necessary because, according to late medieval alchemy, gold was engendered in the earth by the sun's rays. The world's greatest reserves of gold had therefore to be where the sun was strongest. The treasures that had been found in Mexico and Peru, on the fringes of the Tropics, were nothing to what they believed the Equator held in store.

In the late 1530s the Conquistadors finally made contact with the Chibcha civilization, who lived in the highlands around modern Bogotá in the northern Andes. At first they thought they had found El Dorado. The Chibcha were quickly subdued, some peacefully, others violently, but their leader, the Zipa of Bacata, disappeared with all their greatest treasure. When the Spaniards eventually found him again, he was without the riches and the great city was never found. They soon decided that the Chibcha were not the Guianans. The search for El Dorado continued.

There was a ten-year lapse in the quest in the 1550s, however, due to an anti-colonial movement. Since 1539 the Mexican monk Bartolome de las Casas had been in Spain reporting the atrocities of the Conquistadors and trying to put a stop to them. His first achievement was the passing of the New Laws of 1542, which were much more favourable to native Indians, and then, in 1550, the Spanish King Charles I, who was also Holy Roman Emperor, declared a ban on all expeditions to the New World. He called a debate in Valladolid on whether or not Spain should continue to colonize in the New World. He named it the Council of the Indies, and invited many of the most eminent men of the day to attend. The main protagonists were Las Casas and the great humanist Juan Gines de Sepulveda, who believed in the superiority of Spanish culture, and that that justified colonization.

The Council debated for several years. They considered issues such as whether Spaniards should make slaves of the natives, whether they should impose taxes on them, but above all, whether or not it was morally admissible for Spaniards to be out there at all. They came close to banning all colonization and withdrawing the Spanish presence from the New World. But in the end the debate came to no conclusion. It got bogged down in details.

Since 1560 and, after the death of Charles, under the command of the new King Philip II, expeditions had been sailing again. The island of Trinidad lay just off the mouth of the Orinoco and Antonio de Berrio who was avidly seeking the phantom kingdom, saw it as the best base for his expeditions into the interior. But five years after he founded the town of San José de Oruna, an Englishman sacked it. As soon as he could Berrio sent Domingo de Vera back to Spain to find new settlers to help rebuild it.

Domingo was a gentle giant, a charismatic and persuasive man. Within a few months he had mustered over two thousand Extremaduran peasants who sailed across to the New World expecting a ready-made town to be waiting for them. When they found there was nothing they scattered among the islands of the Orinoco delta, where many died. A few stayed on Trinidad and rebuilt San José, which has been inhabited ever since.

Berrio carried on searching for El Dorado until his death, when his son took over the quest.

For the last two hundred years Berrio's town has been called Saint Joseph. It changed name when the British took Trinidad. It lies to the east of Port of Spain and has become an outlying suburb of the city.

Bunny lived with his mother and sister on a hill above Saint Joseph. I climbed up to his house at lunchtime on a windy day. The sky was full of ragged cloud. The house overlooked a great spread of rooftops broken up by sprouting tropical leaves. Beyond were the plains of central Trinidad out of which rose little black pinheads of distant trees. A few ships were anchored out on the sea of the gulf.

Bunny was a cabinetmaker by trade, but he had little time for it now. He made his living from the saxophone. Blue Ventures were one of the few bands in Trinidad with regular work and sure money. They toured America and Canada and the Caribbean and played at least two shows a week at home. Around carnival they got four weeks solid.

'Bobby's a great organizer,' Bunny said. 'He ain't like some of the other band leaders I did play with before. Man, there are people around that like music but music don't like them.'

We sat side by side on a sofa. The big French windows overlooking the gulf were wide open and the wind set the net curtains dancing. We had sheets of music on the floor between us, held down by our feet, and a cassette player, and we played through our parts together. It went fine. After an hour Bunny went to call Bobby. He came back and said, 'You know what I told him? My exact words. This guy is *on* the money.'

'When does he want me to start?' I asked.

'He say first he wants you to see the band play. I'll give you our show list so you can find us.'

Bunny's large, smiling mother brought in lunch: two plates heaped with pelau, yellow fig, sweet potato and calaloo. Pelau is rice and 'peas' (lentils) mixed up with chicken; calaloo is okra cooked in coconut milk with crab; and yellow fig is grated unripe plantain. We sat at the table and ate our way right through the two mounds of food, and then drank down a large pitcher of grapefruit juice.

Bunny told me soca was not his first love. He preferred calypso. But most of all he liked playing Atlantic soul. He warned me that some of the places the band would play were unsavoury. 'You may smell urine and that kind of stuff. And sometimes you get fight and that kind of nonsense,' he said, screwing up his face.

He drove me home early. He didn't want to get caught out at night: there were bandits on the road. You couldn't park a car anywhere or they would rip your wheels right off, or simply take the whole car.

On the way we passed a policeman in his motorbike gear of high boots and white helmet. He was standing in the middle of a junction directing traffic. He waved his arms about elegantly, and he stepped daintily from foot to foot. His signals were like the gestures of Indian dance, or of a conductor taking an orchestra through a fluent waltz.

All the way through the many suburbs of Port of Spain the Northern Range was always hanging there, by turns green and blue and grey, a great bank of wild jungle looming over the city.

 NINE

Carnival is the focus of every art on Trinidad. The carnival season starts at Christmas and rises like a big ocean roller all the way to the two days of carnival itself, just before Lent, when it breaks over the streets. The year is the build-up and the recovery from carnival. In April, after Lent, the calypsonians are already writing new songs for next year. In the summer the big masquerade designers are at work on the new costumes. By November most people have chosen the outfit they will wear when they 'play mas' ' – that is, dance through the streets in one of the masquerade bands – even if it isn't made yet. The steel drum tuners get booked up solid for the next four months. The pan beaters are practising every night in the pan yards all over the island. The soca bands are busy learning the hits of the new season. The air waves get jammed full of calypso.

Carnival arrived in Trinidad in the late eighteenth century. At that time the island was still Spanish, and sparsely settled. The Spanish king Charles III, worried that the English might attack and overrun it as they recently had done with other islands in the West Indies, attempted to bolster the population by passing a decree, the Cedula, whereby anyone could settle in Trinidad provided they were Catholic. His invitation was aimed above all at French planters on other Windward Islands which had already fallen into British hands. Many of them were unhappy under the British yoke and several thousand jumped at the chance to resettle. The population increased sixfold within five years. Whereupon the British promptly seized the island.

The French newcomers brought carnival with them, the two days of wild festivities, the 'farewell to flesh', before Lent. It was a festival of the aristocracy – the Emancipation of Slaves arrived in 1838 but the ex-slaves were not permitted to enter the carnival for another fifty years. When they were admitted they immediately added rhythm to carnival. They danced through the streets to their percussion, their conga drums and shakers.

Throughout the 1880s and 1890s the colonial authorities attempted to keep the black element out of carnival. But they were trying to stem a tide. 'It is disgusting', complained Brierley, a military commander, 'to see members of the white group engaging in the savage orgy that Carnival has come to be in Trinidad.' Soon a singer could declare, 'The whole population – woman and man – playing mas'.' By the turn of the century the black rhythms and dances and rituals, such as the kalinda stick fights, had become part of the festival.

Calypso emerged in the early years of this century from the

chants of the kalinda stick fighting bands who used to walk around the streets at carnival. When they ran into another band they would form a ring and two fighters would take each other on, swinging at one another with their yard-long sticks until one was hurt. While they fought their followers would chant songs to goad them on, from which calypso developed.

The golden age of calypso lasted from the early years of this century until the Second World War. Attila the Hun, Lord Melody, Lord Pretender, Growling Tiger, all sang then. Like the stick fighters, the singers named themselves after heroes. The British wars of the day, the Boer War and the First World War, offered a harvest of soubriquets: Duke Albany, Lord Kitchener, Marlboro.

Since the war the great master calypsonian has been Sparrow. He won the calypso king contest so many times that he was finally banned from it and declared calypso king of the world for all time. Slinger Francisco the name, Mighty Sparrow the soubriquet.

Sparrow's songs are a chronicle of world events since the fifties. He sings as himself and in the guise of dramatic narrators. In one of them, 'Philip, My Dear', he is the Queen of England on the morning after Michael Fagan broke into her bedroom, asking Prince Philip whether or not it was he who had been visiting her in the night. In another, he is the mythical Congo Man, a voracious savage whose appetite for white flesh is inflamed after he spots two white women in the bush.

Calypso has always been a medium for the telling of news. During the 1940s on Tobago radio the news was delivered by a singing calypsonian. It has always been the chief medium of social comment and still plays a crucial role in Trinidad politics.

Eric Williams, prime minister of Trinidad from Independence in 1962 until 1981, owed his long survival to Mighty Sparrow. Several times it was Sparrow's lyrics that persuaded the public of the need to swallow unpopular austerities. When Abu Bakr seized power in his ill-fated coup last year his first act was to set up a permanent calypso station on the television. He played videos of calypsonians who were critical of the government.

Carnival thrives off calypso. The singers compete for the Road

March prize awarded to the song played most on the streets of
Port of Spain during carnival. The calypso tents open up two
months before, halls where entrepreneurs engage a handful of
calypsonians to sing every night. The singers stay with whichever
tent has hired them for the whole season, so the tents become
musical teams. Sometimes they stage matches, 'clashes of the
giants', when two tents meet to outsing each other in a stadium.

Since the seventies there have been two kinds of calypso:
soca and calypso. Soca (soul-calypso) is high-tempo music for
dancing. The soca hits aim at the Road March prize, and during
the carnival season the soca bands like the Blue Ventures take
the year's hits and blast them out at fetes, massive outdoor
parties thrown by outfits like the Metal Box factory, the Carib
brewery and the 'Customs Boys' (the Department of Customs
and Excise). Calypso, also called kaiso (which means encore in
Yoruba and may be the origin of the name calypso), is considered
high culture and is confined to the tents.

Between the wars the authorities started setting up the contests
which have become part of carnival: the competitions for best
masquerade band, for best king and queen costume in a band,
the calypso king, queen and monarch contests, and Panorama,
the steelband competition.

The steelband emerged long after calypso, though its prehis-
tory reaches back to 1884, when the conga drums were banned
from carnival. In their place the blacks used bamboo sticks which
they beat together, the tamboo-bamboo. These became a fixed
feature of mas' bands until carnival Tuesday in 1937. On that
day the steeldrum was born.

Sagiator, the leader of the Bad Behaviour Sailor Band, a masquerade band, was leading his troupe up to the Savannah from the
docks. They had been swimming and then rolling in a heap of coal
to blacken their costumes. Sagiator roused them all on the way:
'We goin up in de Savannah and we go rub up we self and mess
up all dem pretty mas' since dey doesn't give we no prize!'

As they pranced along to the beat of the tamboo-bamboo
two of Sagiator's women discarded their bamboos for rubbish
bins standing at the side of the road. They emptied the bins

and started hammering on them. Soon everyone followed suit: the higher volume was irresistible. Up at the Savannah the new rhythm section won immediate recognition. The Bad Behaviour Sailor Band was called up at once for a prize.

Two years later a bin-beater first discovered its musical potential. It was in British Guiana. Vincent de Souza, an eye-witness, is well known for having been present at the occasion. He chanced to hear one of the boys from the Washboards Orchestra practising on a Trinidad pan and calling out to his friend, 'Boy, come, ah got 'em!'

'Get what, boy?'

'Ah get music, ah get music, come hear for yourself.' The player struck a note and asked, 'Dat ain't D?'

The companion answered, 'Yes, friend, dat is D!'

The player then said, 'If ah get D, ah must be able to get G.'

The young pannist continued to experiment. A little while later, he said with glee, 'Ah get G,' and wrote the letters D and G on the pan.

Shortly afterwards the Second World War began, during the course of which the Americans set up two huge air bases on Trinidad. They brought thousands and thousands of oil drums, enough to stock the many new steel orchestras that sprang up all over the island.

TEN

As I began to see myself with a clearer perspective, away from stifling Britain, I discovered in myself a growing frustration. For the first fortnight or so of travel the overriding experience is generally constipation, which gives way to diarrhoea. This process can plunge all other impressions into shade. You try to ignore your fundamental preoccupation, but in vain.

This must have been the fifth morning. The third, already in despair, I used a laxative. The same the next day. Last night I had dosed myself with Metamucil and Eno's, and again today on rising. Now, three hours later, after several pints of coffee drunk in idle hope of stimulation, my whole body was tingling and twitching. I couldn't write a legible line. My insides were seething.

Maybe the solution is to turn the logic round: it's not that you will know no peace until you unload, but that you won't achieve that until you relax. Deprived by travel of its morning ritual your body is seized with panic. Its reflex is that of the snail, to close itself up. The art is to soothe your body, to persuade it that there is no danger. The situation teeters on the brink of a vortex: as soon as the mind chimes in with its note of discontent, or of fury, the body receives confirmation that it was right to panic. It closes all the more tightly. At which the mind's desperation rises to fever pitch; and so on, centripetally, into the vicious circle, until the mercury blows the top off the thermometer.

I was stuck in a Port of Spain suburb blowing my trombone to a tape. I had been spending all day on a stool in headphones going over difficult phrases again and again (just after 'Poom poom all night long' or 'Gimme more, I want it, I like it' or 'Roll de bum bum') thinking it doesn't make any difference what kind of music it is, only the songwriter has any fun. My mixed feelings about the trombone started welling up again. Every minim was two heart beats wasted. The better you were the worse for you. Musicians were interpreters: uncreative, no matter how talented. They knew this. They denied it, they said it wasn't the notes but what you did with the notes, but the fact was they couldn't choose the notes.

I didn't know whether to carry on playing or to take my trombone down to the docks, blow a Last Post and hurl it out into the waters. It felt like nothing had begun. I didn't know how to begin. I wasn't even sure what I had to begin. Presumably it was a book. But I had clearly set myself an impossible task: to be a musician and a writer. As far as I could see just then it was like trying to move in reverse and drive forward at the same time. I would have to settle for rocking back and forth, getting nowhere.

Playing in a band was hard work. Firstly, talk; secondly, practice; thirdly, performance, which generally happened early in the morning and deprived you of a following day. The kind of exploration that might yield a travel book worth the paper couldn't be done if you were either busy practising music or recovering from the assault of 6000 watt speakers in the wee, wee hours.

My thoughts moved on to my diet. Where had I been going wrong? And then I began thinking about alternative cures. The Cuna shamans of Panama, I remembered, have a delivery method for difficult births that particularly appealed to me. Indian women give birth in the hammock, with the hammock slung under their knees, and this technique is famous among students of maternity for its efficiency. But every so often, inevitably, a woman runs into trouble, and they send for the shaman.

The shaman comes without paraphernalia, empty-handed: no spells, no charms, no medicinal herbs. He squats beside the woman and tells her a story. His voice rises and falls rhythmically, melodically, and engages her attention partly through the soothing pleasure of its sound, and partly through its subject matter. He tells a long story about a mythical Cuna hero well known to her since childhood. He has lost his soul. A devil snatched it and flew down to hell. He has to make his way down there past innumerable obstacles, animate and inanimate, fight the devil, win back his soul, and fight his way up again over the same assault course. The whole ordeal, which the shaman narrates so dramatically that by turns he becomes the hero and the various hostile entities that beset him, takes two or three hours to achieve its resolution. By the time he is safely home a baby has been born, without fail.

It was this shamanic technique that stimulated Levi-Strauss to write his essay 'The Efficacy of Symbols'. With it he began his long quest into the structure of culture. If I ever make it to Panama I may have a word with one of these shamans. Perhaps he could sell me a specially adapted version of the story.

ELEVEN

The next three nights I travelled around Port of Spain going to see the Blue Ventures perform, as Bobby had insisted. On my first night off, when I was waiting to hear his final verdict, I went to watch the women's calypso contest, Woman Rising. It was held in the basketball grandstand of the new Jean Pierre Sports Complex, as Shona had said. On the green silicon tarmac stood a stage and beside it a yellow marquee emblazoned with the Vat 19 rum logo and sheltering the Police Band. All the floodlights were on. It was like being in an operating theatre. Everything, the plastic chairs, the stage, the mikes, the marquee, even the ground, sparkled. Everything except a good deal of the singing.

There were twenty-three competitors, and each did two songs, one in either half of the evening's entertainment, which lasted five hours.

There were hair-raising intonation problems. Again and again the band came in at the wrong speed. But there were a few songs that sent shivers of pleasure down my spine. At its best calypso can be more moving than any other popular music. In no other music of any kind is brass put to such good use. Sometimes the lines, whose harmonic provenance is the nineteenth-century church, are plaintive, and sometimes bright with a primordial joy. The interplay of the brass rhythms with the percussion and the bass sets up a tension which can be turned either way, to joy or grief.

Easlyn Orr, a statuesque young woman with her hair bunched back from her face, sang 'Woman Respect Yourself'. She had a fine, clear voice, impeccably in tune and sang with conviction about women's plight. She exhorted women to stand up for themselves because that way men would have respect for 'all of we'. She is a successful calypsonian, singing regularly in Lord Kitchener's Revue, a calypso tent.

There were two white singers: Colleen Ella, a blond BWIA

air hostess in headband who sang about racial discrimination in her song 'The Rainbow'. In the earlier rounds there is a custom that ladies of the audience throw lavatory paper at singers they don't like. Ella had got through by cunningly invoking in her chorus the rainbow, the symbol of racial harmony with which Bishop Tutu blessed the island. The rainbow is the right symbol, it encompasses all the colours: mainly black and Indian, but also Chinese, Syrian, European, and the many magnificent achievements in eugenics from the multifold mixing.

The other was Denise Plummer. She sang her song, 'There's a Storm Coming', stridently, superbly. It belonged to one of the calypso sub-genres, the prophetic, millennial song. Her voice was strong and right in tune. She wore lavish showbiz outfits – a gold Cleopatra headdress, a huge lime-green toga and heavy gold chains. Her black ringlets cascaded down her back and whipped about as she furiously paced the stage. She was a great presence. She won.

The weaker singers made up with show. In 'Education is a Must' a teenage girl in dishevelled school uniform sulked onto the stage and sat on a chair at the front listening to a Walkman in a pair of luminous shades. The calypsonian entered, in scarlet satin gown and matching mortarboard, and proceeded to scold her unmusically, breaking atonally into platitudes, like the title, at every chorus.

In her party song after the interval Lady Irie won several standing ovations by coming on in a skin-tight body-suit. She was a clear twenty-stoner. Every time she turned her back on the audience and shook herself, to set all the bulges quivering, people stood up and roared.

Otherwise it was a restrained audience: this was a calypso evening. People drank, but no one got evidently drunk. Bottles of Vat 19 and cans of Coke nestled among the chair legs. Ice and nut vendors in ill-fitting white suits walked the aisles, to help the drink down.

Afterwards I was hungry. I strolled round the Queen's Park Savannah to a row of shacks that sold food. One was open. A middle-aged rasta woman was smoking a fat joint inside,

behind the grill. Her cheeks were faintly pockmarked and her
eyes sparkled. As soon as she saw me she called out, 'What
happen? Food? You want food?' She was smiling broadly. 'I
got rice and chana.' Chana was chick peas.

I said OK. She made no move to get me a plate but carried on
talking. She told me her name was Zebelon. She had a brother in
London with whom she had lost contact. She had two teenage
sons. She called out to them, and they emerged from behind
the hut. She wanted to show them to me. They both had huge
innocent eyes and huge woollen hats.

It was the night of some round or other of the Calypso King
contest. It was being held in San Fernando, the big city of the
south, and Zebelon's husband and various other men were in
the shack next door watching it on TV. We could hear the music
clearly. I was starting to feel bad. The women calypsonians had
taken my mind off it, but now I found myself thinking about
Bobby Quan, who hadn't yet called me as he had said he would. I
was wondering what on earth I would do if he didn't take me on.

Zebelon told me to go and sit in the other shack and eat my
food. Someone indicated a beer crate for me. It was in here that
they kept the family sound system, a stack of several speakers
that they set out on the street on holidays and weekends, and
during carnival. Sugar Aloes was just then singing his moral
number about AIDS. He sang that it was never meant to be,
that man was supposed to live in harmony with woman as his
companion. A few grunts of approval rose up from among the
boxes and speakers each time he sang the chorus.

There is a reactionary side to Trinidad society. It goes hand in
hand with eroticism. The duality is expressed most succinctly in
the person of the calypsonian. Calypsonians sing two songs in
each round of the contests. The first is serious calypso, a stinging
attack on a politician or a general complaint about the state of
society, and the second is a party song rich in *double entendre*.

After eating I had another wide-ranging chat with Zebelon.
The most important thing in life was how you brought up
children, she told me. Discipline, Zebelon said, discipline was
what you had to give them – perhaps a surprising message, from

a dope-smoking, vegetarian rasta. Then I remembered that rastas are not hippies, they are religious devotees.

While walking home near midnight I passed several lost souls wandering around the Savannah. It was the city's Lonely Street. I was still feeling bad, but suddenly I realized out of the blue that I was missing my friends and family, and worse, that I felt immoral and guilty for having left them. Was I running away from love? Was I a man who didn't know how to love? I went to bed, alone with my loneliness and doubts.

TWELVE

The next night I was leafing through Dr Chow's stack of large colourful books on carnival when the telephone rang. It was Bobby Quan.

'We need you Saturday,' he said. 'And every night from now till carnival. You're gonna be on the truck with us right through carnival. OK?'

'OK.' Relief flooded through me.

'And if you're in, you're in,' he added. 'I want continuity. I don't want to see you Wednesday and then not till Friday.'

Just then Dr Chow came in from his evening run round the Savannah. He drank two glasses of water, slumped at the kitchen table and called out to me.

I didn't catch what he said. I kept having trouble understanding him. He spoke quietly, intimately, with the soft modulations of the Trinidad accent. He called out again, 'Would you like to go to Crosby's Launching?'

Crosby's Launching was an important event in the calypso calendar. It was when most of the calypsonians first appeared on the same stage singing their hits for the year. Crosby's was a big record store in St James, a residential district of the city, that put up a stage on the main street outside the shop. Dr Chow had friends who owned a hardware store directly opposite, the Limchoys. They held open house each year on the night of the Launching.

'You know what?' I said to him. 'I'm in.'

'In? You're in Crosby's Launching?'

'No, no. In Blue Ventures.'

'You mean you're going to be on a truck in carnival?' He shook with laughter. 'You'll be able to watch us all have fun on the street.'

When we got to the Launching at around nine the street was thronged. It was a long wide street running from downtown out west, lined with shops and bars. Several blocks were jammed thick with people. This was the biggest event that night in Trinidad. Ten thousand, fifteen thousand, twenty thousand, people said. Whatever the figure, we had to get through half of it. It took us most of an hour. The crowd was solid. Finally we lunged between the last few shoulders to reach the metal gate of the hardware store.

People grudgingly pulled one another out of the way so the gate could open enough for us to slip through and up a cement staircase into a large living room with two black sofas. Against a wall was a big TV with something I didn't recognize on the screen. There were two people facing it, a boy and an old man, both holding little boxes in their laps. I realized they were playing a computer game. We went into another room, dark, overlooking the street. Shelves on the walls were fully stacked with goods: Black and Decker drills, outdoor lights, all in their boxes. The apartment, right over the shop, took the excess of the stock. They were like medieval merchants, living over their warehouse.

We climbed out through the window onto a ledge. From up here the crowd seemed thinner, relaxed, pressure-free, because you saw only the heads, not their bodies jammed together beneath. There were several people already out on the ledge in the darkness. A hand thrust a bottle of rum out of the window for us. Plastic cups followed, then a big bottle of ginger ale, an ornate ice bucket, a big metal bowl of sweet scones. More people climbed out of the window. Soon there was a small party hanging above the street. Some sat, some wined gently, some vigorously, some stood. The show had not yet started.

I got talking to a breathtakingly beautiful girl called Terry. She spoke very directly, fixing me with her eyes, which were soft brown. She was a graphic designer who studied for three years in London. She was born and raised in Trinidad and had returned to live and work now. She had glowing skin, fine high cheekbones. I told her that I would be playing with Blue Ventures in carnival. She gasped in admiration and touched my arm. My heart missed a beat, but then she started talking about her boyfriend, who was currently in California. He was the son of a Scandinavian shipping tycoon, in another league from a mere trombonist.

The records stopped, the MC was out on the stage in a scarlet suit plugging Vat 19 rum, who were sponsoring the show. 'Vat 19 rum totals Trinidad and Tobago,' he declared. Then he was into a joke which I couldn't fully understand over the PA. A woman wants to play with different parts of a man's clothing. You play with me shoes next ting play with me hat next ting play with me shirt next ting play with me trousers next ting play with me underpants and then I got to find a place to put what dangling. The crowd roared, so it was the punchline.

Twenty-five singers performed tonight. Each came out onto the stage to sing along with their hit record. You could tell they were really singing because they didn't always pitch as they did when they recorded. But you could also tell that the record was playing because sometimes they failed to get the mike to their lips in time. This happened particularly with the more theatrical calypsonians, who liked to climb up onto the frame of bars enclosing the stage and sing right down at the crowd.

'Theatrics, dramatics, a lot of show business coming into calypso,' said the MC, when introducing Batman. Fully done up, Batman climbed right up onto the frame and perched there singing about the virtues of Batman. In the chorus he called on the crowd to shout all together 'Batman'. The rambling lines of his song illustrated the one rule of scansion in calypso: you have to fit in as many or as few syllables as you like.

Another heavily costumed performer was the Commentator

Dragon. He had a skin-tight silver suit that extended into a
long tail replete with scales. He also had a large matching
dragon's head which he took off and held under his arm while
he sang. With this occupying one arm and the mike the other
he was somewhat hampered in his attempts to climb all over the
frame like a parrot inside its cage. He tried anyway, with some
ungainliness. The crowd loved it. At one point he got into a series
of deep thrusts with his silver but otherwise unconcealed loins,
which sent waves of laughter spreading across the street.

Even Blue Boy, a good calypsonian, succumbed to the tempta-
tion to make a show of his song. At one point in his endless song,
'We're Having a Nice Time', repeated ad infinitum, he summoned
on stage a troupe of Red Indians, each with a bow, a spear or a
tomahawk, who danced unchoreographed for a few rounds of
'Nice Time' and suddenly found themselves caught high and dry,
the record finished.

Sugar Aloes, slick, necklaced, in a safari suit and a cold glint
in the eye, sang his soca number, 'Fete', a song that had all the
ingredients but never quite took off.

After him Poser came on. In a red boiler suit and a derby
perched on the back of his head he looked like a cross between
the salesman in the forecourt and the mechanic in the back. In
fact he is a bus conductor, as everyone knows, and as he says
in his song, 'The Bus Conductor'. In its chorus he declares his
desire to work only on buses with woman drivers. He wants to
work on 'Janet Bus' and 'Sarah Bus', but not on 'Isaac Bus'. He
does 'feel to cuss' when they put him on a 'man bus'.

Trinidadians drop final consonants. They say 'mas' for 'mask' (for
'masquerade') and 'las lap' for 'last lap'. That was the point of Poser's
song: it fell into the sub-genre of songs in which you give yourself a
cover for saying something otherwise inadmissibly direct. He sang
with a big smile under his moustache. Another example of this
thinly veiled coding was the lines of the song 'Good Screw'. The
singer wonders what is happening to all his furniture that keeps
falling apart, and needs some good long screws.

Lennox Picou, who lives in Brooklyn, was another favourite
with the crowd with his hit this year 'Don't Bother Me Now,

Don't Hassle Me Now'. They are the words of a woman whose boyfriend raises some grievance at a party. Everybody knew the song well enough from the radio for him to hold the mike out over the crowd for some of the refrains. He wore steel rim glasses and a suitable expression of carelessness, eyebrows raised, grinning, and danced in loose steps kicking his legs out backwards, arms dangling.

If anything more people packed the street as midnight passed. There was no hint of the show flagging. On our little ledge people were dancing with dangerous abandon, pumping directly at the singers clean over the heads of the crowd.

Above Crosby's store a yellow Vat 19 banner reminded everyone what the spirit of Trinidad and Tobago was. Above that was the apex of a wooden roof; above that the Northern Range, a blackness prickling low down with lights, bare and undisturbed higher up. It was like an inkspill on the sky. Riding high along the street, from east to west, was a moon just past full. It was very far away, very small.

THIRTEEN

The first time I played with Blue Ventures I had to sit around waiting and waiting for the sound check to start. I was feeling nervous and was reading *Robinson Crusoe* in an attempt to distract or even instruct myself. I was hoping to learn how he had overcome his fears and pessimism. Nearby Tobago claimed to be Crusoe's island: it was an island more or less in the mouth of the great 'Oroonoque river'.

I dutifully arrived quarter of an hour early, at quarter to twelve. I found the stage easily enough: it was in a huge room opening onto verandas at either end, in the Country Club. The sound system and mikes were all set up. I was at the right place on the right day, but the only person around was a security guard. At one o'clock band members started rolling in. By two most were there. But Bobby and the sound man didn't arrive till four. I moved from table to table trying to read, trying to calm myself. The only people I knew were Bunny and Michael, the other trombonist. They were cool, it was just another wait for a sound check. Bunny beckoned me over to a table where he was sitting with Adrian and Adrian's ex-wife, who had flown down from Brooklyn for carnival with their ten-year-old son. They were discussing what to eat for lunch: Kentucky or rotis or pizza, all three of which were available in a shopping mall across the road. The son was counting out one-dollar notes. If he got it right he could have the money. There were fourteen. They were faded and messed up, difficult to open flat. He stared at them intently as he leafed through them, his tongue protruding through his lips. He got it right the second time.

Having invited me to join them Bunny did not then talk to me. Their table was just a place for me to be. I listened to the intermittent conversation for a while then took *Robinson Crusoe* out again. I was hungry for the story of his conquest of anxiety. Fear and pessimism were never necessary, never helpful. If you had faith things always worked out. I needed to be shown this again and again. Look at me now, I kept saying to myself: a nervous wreck. Why? Because I'm waiting, waiting; because this will be my first time playing with the band; because if I make a mistake they might not have me again. It was ridiculous, but I was having the kind of pre-performance nerves I used to get years ago. What bothered me most was that there didn't seem to be a mike stand for me. I went to check the stage countless times. An extra mike never appeared until Bobby was actually calling the band onto the stage. Larry the chief roadie quickly set one up for me. At least I was next to Bunny, I told myself as if I was undergoing some real ordeal.

After the sound check Bobby announced what we were to wear and said he would bring a shirt for me. 'You got white pants?' he asked. I was wearing cream trousers. I tugged at them. 'White enough,' he said, and everyone laughed.

When I got back from supper that night and we were about

to start, the two male vocalists went round the band knocking fists with everybody. At first I thought they were going to leave me out, but they didn't. They gave me good hard knocks accompanied by welcoming smiles.

Blue Ventures was a big band in every way. Financially they did better than all except one, Charlies Roots. They had been around for twenty-five years. Big calypso names sang with them. And there were eighteen members.

One of the keyboard men was a big, tall man called Skies. He had a mass of long frizzy hair, a little patch of black beard under the lip and a moustache. He did the arranging and stood next to the horns on stage. The other, Patrick, was a computer programmer. He wore glasses and a full beard. He stood on the other side of the stage and counted the band in at the start of each number by waving one arm out to the beat with a single finger extended, then again with two, and so on: one, two, one, two, three, four. Generally the horns opened the songs, usually with the theme of the chorus, sometimes with a counter melody that established itself as a kind of signature tune of the song. So before each number Patrick would turn to the horns from the far side of the stage, a faint smile on his cheeks, glasses flashing with the lights, and fling out his arm looking around to make sure everybody saw it.

There were four horns. They stood in a line at the side of the stage. The trumpeter, Mike, was young and short. He greased his hair down and wore tight tee-shirts. He told me later that when he wasn't playing with the band he sold clothes on Independence Square. He became a trumpeter because he grew up in an orphanage. Most Trinidad brass players came from orphanages, which always owned several trumpets and saxophones that the children were taught to play.

Michael, the other trombonist, was so tall that when I stood next to him I barely came up to his shoulders. He often smiled, and he played his old instrument reliably and very loud. At the end of every concert he would climb into his tiny Honda car to drive home. You could see his knees up around the steering-wheel.

Trevor played tenor saxophone. He too was tall and slim. He had very short hair and a smooth face. He stood very still while he played, occasionally leaning closer to his microphone for a mellifluous passage. Beside him stood Bunny, who played alto and who, as the leader, initiated the tuning of the brass section before each concert.

There were two guitarists, Bobby Quan and Roddy, who always wore a cowboy hat. The two of them fooled around together, marching from side to side of the stage, bouncing up and down, doing square-dance steps in time to the soca beat.

But the largest section was the percussion. They were all crammed in at the back of the stage either side of the drum kit. The conga-player, Dacueil (pronounced 'Dakay'), grinned wildly as he beat the drums, and beside him Sergeant Keith Coombes of the Police Band played timbales vigorously and deafeningly. There were three or four ironmen who clanked away at their old brake drums giving the rhythm its distinctive exhilarating drive.

The three singers were Nigel, Adrian and Natalie. They took it in turns to sing lead, but mainly it was Adrian who sang the verses. He was a strong man, solidly built and tough-looking. He wore jeans and sneakers and shirts unbuttoned to the navel on stage. His hair was in short curls, and he had a moustache. He sang and moved simply, now and then allowing his hips to go through a little dance routine of their own. Women found him attractive. After concerts he often disappeared into the car park holding hands with someone who had introduced herself at the end of a set. Once I saw a woman right at the front staring straight at him and grinding her loins against one of the supports of the crowd barrier.

Nigel was more flamboyant. He was tall and slim, and wined outrageously on stage. Sometimes he wore his braids, sometimes a little round hat, and sometimes he kept his cropped head bare. Mainly he sang backing vocals with Natalie.

Natalie was beautiful, with large wide eyes and high cheek-bones, and she had a superb voice. She danced around the stage wining and pumping and smiling throughout. She would go to the front of the stage and sing down at the audience, bending close, and hands would strain up towards her. She wore miniskirts or leggings. Her face had an open innocence that magnetized the crowd.

At the end of every set the band played a short closing number that I finally realized was an advertisement for Carib beer, in exchange for which Carib provided the band with tee-shirts, a grant and three cases of beer for each concert. After the final drum crash hands would reach into the freezing water of the band cool-box, groping around for the bottles of Carib and cans of Sprite to mix with the rum and scotch that Bobby always provided.

The set started with an avalanche of percussion, which settled into a driving beat. All the horns lifted their bells to the mikes at the side of the stage and blasted straight at the rest of the band. They couldn't hear us, and we could barely hear ourselves, partly because the whole system was so deafeningly loud and partly because they were all wearing ear plugs. I found to my surprise, and to everyone else's, that I did seem to have learnt the parts correctly, but I could tell only by looking at the way my slide work corresponded to Michael's, the other trombonist's.

The one thing that kept worrying me as we played was the absence of a set list. I never knew what song was coming next. Once we got going the percussion section – all six of them – never stopped. Between songs they kept driving the beat on until suddenly the band came crashing in over them with the next number. I understood when to come in: we had to watch for the signal from Patrick, the keyboard player. The problem was what song to come in with.

I kept screaming into Bunny's ear, 'What's next?'

He would hold his airport headphones away from his ear to allow my voice in, and then make some meaningless gesture. He would tug at his shirt, or point to one of the blue streaks in the shirt's design, or twirl his finger at his temple to indicate madness, or point to his behind. At first I was completely perplexed, but by the end of the set I had figured it out. The band had invented its own semaphore. The tug on the shirt chest indicated a bust. Hence, it meant Poser's song 'The Bus Conductor' was coming next. The blue streak signified Blue Boy, whose song this year was 'Nice Time'. The madness finger to the head of course indicated Crazy, the mad calypsonian – his song was 'Gimme More, Gimme More, I Want It, I Like It'. And the behind signalled a song called 'The Congaline', an old hit by the Barbadian band Spice. Its chorus was about 'bumping and wining', which required the dancing partners to bump behinds.

For the first few numbers I stood with my horn raised and ready to play and had to wait for the opening phrase to discover what song we were doing. But towards the end of the set I was figuring it out.

It had been a while since I last performed, and it was good to be up there again with a mike in front of me and an irresistible rhythm surging from the back of the stage, and a thick crowd bobbing up and down as they danced in the darkness.

After the third set, at three in the morning, several players had shaken my hand and complimented me. I felt happy.

Over the next ten days right up until carnival the band played all around Port of Spain – at private parties, at the PNM's annual bash (PNM being the political party in power), at the Customs Boys' fete, in Soca Village, at the Carib Beer factory. My initiation into the band took place at my third concert. We were playing a private party out in a wealthy suburb. The hostess was the owner of the Solo soft drinks factory and every year she held a fete in the back garden of her luxury home. For several blocks around there were Nissans and Toyotas parked along the streets, immaculately clean streets with pavements for the gardeners and maids. Her garden wasn't big, but she packed the guests in and she had hired the full Blue Ventures PA, as well as a big DJ sound system. It was at this show that I also got initiated into wining.

After our first set, while the disco was pounding away, I jumped off the stage to use the food and drink tickets I had been given. There was a bar serving draught Carib in giant paper cups, and next to it a stall for rotis and doubles, both of which were stuffed

Indian pancakes, but folded and stuffed in two different ways. Just as I was launching myself into the crush Mike the trumpeter touched my shoulder.

I was expecting him to say he would join me in a drink, but he didn't. Instead he told me that there were two ladies who wanted to meet me, and he led me round to the front of the stage.

One was a tall Indian woman with short curled hair and a fine smooth face, the other a thin long-haired, Chinese woman with high cheek bones. Mike vanished as soon as he had delivered me. We shouted a few exchanges which none of us heard. They said something about watching me play. Their names sounded like Merle and Lee. The only message that came over clearly was that they wanted to dance. We forged into the throng.

I was keen to be taught some wining skills, and was about to ask when right away Merle was in front of me reversing hard against me and locking tight. Meanwhile Lee's backside found mine and pushed. I was firmly lodged between the two of them. The music was ripping through me. The whole throng was flexing to the beat. All I had to do was relax my abdomen and allow my loins to be danced by them. There could be no better way to learn. We kept going for half an hour, changed positions a few times. I figured out that wining was one of those things you can't do if you think about what you're doing. As long as you keep your mind quiet it worked by itself, which I found was not difficult to achieve in my circumstances just then.

Wining began as a dance done by several people: the participants pressed front-to-back in a long conga line, synchronized their loin thrusts and went snaking around the dance floor. Then it became a far more potent dance for couples. The skill is all in the hip rhythm – the pattern and the speed and the extent. Small swings, wide swings, rapid pumping with just the loins, and slow deep pumping with the abdomen too. A good couple pick up the same signals from the music to move on through the repertoire.

There are four basic wining positions: both facing the same way with either man or woman behind; facing opposite ways, either towards each other or back-to-back. This last is often the initiatory position. You suddenly feel a rump against yours, fumbling to find your rhythm and then pressing more firmly. If the feeling is good, after a while one of you turns round.

When one partner is behind you can start jamming. Jamming is squeezing up tight together, especially when the man is behind: 'Jam she in a cosy corner,' as an Antiguan band puts it, and you should press hard so the woman can feel 'the pressure'. There are different ratings. They begin where Lambada, Brazil's 'forbidden dance', ends. Lowest of all is when you face each other. You see photos in the papers of ministers and their wives or friends wining like this at parties. It may be like being belly to belly with a belly dancer, but it's respectable. It's still respectable when a woman is in front of you arching her back and pulling you hard against a protruding rear to ensure you don't miss any of its contours. But some steps you don't see photos of ministers performing. An example is when you 'get on down', that is bend your legs, loins doing their stuff all the while, so a girl can lean out in front and get her hands on the ground, legs spread wide. She may even drop close to all fours. Another is when you're facing each other and a woman drapes her leg over your hip.

After a while Merle suggested we stop for some drinks. They drank rum. We stood against the fence furthest from the speakers so we could talk. Merle was married. Her husband, who owned several businesses down in Mayaro, a beach resort in the south-east, had stayed home. She said, 'This is Trinidad,' and gave me a phone number.

It was in the second set that I went through my rite of passage. Bobby kept glancing at me and making signs about me to Nigel. Suddenly during a percussion break Nigel was beckoning me out of the row of horns and into the middle of the stage. Meanwhile I made out the voice of Adrian saying, 'We got a new member for you today. You want to see how he can wine? You wanna see him wine?' An affirmative cheer rose up. Nigel came back to take my arm and lead me up to the front of the stage. 'You ready to wine?' he asked me, talking into the mike. The percussion was still driving on. The whole gardenful of people was staring up at me.

I said, 'Oh no, look, I'm only a trombone player,' into his ear.

'He say he only a trombone player. You wanna see him wine?' Another cheer. 'All right. You gonna see him wine. You ready?' To me. 'One, two, one, two, three, four.'

He began a slow rotational grind on the downbeat. He gradually speeded up, getting lower and lower. I followed him as far as I could, and finally got left behind. He had bewitchingly flexible hips. He could move them so fast you could hardly follow them with your eyes, let alone with your body.

'OK, OK.' He stood up straight. 'You wanna see him wine some more? All right. Put the horn in the air.'

I held the trombone up over my head and we wined down again.

'All right. He wine good?' A cheer from the crowd. 'All right.'

I stepped back over the monitors, between the mike stands, into the horn line, full of gratitude for everyone, and particularly for Merle and Lee.

Suddenly half the band was reaching across to shake my hand, laughing and grinning. Bunny and Michael knocked their fists against mine.

I had a further deeper introduction to wining two days later at the PNM party. A girl was standing at the front resting her elbows on the stage right through our first set, and I was acutely conscious that she hardly took her eyes off me. I was not only embarrassed about this, because it must have been so obvious to all the other horn players, but also scared. I was thinking that she must either have been a hooker – who else could be so brazen – or crazy. I was dreading the end of the set. When it came I headed straight for my trombone case at the back of the stage and started on a long thorough cleaning of my trombone slide.

'You're wanted,' someone called me. I had been waiting for it. I turned round. It was Mike again who was hooking me up. He pointed down to the side of the stage. There she was, still staring straight at me with her large, wide eyes.

I didn't seem to have any choice. I jumped down off the stage. She walked up to me and took my hand without a word and

pulled me out into the dancing crowd. Shandileer were just
starting their set. She then showed me what wining was really
all about. She got in front and started grinding her rump firmly
into me. I wasn't sure what to do with my hands, so I held
my arms out to either side as I had seen other people do. She
reached back and grabbed both of them and pulled them first
onto her belly, which was bare because she was wearing only a
short loose top, and then directly onto her breasts. Meanwhile
she arched her back and speeded up her hips. Then, when she
had had enough of that, she pulled my hands down to the top
of either leg. She looked back at me over her shoulder coyly, and
then steered my hands home.

I couldn't believe it. All this out on the dance floor in front
of everybody. The next tableau involved her reaching gradually
forwards until her hands were on the ground. Her legs spread
wide as she went down. She kept her hips grinding or thrusting
or rotating all the while. She was almost on all fours. I was left
high up above her facing the crowd of dancers. It was like being
caught in the act. I felt like shrugging my shoulders at them and
apologizing.

Just before the second set Nigel took me aside and said into
my ear: 'If you planning to work on that girl protect yourself
good.' He looked at me checking I had understood.

'No, no,' I replied. 'I'm not planning to.'

At the end of the second set he pressed a small package into
my hand.

There was one musician I met at several of our concerts, Wayne,
who was the best trombonist on the island. He played with
Sound Revolution, one of the big soca bands. I had met him
first at an afternoon concert in the Cruise Ship Complex down
in the port area next to Independence Square. The complex
was a small shopping mall of knick-knack stores. The adminis-
trators were hosting a party for employees and friends. There
were three bands due to play and none had yet started. No

one knew who was supposed to play first. I was outside on a stretch of concrete overlooking the water at the back. Some welders were working on the side of a ship nearby. Cruise ships had only begun calling at Port of Spain a year ago, when the government had knocked up this arcade to receive them and their money.

Mike and Michael were with me. We were playing through some of the parts. They didn't play in tune with each other, which didn't matter because it put a bright sizzle on the sound, and I was practising my compromise. Some horn men from the other bands gathered around us. One of them was Wayne.

He was a rasta with fresh, short locks. He had a smooth, soft complexion and finely carved cheeks. His eyes glistened with an inner intensity. He asked to try my instrument. He blew some fine jazz riffs, some loud, fast soca lines, and some pedal notes. He pushed the slide all the way down to the socks and blew a fat note, fantastically deep.

'That E flat,' he said. 'Pedal E flat.' It sounded good.

He looked the trombone up and down, holding it at an angle, and said, 'That a sick horn. A *sick* horn.'

I next saw him at the PSA concert. Every year the Public Services Association gave a huge fete a few days before carnival on their sports field just up from the Savannah. The ground was enclosed by a high wall along the road and otherwise by wire fencing.

Two of its floodlight towers were switched on. Four stages had been set up, one for each band. Sound Rev, Charlies Roots, Blue Ventures and Pan Vibes, a cross-over outfit somewhere between a steel and a soca band, were playing. All the stages were a pair of truck trailers, one for speakers and one for the band. There were also extra stacks of speakers on the ground.

I was getting used to the impossibility of checking your intonation at the volume level we put out. The decibels played around with the acoustics of the ear. You would suddenly hear yourself playing a semitone flat, and then wonder if in fact you weren't a semitone sharp, and then decide that you couldn't be so far out either way and leave your tuning as it was for want of any clear idea of what else to do. The sight of all the speakers, and the anticipation of the deafening sound they would produce, excited me now.

While Sound Rev were playing their set, all in red tee-shirts with the band logo and white trousers, I went over to watch from the side of the stage. The trucks were parked in an arc along one side of the field. Behind them was a wide strip of long grass, and then the wire fence. You could walk freely along here, and it gave you a sense of spaciousness in the yellow wake of the floodlights' glare directed at the other side of the trucks and the dense throng of people reaching all the way to the road. To my surprise I found Wayne standing in this margin of peace behind the stage.

'It have a next feller does play some time,' he explained. 'The band have two trombone. Two trombone,' he emphasized, in case I didn't understand. Wayne was wearing the uniform. He would be playing the next set.

We watched the other player from below for two songs, talked a little about technique, and strolled out into the longer grass. Two men came running along on the other side of the fence until they found a slit in the wire and slipped through. A moment later a security guard with a Doberman and a torch walked past briskly, pulled by the dog. The two were already lost in the crowd.

Meanwhile Wayne was explaining his philosophy to me. He believed in astral projection. Enlightened souls could leave their bodies through meditation and in dreams. They could fly wherever they wanted and there were certain desolate planets where they would congregate. Neptune was one. A person could meet someone down here on Earth whose soul they had actually been meeting regularly on Neptune. If they were enlightened, that is. If they were very enlightened they would recognize one another. Wayne read books which explained all these things, and how to join in the action.

I asked him if he found the trombone frustrating musically.

'I play other ting,' he said, laughing. 'Yes. I play other ting.' I couldn't tell whether it was a knowing laugh, as if what he said was charged with arcane significance, or simply one of modesty. It must have been the latter, because when I asked him what else he played it seemed to be the question he had been waiting for. He delivered the list evenly. 'Bass, keyboard, guitar, percussion, saxophone.'

'What? You play everything?'

'The onliest ting I don't play is the trumpet. I won't touch the trumpet. No.'

'Why not?'

He turned away for a minute, and then round again to offer me a beer from the band cool-box. He bit the top off and handed me a bottle.

'I play the trumpet before. Long time. When I lived in Germany.' He was smiling at me curiously.

'When was that?' I asked.

'Before Hitler and all that.' His smile became a grin. 'I played in a brass band in Berlin. In another life, man. So I play a next ting in this life.'

'Have you always been a musician?'

'My last three lives. Now is enough music. Next time I come back a millionaire.'

 FOURTEEN

It was the afternoon of Dimanche Gras. Carnival began the following morning. For the next two and a half days we were going to play with hardly a break. All that time we would be on a truck, winding through the streets of Port of Spain.

The whole band, all eighteen of us, had gathered in the car park of the Oval cricket ground under two enormous cedar trees waiting for the truck to arrive. It was late. A wall thirty feet high enclosing the ground offered no shade. It was still early afternoon, and hot.

Three men had been busy setting up the drinks stall for the

fete that was being held in the cricket ground that night, but something had stopped them half-way through the job. They had got the tent up, and a few trestles. Nothing more. Some members of the band were lying on their sides on the tables making them sag, in the shade of the tent. They were laughing and joking loudly. I had moved towards them in a daze induced by the stuffy heat, the direct sun and ten short nights. I had been getting to bed at three or four, my head reeling from the decibels, and waking up at seven. Every household in Trinidad was moving by six, and the bustle always woke me up. If I took everything easy and had a siesta I got by. That was my problem now. It was the afternoon. I needed to lie in a breeze and read a book until I fell asleep for an hour or two.

Dacueil the conga-player was sitting on a beer box under the tent. He called me over. 'It have Carib,' he said, 'but hot. You want?'

'Thanks.' I didn't really want a beer, especially not a warm one. But I was afraid of refusing. I hadn't adjusted to the pace.

One of the men setting up the drinks stall, in jeans and a blue woollen hat, opened a box beside the one he was sitting on and got up to knock a bottle against a table edge to open it. He gave it to me. 'So how he does play?' he asked Dacueil.

'All right,' said Dacueil as if he'd just received the answer to a question, lingering on the second syllable.

'He play soca?'

'Eh,' Dacueil's voice fell. 'What you think the Ventures does play?'

The drinks man muttered something I couldn't understand and the other people then broke into laughter. 'No, no,' he added, 'dey is a sick band. A sick band.' More laughter, this time at the use of the word 'sick', which was about equivalent to the British slang use of 'wicked'.

I took a swig of the beer. It was warm and bitter and sweet all at the same time. I was standing there with the beer in my hand and my trombone case over my shoulder. I badly needed at least to sit, if not lie down, preferably somewhere where I wouldn't have to make conversation.

The man who gave me the beer asked me: 'What you think? Dey is a sick band?' I laughed appropriately and said sure. I really wasn't in the mood for talk.

I walked out into the sun again. There was a narrow slip of shade along the high wall. I was thinking of going over to lie in it, on the stony dusty ground, when Trevor the tenor saxophonist called out, 'Hey.'

He was sitting in his car, a luxurious air-conditioned Datsun saloon, parked beneath the high cedar branches. Trevor was tall and slim and something of a ladykiller, although married with two boys.

'Climb in,' he said when I was closer. His car had an uphol-stered bench seat in front. I joined him in the cool, and immediately felt better. I realized how tense I had been. I rested the beer between my legs, leaned back, closed my eyes and awaited Trevor's charm.

'What you were saying the other day,' he said in the high-pitched voice with which he opened his conversations, 'about getting away from it all, I was interested, very interested in that. You say you found a kind of paradise for you up in the mountains, the, what do you call it, the Andes. What I want to know is what do you believe is the value of a life apart from people?'

He was sitting with his head rested right back on the seat. He rolled it round to look at me. His eyes were bright and keen.

'I'm not talking about getting away from people,' I said.

'I mean the people who matter to you. You see, I believe you find yourself in your relationships. OK, lemme ask you a question. What kind of relationships are you going to find up over out there in the mountains?' He waved limp-wristedly at the prepositions.

'I'm not talking about going for ever.'

Just then Natalie the singer appeared. She looked at Trevor and fanned her face with her hand, showing what a hot afternoon it was and also implying that having to wait made it hotter.

'Natalie, I know I does get you hot but you see I can help you. I am your cure. I know how you feel, Natalie. Why don't you let me help?'

'The day I have a problem you can cure I will let you know, Trevor.' Natalie was smiling, her eyebrows raised.

'Natalie, why you does pretend and stifle your feelings so? I admit how I feel, why can't you?'

She laughed. 'What I feel now, Trevor, is hot. Hot from the sun. And thirsty. I'm not doing any pretending about that.'

'Well, come and let me give you a little cooling.'

'Trevor.' Her eyebrows frowned while her lips smiled.

'Natalie, when are you going to respect my honest love?'

'Honest? What kind of respect am I going to have for a man who says he fall in love as soon as he turn his back on his wife? I'm going for a Coke.'

'Natalie, Natalie, come and cool down here. Just move the things.' On the back seat were his sax and my trombone. He reached back to clear a space.

She accepted with mock reluctance. As she sat she flashed a glance at me. My heart kicked. In my beery, sweaty light-headedness emotions came strong. From where I stood during the show, at the side of the stage, I always had an unob-structed view of the singers. Natalie was a magnet for the eyesight. The lights and the adrenaline, her own and mine, cloaked her in a radiant nimbus. All the horns except Bunny confessed to a weakness for her. I had talked to her before, not much, and fantasized that I detected a seed of mutual feeling in her smile. Now when she smiled straight at me she winded me.

Trevor came on with more outrageous verbal flirtation which Natalie parried wittily, defending, I imagined in my bleariness, the bud of love we shared.

'Next time I see your wife I'm going to tell her the things her husband does say. That's enough, Trevor,' she said brightly. She turned to me and said: 'So which part do you live?'

'London.'

'That's a great place,' she cried. 'Which part?'

'Different parts. You know it?'

'Plenty,' she sang high. 'I got three aunts in England. One in Wolverhampton, one in King's Cross and one in Brixton. When

I go I go and stay with all three.' After a little pause she declared in a kind of cry, 'I love it.'

'You bring back all your lovely things,' said Trevor. 'Your lovely clothes and necklaces and shoes and sunglasses.'

'Trevor, do you know where I buy my things?'

She was smiling and talking emphatically, excitedly. It suddenly occurred to me that as a singer in a big soca band she was probably used to a lot of attention, and was a natural flirt. There was probably nothing between us, her brilliant eyes meant nothing personal when they caught mine. As if in confirmation of this she opened the car door and finally did what she had been threatening to do all along. She climbed out to go and buy a Coke.

Trevor shook his head grinning and cried out after her, 'Oh Natalie.'

She turned to frown just before she walked through the gate out of the ground.

Trevor and I got into a discussion about marital fidelity. He told me, using the general, second-person pronoun, that he had affairs on the side without any hassles. You had to be discreet and careful about the girl. You had to be sure she wasn't going to create problems and start calling you at home, so you took it very gently. A girl might approach you after a band set at a party. You would get talking and if things worked out maybe you would think afterwards, 'Hey, that was good,' and give the girl a call in a few days and say, 'Hey, what you doing next Wednesday?'

I said, 'How would you feel if your wife was talking like this?'

Trevor laughed briefly. 'Your answer is in that word I used earlier. Discretion.'

'As long as you don't know you don't mind?'

'Well, truly I think it's a question of opportunity. I don't think she would get the opportunity.'

Natalie was back with two bottles of Coke in her hand. She came to my side of the car and handed me one through the open window – it was exactly what I wanted.

'I thought you might need it,' she said. 'Nothing for you, Trevor. You're a bad boy.' She was grinning at him.

'Is it my fault they built you perfect, Natalie?'

She threw back her head laughing and walked away.

The truck was already three hours late. We had been told to be here at one. Now the shadows were lengthening, the light was mellowing, and the truck still hadn't shown up. Nobody minded. The afternoon had become a pleasant lime, a session of hanging out and chatting. The other band playing that night, Triveni Brass, had done their sound check. The DJ system, with some of its speakers high on the end of the grandstand, had been set up. The drinks tent was all ready. We were supposed to have reached the Carib factory out of town by now for an afternoon fete. We wouldn't make it before dark. And by the time we were through there we would have to head straight back here to the Oval without the planned rest of three hours. We would then play on and off until two or three in the morning. And all that on the eve of carnival, of two days of playing for eighteen hours without a break. I was anxious. It might be fun, but it was likely to be an ordeal too.

It was approaching six o'clock when the truck appeared at the gate. The top half of it caught the late sun and was shining scarlet. Two silver air horns gleamed on top. Above them, roped into position, loomed six black speakers. The front of the truck nosed through the entrance to the ground, then withdrew. And again. The driver was having trouble making the turn. And again. Finally it kept on coming, pulling in a long, tall trailer. There was a Blue Ventures banner on either side, blue letters flying at you from a vanishing point and flanked by yellow Carib bottle tops. The front and back of the trailer were walled with speakers. Along either side was a low fence of speakers, and speakers hung at intervals from the top bars of the iron fence that ran the length of the truck. There was a roof of boards, and on the roof were more speakers. In all the gaps between the speakers you could see microphones, on stands, hanging from the roof, taped onto bars. It was one huge machine waiting to be loud. It was waiting for us.

FIFTEEN

Vitamins B and C in perilous dosage, mugfuls of liver tonic, a regimen of fruits and steaks, and brave swigging throughout the day of malt drinks warmed by the sun to emetic sweetness, made not the least impression on the ghostly daze of the next three days. My body shrugged them off as little nuisances. What I was learning about Trinidad carnival was of questionable interest, but I was getting some valuable insight into a celebrated Haitian phenomenon. They weren't normally found in Trinidad, but on carnival Monday and Tuesday there were several zombies in Port of Spain. They were being towed around the city caged in a truck for the crowds to look at.

I looked back too while mechanically playing lines that by now, after one or two thousand times, had replaced my personality. I had one thought every now and then, and it was that I was in a voyeur's paradise. The streets were thronged with women of breathtaking beauty, all of them wearing skimpy, glossy leotards adorned here and there with a frill or a few shreds of colourful cloth, and they were all either wining or chipping, the masquerader's step to the beat, also called prancing. In shades and earplugs, the horn section uniform, I felt invisible and inaudible, encased in my own protective bubble. I could study the anatomies of Trinidad in complete peace. When I wasn't a zombie I was a satyr. This was an extended *après-midi d'un faune*, a leisurely oscillation between dozing and lust. Except that all I could do about it was blow my trombone.

We were playing in a mas' band of three or four thousand people called the Witches' Brew and it was one of the biggest. Every band has a king and a queen, a pair of vast and elaborate costumes, generally on wheels, which the wearer pushes along from inside. The Witches' Brew king was a huge red and gold porcupine-like costume with twenty-foot quills. It had won the Kings Contest on Saturday. The sorcery theme of the band was suggested by mascots on the ends of staffs that everyone carried.

There were eighteen sections, each in its own colour, carrying orange cardboard pumpkins, silver skulls, black and gold bats, giant spiders on tiny webs, black cat faces with long whiskers, and some three thousand people in all. The women, and they mostly were women, wore the regulation glistening Brazilian swimsuit, in a variety of bold colours. The men wore shorts. They chipped along and when the truck had to wait for crowds to move they wined beside it, enjoying a dose of decibels that would have slain more sensitive creatures. The city was an orgy or an inferno, depending on your rum intake, of rhythmic noise and human flesh. The only intoxicant I had working for me was fatigue, which did nothing towards heightening my perception – it simply made me tired. Mike had said he would bring some under-the-counter bathtub rum but he didn't. He brought large bottles of Lucozade. But, for me, a few images of carnival squeezed between the zombie and the satyr to find the man.

It all started on the night of Dimanche Gras, the day before Carnival proper began. We were to play a late show and then catch three hours' sleep to be up early for Carnival Monday. We would play all day Monday and Tuesday, and late into the night at the Country Club afterwards. It would all end at midnight on Tuesday, when the band would shake hands and go home, but without a sense of common achievement or culmination because the next concert was in only three days' time.

At three o'clock in the morning on Dimanche Gras as we were hammering through Kitchener's 'Iron Man' in the Oval car park, before we moved out onto the streets, a fight broke out. Suddenly a circle cleared in the throng near the truck. From our height I could see the space open and move a little and close again, like liquid. Someone had grabbed a broken chair that had been lying around and made a few lunges, and been disarmed. It happened again half an hour later, while the sound system was thumping out a song by Drupatee, an Indian girl, about all the men who want to 'throw her down', but who doesn't fall down 'so easy at all'. The words were coming out in her clear young-sounding voice, bright and high above the soca beat. She was singing about men chasing

her, but the lyrics got inextricably interwoven with fighting in
my mind.

The Oval was on the main street of St James. When I left at
four the street was a thick crowd. People were still queuing for
the Oval fete and a sound system a few doors along had drawn a
crowd that completely blocked the road. Out of the crowd came
Billy Chow, who was on his way to the Phase Two pan yard to
help push the drums into town while they played. J'ouvert was
about to begin, the dawn romp that opens carnival. He asked
me along.

I was exhausted. I hoped to catch four hours' sleep before the
marathon. But it was carnival. This was carnival about to start.
My heart heaved and groaned and for an instant I wondered
whether I was doing the right thing: it was possible that for the
next two days I would see little more of carnival than a trumpet
bell and a pair of distended cheeks. But I decided that whatever
happened I would need all the sleep I could get. Billy disappeared
into the throng.

Then I changed my mind, too late to find him. I walked quickly
into downtown anyway.

At J'ouvert the mas' bands were all throwing paint and dye
over one another. People were laughing and drinking. I walked
around watching for a while and got to bed as the sun rose.

Our truck left from the same district, near the Oval. When I
got there three hours later it had already moved off down the
street. I had expected the habitual period of time-killing. I had
to force my way past masqueraders prancing to the din coming
from the truck.

Bunny pointed out the chip chip of the masqueraders' boots,
audible under the weight of noise we tried to smother it with.

We passed a long cemetery and over its wall, across a field of
white tombs, I could see to an ice factory, and beyond that some
dockside derricks and chimneys, and a glitter of water. The sun
shone and all colours were bright and rich. We drove into town,

and up to the Savannah, where, after a three-hour wait during which we continued to play, we accompanied the mas' band across the stage of the grandstand for judges and audience. We then drove back out to St James. At five we parked in a small square and had a half-hour break. I ate two beef sandwiches from a stall, drank two beers, chatted to a girl who had been giving me the eye from the street and who introduced me to her boyfriend.

We did another two hours in the dusk. After sunset a new moon, brilliant and fine as wire, hung over the hills, a bright hair caught on a lens. The band enjoyed that last bout of the day, when there was no long sunny afternoon to play through. Now and then someone climbed down and pushed through the flowing throng to buy an armful of cold beer. People called to each other, made jokes.

The next day my mind had all but closed down. I remember seeing boys sitting on the tops of walls, at the same height as me on the truck, who held hosepipes in their hands and sprayed anyone who asked. People would stop in their tracks and call up, 'Yeah,' and get a quick, complete showering from above, costume and all.

Glances from the girl I had met the day before were what sustained me. She pranced along beside the horn section most of the afternoon in her shiny black leotard, flexing her body to the beat. She smiled up at me at every horn riff. She had a bright, pretty face and a slender physique and she seemed unmistakably to be offering me something to look forward to. There was no sign of her boyfriend. Maybe he hadn't been her boyfriend after all. Because of her, eight o'clock in the evening, when we would take a break, became a target, something that I was aiming for.

By the time the appointed hour came around I had developed, in my fatigue, a fully fledged schoolboy crush on this girl. I had two hours free before I had to play again. As soon as I climbed down off the truck she took my hand and gave me a kiss on the cheek, then smiled at me for a long time. She had dark eyes that shone and sleek, high cheeks. Her hair was a mass of braids pulled back into a ponytail. We wandered around in one another's arms, dancing to steel bands, talking and laughing. I had arrived in some dreamland between waking and sleeping where you could have whatever you wanted. I had arrived at the heart of carnival.

We finally wound up somewhere on the Savannah, which was strewn like a battlefield with bodies, some single, some double. As we started to kiss, warmly and deeply, it felt like true love. It felt like stepping off a hot beach into cool water.

I woke up the following afternoon alone and I couldn't remember anything of what had taken place where I lay. We had played a concert somewhere that resembled the Country Club, I remembered a lot of handshaking among the band when we stopped playing at midnight, I remembered having seen dawn, and for some reason the face of her boyfriend or friend stuck in my mind. I had a headache so all-encompassing that the pain had spread throughout my body. I had passed through headache and now reached another little-known land, an empty place where there was nothing but a wave of acute pain that swept round and round like the beam of a lighthouse, sweeping across a desolate sea. I had to lie still.

PART II

Islands

SIXTEEN

Luther kept the lighthouse on Galera Point, out on the far north-east corner of Trinidad. He was standing in the shade of the bushes that grew on the slope beneath the lighthouse when I met him. Below, two men were fishing off the black rocks.

'What happen?' he said when he saw me come down the path. 'I'm jes' chillin' here.'

I said hello. He gave me a long smile like he wanted a conversation. He looked barely out of his teens and wore a green, woollen commando cap. He had a friendly face, a big round jaw and a gap between his front teeth.

'You want to see the light?' he asked me. 'I keep the light.'

'Thanks.'

'Leggo.' And just as he started striding up the path he cried out, 'Eh. Look. It have a fish.' He ran down out of the bushes onto the black rocks, out into the sunlight and the dazzling light of the white spume. 'Look at it one time,' he called back to me.

I followed. It was a fat fish, half head, a giant angel fish, striped blue and orange but its colours already fading, blurring as it lay on the rock under the sun. The man had to use a knife on its mouth to get the hook out. At every wave blow holes in the rocks roared and gasped out a breath of spray, like steam, which blew over the dying fish and briefly summoned the ghost of a rainbow.

The green swells rolled over the rock next to the fishermen and turned it white, snow white. Every few waves one came that curled in just the right place to knock hard on the overhang beneath them and send up a sheet of spray which showered the two men. Neither of them minded. The man who had caught the fish took off his shirt after the big sprays and wrung it out. In the warm wind that drove the waves in his torso lost its shine even before he finished with his shirt. He fished in front, lower down the rock than his partner. He had a large bald patch on the crown of his head that was a rich burnished copper colour, like a blood orange. It was a beautiful colour, all of him was a beautiful colour, a deep ruddy copper.

The other man, in a linen boiler suit and sunglasses and cropped grey hair, stepped back a pace or two, economically and relaxed, whenever a big wave came. Fans of white spray rose before his eyes and were tugged sideways by the wind. Mist would fly at him a second later, which he didn't mind. The stiff, hot wind would dry out his thin suit long before the next big wave. Just then he too caught a fish. It was big.

'Luther, Luther,' he called. Luther was a known expert. He ran from my side to take the line off the man and played the fish. He pulled in when he could. When he couldn't he tweaked the line, pulling with one hand and letting it go. When he let the reel go it whistled. 'You got a nice snapper there, boy. It have a nice one.' It was too heavy to haul directly up onto the rock where they stood. Luther moved round to the side of the rock, taking careful steps, stooping, watching his footing and the line at the same time. When the line was hanging straight down out of his hand he called to two youths further up the rock. One of them clambered down to where the fish was, in a rockpool, a small tub which the waves broke into, a landing basin. The youth timed his approach, scrambling down as a wave broke so it would be receding when he got there. He cut the line and brought the fish into view and up onto the high slope of the rock from which they fished. It was a yard long, pink, striped red, its pupils wide black discs ringed with gold.

'Yes sir,' said Luther. 'That a fine snapper.'

Its gills were great flaps. Half an hour later they were still working, working, slowly and steadily. The blow-hole spray slowed the death, roaring like gas bottles opened then closed tight again.

'Look over there,' Luther pointed. There were fish, good size, brown fish, half a yard long, swimming down the slope of a wave, within its glassy, green face. The men were fishing the Caribbean. If they cast from the other side of the head-land, beyond the submerged crest which kept the deep blue ocean water and the green sea water apart, they would have been fishing the Atlantic. The Atlantic meets the Caribbean at Galera Point.

Flung a quarter of a mile off the Point is a rock which the big waves smother in their snow. The Americans used it for target practice in the last World War. They flew their planes low over it and dropped small bombs, sprayed machine-gun bullets. You can still see where they had their emergency runway, a long treeless field reaching back from the lighthouse towards Toco, the nearby town. This north-east corner is an outpost of Trinidad, which is itself an outpost of South America, so that that rock was like a vanguard of the whole continent.

I watched the big seas roll in and throw up their white hands. The sun was beginning to glitter on the water out near the horizon. It took me back to another ocean, another late afternoon, eight years earlier, when I had been on an island off the coast of Ecuador. Then the dropping sun had spread a silver path across the ocean, a highway out to the bow of the horizon. I had stared at it. All thought had melted in the fire of that blinding reflection, until the brilliant coruscation had suffused itself into my mind, made my mind its mirror. Suddenly I had found myself living in a radiant body in a radiant world whose life was one with mine, living in bliss.

The sensation may have lasted only a minute, perhaps even less. It didn't matter how long. I had glimpsed an eternity.

It was not until now, on Galera Point, that I realized I had been searching for it ever since. It was to recover that moment that I was travelling now. And at the same instant I realized that wherever I travelled I would be looking in the wrong place. It dwelt inside me.

Luther took me up the lighthouse. The top floor was very cramped, with the ceiling so low that we could not even enter it crouching. We had to crawl. Both floor and ceiling were of rusting iron. In the middle was the great iron pole supporting the beacon itself, still there from the days when the light rotated. We climbed out through a small hatch onto the ledge that ran around the top of the white edifice. It had white railings. Above rose the structure of the beacon itself. He showed me Tobago,

a faint stain resting on the horizon. Behind were the blue hills
of the Northern Range, shining palms and forests, and the old
airstrip. He showed me where the ocean and the sea met.

There were vultures on the beacon. One perched on the very
top of the light. Another launched itself into the air, its two white
feet quickly resting up against its tail very tidily, like undercarriage
retracted.

Over the sea a pelican was out fishing. It stretched out its long
nose as it flapped, and then while it glided the nose swivelled
down and hung like a dart poised for the drop. It opened its
wings wide, bent them at the elbows, started to fall, opened them
again, dropping, twisting, shifting its body awkwardly from side
to side, its wings shrinking and opening to keep the course true,
until the final drop into the water. The wings folded back for an
instant making the entire bird a dart, and then there they were
flopping out on the water in relief. The bird rode the swells a
moment, bobbing, resting, then flapped itself airborne again.

Luther liked to read. He had read Eric Williams, Earl Lovelace
and Samuel Selvon, all Trinidad writers. Lovelace was from the
nearby town, Toco. 'Sam Selvon does curse and ting,' said Luther.
'He really something.' If you didn't read you were helpless, he
told me, looking me straight in the eye. The sunlight was catching
his whole face, making it shine and his eyes were bright white.
'Reading lets you know what's really going down,' he said.

I was whistling a calypso from this year's carnival when we
walked out of the tower. He laughed and said I whistled good.
'That a carnival tune.' He laid great emphasis on the 'car', so it
sounded like a snarl. But he was smiling.

'You did play mas'?' he asked me.

'No. I played with a soca band.'

'Which?'

'Blue Ventures.'

'Ha!' He let out a loud laugh. 'Yer does play with Nigel. Nigel
from here, he from Toco, man.'

Luther unlocked the padlock on the door of his house beside
the light and fetched two coconuts. He carried them by their
stalks. He offered me one, hacking off its crown with a cutlass

then gouging a hole in the white cartilage with the tip of the blade.

We drank from the coconuts, spilling juice all over our faces and shirts. It was tepid and not quite sweet. The nuts were lime-green and brimming with milk, not yet ripe. The copra was still soft and thin. We swung the empty husks into the bushes, disturbing a thin black cat that shot out from its hiding place past us.

SEVENTEEN

It had taken three days of feeding and resting before my mind again became aware of its surroundings after carnival. I had lain in a hammock in Dr Chow's garden reading and dozing. The weather was so hot I had been sweating all over, wearing only a pair of shorts.

I had drunk tea brewed with lemon grass cut from clumps that grew in his borders. He had shown me how to slice off a handful of blades and tie them in a knot so they would fit in the pot.

As my strength and consciousness had returned I had developed once more a powerful urge to move. I was through, not only with carnival but also with the band. It was time to move on, to see the rest of Trinidad. At last I was free to explore the Northern Range.

The north coast of Trinidad is a neglected corner of the Caribbean. From Toco in the east the road passes through Grande Riviere as far as Matelot and then stops. From Matelot there is only the wild Northern Range leaping down to the blue sea. A little path leads through the bush and across beaches, all the way along to Blanchesseuse, which amounts to a day or two's walking. There, in the next town to the west, you can pick up a road again.

The road climbs out of Toco, swinging back from the sea. You reach a pass, a saddle in the ridge, where there are a few tin-roofed houses that form the village of Montevideo, and then wind down again and finally cross the big river, which is only a shallow stream, that has given its name to Grande Riviere.

Boys play basketball in the streets of Grande Riviere. They have a basket up on the main corner. Above that is a wooden house with a banner saying, 'Roots and Branches'. It is the band room of the band that Nigel used to sing with. Their leader is Roots, Roots because he's a rasta.

I climbed up to the band room. They were rehearsing. They nodded me inside. They were putting out a good soca beat, and while they played I looked out of the door, down at the main street below, with the basketball players and electricity wires, and up at the forested hills above. This was the kind of view I had come for, I said to myself, this view and this beat. I had a moment of peace.

Roots had long, thick, matted locks. He was missing several front teeth and he grinned more or less continuously. He was small and lithe and skanked gently to the beat while he played his guitar, sometimes inserting some wining moves into his dance.

'Lewwe go and get a drink,' he said at the end of the song, taking off his guitar. We scrambled down the hillside to the village rum shop, a wooden store selling general groceries as well as having a long, wooden counter for drinking.

Roots had grown up in Grande Riviere. His family had lived here for as long as anyone could remember. He had his own house not far from his parents', where he lived with a girlfriend and two sons. He worked for the County Council repairing roads and clearing rivers of debris that encouraged the proliferation of mosquitoes. He had been playing music for years. His father had taught him his first tunes, old folk songs, as a boy.

A small man with his face creased up, as if constantly laughing at some private joke, came in and ordered a rum. The barman ignored him and the man didn't seem to mind. He just beamed on and rocked a little sometimes with quiet laughter. His face shone alcoholically.

'That Diggydown,' Roots told me. 'His woman leave him long time and he still on the bottle.'

Diggydown sang bongo songs, humorous party songs sung at funeral parties and wakes. For a living he caught crabs and fish, eating what he needed and selling anything left over.

'Sing we some bongo and I get you a beer,' Roots offered.

Diggydown turned round and looked at us for a long minute and then still looking at us started into a song. He sang softly and gradually got bolder with his voice. He was half-way into the verse before we noticed he had started. Then everyone at the bar started hitting their shot glasses down onto the counter to give him rhythm, and chanted the choruses. But he kept doubling up in laughter, or breaking into a different song, or calling for a second beer, to which the men, either Roots or his brother or someone down the bar, would gravely murmur a negative. His eyes were like brilliant lights in the dim, yellow, rum shop. His mouth was set in a permanent rictus. He got bored of bongo songs. The right place for them was a wake with a crowd of people drinking rum. He staggered out into the street saying he was off to the beach to watch turtles lay eggs.

At one end of the counter there was a small room with a juke box. Kids ran in with coins to play reggae. The juke boxes in Trinidad never had soca or calypso numbers on them. Reggae and soul was what the suppliers supplied, though you only heard them in Lent, when the radio stations weren't supposed to be playing soca. But the lenten prudishness of the DJs usually wore thin after only a week. Barmen would tell you no one played soca in Lent because it was kind of horny music, and then promptly get a soca number blaring from behind the bar.

The next morning we met Diggydown on the beach. He had a great clump of blue crabs hanging from his hand, threaded on a piece of string. He took us along the beach to show us the turtle tracks. The turtle had dug a great spiral down into the beach, and messed up a wide area around it. The spiral was probably a decoy, he explained. Last night he had fallen asleep before the turtle arrived.

Roots took me to Matelot, at the end of the road, to hear parang and folk songs. The lady who ran the shop up the hill at the top of the village closed up her door and slowly walked

to a bench nailed to the roots of a huge tamarind tree. Her son
fetched her guitar.

She had a moving voice, clear and pure like a child's. She sang
perfectly in tune with a very even tone. A man who sang parang
joined us under the tree to show me what parang was like. He
took the guitar and sang a song. It was a Spanish aguinaldo, a
serenade sung outside people's houses at Christmas time. Parang
is Christmas music, originally from Venezuela. A shak-shak player
who heard the singing came from his house nearby on the same
hillside with his maracas and joined in.

A breeze was coming off the sea. We spent the afternoon in the
shade of the tree. The woman and the parang singer exchanged
songs. Between performances, when no one was talking, you
could hear the surf at the bottom of the village. It pounded on
the beach with a deep reverberating bass.

EIGHTEEN

It was in Matelot that I met Jimmy Bengochea, a man
of Basque descent. He was in a store drinking a beer
and talking loudly, between swigs, to the store-owner
about the size of a snake he had seen in the bush. His
voice was smooth and nasal and resonant all at once, and he had
a smooth, round, bright face. His hair was cropped and he had
fine stubble around his jaw. He looked like an unusually tanned
and suave Mediterranean.

Soon after I walked in he asked me where I was from. I
told him, saying also how I had been playing in the carnival and had come to see another side of Trinidad and to
relax.

'This man need Tacarib,' he said. The store-owner laughed
from behind his counter. He was a tall man and he was leaning
back against some shelves.

'What?' Bengochea challenged. 'That not another side of T and T?'

'Oh sure,' the owner murmured, and chuckled again.

'And relax,' added Bengochea. 'Why you don't come? I leaving to go just now.'

I asked him what Tacarib was.

'Paradise, man.'

At the age of thirteen Bengochea had walked from Arima to Tacarib, some forty miles through the Northern Range. Tacarib was on the coast half-way between Matelot and Blanchesseuse. Then it had been a small bustling village at the centre of several thriving coconut plantations, businesses that had fallen into neglect over the years. The population had steadily dwindled to Bengochea and a handful of others until a year ago when even he had been forced to leave. Two outlaws, one a rapist and the other a murderer, had escaped from jail in Arima. They had gone into hiding in the Northern Range, in the remotest part of it: the bush around Tacarib. Their first gesture had been to burn down every dwelling in the area, to clear it of human inhabitants. Bengochea had reluctantly withdrawn to Port of Spain. Now, a year later, the outlaws had been caught again.

We walked along beaches, up hills, through jungle, mangrove, palm groves. Bengochea was a lithe, energetic man, and he walked fast. In the dark jungle, brilliant mauve butterflies the size of blackbirds flapped at us, and sometimes a bat the size of a cat would accompany them in confusion, tempted out by the thick obscurity under the forest canopy. Every few paces an ant highway would cross our path. They were made by the leafcutter ants, and were several inches wide and miles long, and were kept immaculately clean by the ants. They were the canals of the jungle. Fleets of emerald green sails floated along them.

Bengochea started telling me the Trinidad bush lore. He talked the same way he walked, quickly and so energetically that he sometimes tangled himself up in his own eagerness to introduce new subjects. 'It have who is I believe does do so . . .' he would begin.

He told me the local insect lore. 'I did hear a story any time you see hunting ants it gonna rain.' When the ants hit a house they clean out all the cockroaches, no matter how they hop and fly and try to hide. The ants cover the whole place. When a battalion gets busy on a cockroach they dismantle it. You see a long pair of antennae, a hairy leg, a wing shield, slowly making their way across the floor, borne away like trophies. The leafcutter ants can't resist the leaves of an orange tree. They are too delicious. The woodlice won't touch cedar because they find it bitter.

The moon was the heart of the agricultural calendar and this threw up another set of rules. On the day of the changing of the moon it will always rain all day. If you plant a fruit tree when the moon is full it will never bear fruit; you cut bamboo at the dark moon if you don't want worms eating it within weeks. Squeeze coconuts for oil during the new moon, at which time four nuts will give you the normal yield of ten. At the full moon the armadillo does not run far because it has a swollen liver. The best time for hunting is the new moon, when the animals come out to feed early.

This was the warehouse jungle, the jungle where a person who knows it well can live, build a house, cook food, plant a garden, spend the rest of their days with no more equipment than a large knife. Yams, fruit, fish, small mammals for food, coconuts for oil, bamboo and palm fronds for bed and shelter.

There was a lot of hunting lore. Wild hogs spray their scent oil into the air and when the hunting dog runs through the mist it goes mad. Bathed with the leaves of a certain bush in a stream, a dog can be made to run fast; another bush makes it fierce; another makes it find the lapp, a small forest mammal, right away. Bengochea once washed a dog in all three and set it off. Soon it was barking deep in the bush. He ran after it and found it chasing a lapp in a big circle. Finally the lapp ran to a stream and tried to hide under water, in a pool. The dog stood frothing on the bank. It was the very pool of the very stream in which Bengochea had washed the dog.

The beach at Tacarib rises and falls each year. In August the sand is four feet higher. By Christmas it has receded and laid bare the rocks again.

The owner of the land at Tacarib was having a home built. The outlaws had burnt down the last one. Now that they had been arrested he thought it safe to build a new one. Bengochea was his supervisor. There were several men out there living in a barrack, a tin-roofed shelter with foam bunks. One of the men was called Bones, a brilliant hunter who had three hunting dogs. He had long, black hair and a smooth, pale face. From far off he looked like a Mayan Indian, except that he always wore shorts and Wellington boots. He kept his dogs in a kennel, really a cage, across the clearing from the barrack. He had trained his dogs so well that when he went hunting he rarely returned empty-handed.

'That man have a compass in his head,' said Bengochea. 'It don't matter which way he walk into the bush or how deep he go, he gonna walk back down the exact same way.'

There was Hinkson Beatrice, who lived in Blanchesseuse and had a gun licence because he owned a small piece of forest. You need a land title to get a gun licence. He kept his gun with him all the time, slung by a rope over his shoulder. It was a single-barrel shotgun, a very simple, plain gun: a wood stock, a barrel and a trigger. Hinkson was the oldest man there, with friendly wrinkles on his face, pulled wide across his cheeks and eyes that were narrow but glowed warmly. He wore a trilby hat and a plastic windcheater and boots. His voice was a soft, melodious drawl and there was a hum that kept going beneath all his words, like the nasal humming of the Mongolian sinus singers, or like the drone of a bagpipe.

Another of Bengochea's men was Mike Hawkins the chief carpenter (the house they were building was entirely of russet cedar boards). He had his bunk at the end of the barrack. He would sit on a stool with the papers of his year's accounting spread over the bed and put on his glasses to inspect them and make pencil marks on them. If someone called out to him he would look up, turn round, sit back against the wall, take off his glasses, and happily chat and be drawn into the joking. For a while his gravity would evaporate in laughter. And then he would put his glasses on again and get back to his figures.

Bengochea was a joker. He was tirelessly happy in the bush. The bush was where he belonged, his natural habitat. He didn't like not being able to live for free if he chose to. He didn't like the hassle of the city, the fear, the danger. The only fear in the bush was when you were far out in it after the moon had set and you thought you were lost. Once he got lost for a whole night and a day. He said that at one point, in pitch darkness of the forest night, he had heard a sharp breath by his shoulder. He span round. There was no one there, nothing. It was Papa Bwan, who leads people astray so they are never found again. Bengochea got out that time, but he said he had heard that breath again on other trips. Bones explained to him that it was some bird.

Jimmy Bengochea was always bragging about his success with women. 'I got lots of chat,' he said. 'The women like my chat.'

He claimed mutual fidelity with his girlfriend. 'It have some women does have a long eye,' he told me. 'But not mine.' She was a teacher in Port of Spain. Because she kept her mind busy she wasn't led astray by her natural heat, like most Trini women. They were so hot it ruled them, he explained. They had nothing in their heads.

There was also Mark Gilby. Gilby talked a lot. He listened to the radio and read the papers and opened conversations on current affairs and sports. 'That Chamorro is gonna have some problems, I believe,' he would suddenly throw into an evening silence. Or, 'I think it's sixteen years.' It was like a test. Did you know he was talking about the imminent English cricket victory, it having been sixteen years since they last won a Test Match against the West Indies. He talked late into the night from his bunk. You answered one another with long sentences in the darkness which never quite strung together into cogency. They were like the white dashes in the middle of a road. You each had the pleasure of formulating your own paragraphs of thought.

I helped Bones make coconut oil. We picked the copra from the knife-cracked shells with the tips of blades and grated it into bowls. He mixed the gratings with water and left them to stand overnight in the moonlight. Next day Bones scooped the cream that had formed on top, a deep layer of curd, into a pan, and boiled it on the fire for a few hours. It separated into oil and a lumpy brown mass that turned gradually browner. When it got no browner he spooned it out and the oil was left behind. He left it to cool. They used the oil to fry the bakes in the morning, lumps of dough eaten with chocolate or tea that smelt and tasted of fresh, succulent coconut because of that fresh oil.

Bengochea and Hinkson Beatrice went hunting at night. They would search the bush at dusk for the right kind of fruit trees for the animals and for the right tracks on the forest floor, and then cut two long bamboos and set them up on forked branches leaning against tree trunks, one two feet above the other: a bar to sit on and a bar to rest the feet on. They called that a sentry. They sat on the sentry waiting for the moon to set and the animals to come out to feed. They went two nights. The first they were through by three, the next at five and they didn't shoot anything. The first night they had an agouti and a manicou.

In the day Hinkson muttered to himself in his quiet melodious voice as he skinned the animals. He had a pot of water boiling on the fire, which had been set on a big sheet of metal. There were two sets of stones to rest pots on and build heat. He plunged the agouti headfirst into the pot. It was a small, brown, furry mammal, something like a badger or a rabbit. Its rounded rump stuck up into the air out of the pot. Hinkson scraped the boiled part with a knife. The hairs, long and bristly, came away leaving white, bald skin covered with little blue dots. He had to press and scrape hard. Then the rump sat in the pot, the shaved head, mouth open enough to show the ratlike incisors, staring at the tin roof with the little front paws under the chin. When he had it fully shaved he started on the manicou, a huge, dirty, white rat, an opossum. That needed a lot of boiling and very hard scraping, scraping against the grain. At one point he pressed too hard and a sickly sweet smell drifted through the barrack. Two little bubbles of gut had broken through the white skin.

When the animals were both ready he laid them side by side on the ground in the sun on a piece of iron. He gutted them and cut them up. He was going to take the manicou back for his wife. It was the only wild meat she liked.

Bengochea cooked the agouti. He was an excellent cook. In the clearing by the barrack they grew garlic and onions and peppers, as well as fruits and vegetables. He threw everything in with the flesh and made agouti stew, rich and nourishing. A thick natural gravy formed spontaneously in the pot.

Pelicans cruised the shore by Tacarib. At dusk they flopped into the water one after another. They liked the north coast.

Bengochea and I walked to Blanchesseuse together to pick up the road again for Port of Spain. As we entered the last, short valley before the town a volley of trumpeting startled not only us but also a fleet of parakeets, which rose from its many hidden perches in the foliage below and flashed briefly into view crying, before plunging back into the green depths like a school of flying fish. High trills and scales ripped through the air. It was unmistakably a trumpet, blown in the local style, hard.

The noise stopped as we moved closer to it. Finally we were walking down the path to Roy's house, a small, new house perched on the valleyside. Roy was a friend of Bengochea's. 'This Is Paradise,' a notice above the door announced, 'Respect It.'

On the porch, leaning back in a hammock, was a man with long, grey hair gathered into a pigtail and a long beard. He was wearing shorts and nothing else. He had several gold teeth and on his bare knees rested a silver trumpet.

Roy, tall, slim, polite, with carefully greased and parted hair and a clipped moustache, offered us sorrel juice. He introduced the musician: Fortunia (pronounced Fortunay) Ruiz O'Reilly. After carnival he liked to cool out for a few days in the peaceful bush, he explained, enjoying the birds and trees and flowers and the peace, sometimes taking a little stroll down to the beach, sometimes blowing a few tunes. He was freelance. He played the tents, as did his two sons, a bassist and a keyboard player. He had played behind all the big names of calypso and was moving gently towards retirement. This was what he was heading for, he said gazing out over the jungle valley. Living peacefully out in the bush, he and his trumpet at one with the birds and the trees.

NINETEEN

The blue, forested mountains project themselves out over the sea, the still sea when seen from high up with the cliffs and great flanks of foliage falling away beneath you. They stand out over the ocean, affirmative, big, real, more than real, they break through the skin of your reality and stand there like a revelation. There is a world out there that you don't know about, a world to explore. There is an uncharted life ahead of you. The grace and majesty, the splendid composure of these mountains in their green and blue robes, which make the sea look small and calm, rouse you to action. You don't have long.

Trinidad is a modern place. Mostly it is part of the world economy. But the society is bewilderingly diverse. There are rastas who have left the system and live in shacks in the mountains eating fruits and vegetables, there are plantation labourers who live in rows of cheap cottages beside the absentee owner's villa, there are oil technicians and bureaucrats and all the usual personnel of a modern economy, and fishermen who go out in diminutive craft at night with paraffin lamps hung over the stern who will be back by seven or eight in the morning or else their colleagues will know they have run into trouble, and children who walk three hours to school in the morning and three hours back in the afternoon along tracks in the bush.

I go out walking on a plantation in the middle of the island. Things behave as you want them to in the tropics. A bird's whistling rises up to a repeated note and falls again, rises and falls. I want to see the bird. It continues to flute as I approach. It sings, I see it, I walk closer, it still sings.

I'm wondering what growing cocoa looks like. I have a vague memory of there being such a thing as a cocoa pod. Many bushes around have yellow and red pods hanging beneath their leaves. I hit one pod at the stalk with a stick. It falls at my feet. I flick it onto the path, where I whack it in the middle. The cask is thick and hard and breaks in two. I pull away the upper part, from which hangs the contents of the pod: a cluster, like a small bunch of grapes, of white beans. A white slime covers them. They smell delicious, of custard, wet paint, white chocolate - somehow of all of these at once. Sure enough, it is cocoa. Strangely, the pods don't grow like other fruits from the ends of twigs. They grow from the trunk itself, sprouted out of the otherwise barren, vertical trunk, hanging there like a suckling litter.

That night I went to a rum shop called the Playboy Bar. It was a garage with a jukebox and one table, the only rum shop of Pepper Village. There I met Issa, who had changed his name from Tony when he became a Muslim. He was nineteen and had converted because he knew no love at home. One night he had woken up to find his room on fire. He had clambered out of the window and discovered that the whole house was burning down. His mother and stepfather were standing on the grass watching the blaze.

Issa wore a green wool cap and had nervous, sorrowful eyes. He had been taking on jobs here and there and acquiring a reputation in Pepper Village for being only one step ahead of the law. His Islam, a peculiarly mild and mystical brand, was giving him solace. He had a friend on a nearby plantation who had also converted, Daoud, and they had a little room where they made their meditations, burning candles and sitting on straw mats, that was smaller than the average cupboard under the stairs in Britain. Two pieces of driftwood, fine, smooth, twisted shapes that Issa had painted with rich, green gloss, rested against the wall. They found peace in this tiny cell, shelter from a loveless world.

Issa sang dub. Daoud's brother would ventriloquize the bass line through his teeth and lips and Daoud would do the drum sounds while Issa sang a plaintive line full of syncopation and yearning. He threw his young heart straight out into the song. He had hours of poetry, but no one to listen.

TWENTY

The Caribbean is a sea encircled by land, with the continent to the west and a chain of islands arching round to the east. You might expect travellers simply to make their way round it, logically taking each island in turn, moving in one direction or the other. But all the time I travelled I met no one who was doing that. Everyone had been jumping islands, retracing their steps, crossing corners of the sea only to cut back across half of it. On every island someone would ask, 'I guess you're what they call island hopping?' as if that were the normal thing to do. But to island hop is complicated and costly. You can enter no island except on a return ticket. Some islands regularly insist on your having a return ticket all the way home. Every time you move to the next island you have to have your tickets altered to satisfy the new officials.

Boat captains won't take you unless you have the right tickets for the immigration authorities. Not only that, but boats don't simply work up and down the island chain. The schooners of Carriacou, for example, sail to St Martin and back; they stop nowhere else on the way. In Dominica many boats go to St Kitts, but stop at neither Guadeloupe nor Martinique, the neighbouring islands. It would take great patience to island hop without hopping over islands.

Sometimes it works out quicker and cheaper to fly to some distant airline hub and then nearly all the way back than to fly to an island two or three along the chain. You might fly from Grenada to Antigua to get to Dominica; or from Martinique to St Martin via San Juan – in both cases this involves travelling two long sides of an isosceles triangle. It's the same with boats – unless you have your own, or limitless time, you have to travel along the popular trading routes.

It was hard for me to move on from Trinidad because I had not yet decided where I was going next. The six weeks Immigration had given me were all of a sudden nearly over. To extend my stay would have cost me a day in a waiting room and a few hundred dollars. I had a press visa for Cuba that would expire in a month, but Cuba was the opposite corner of the Caribbean and I did not feel inclined to climb into an aeroplane and miss all the islands of the Caribbean that lay between here and there. On the other hand, if I tried to go by boat around the islands or by bus through South and Central America within a month, I would have to travel through the towns and villages at such a speed that I might as well be flying over them.

I decided to forgo Cuba for the time being, hoping I would be able to renew my visa later on if I wanted. I would remain in the Antilles to visit three islands I particularly wanted to see: Grenada, Carriacou, a tiny Grenadine, and Dominica. They were all said to be unspoilt islands with their traditional cultures still alive, islands not overrun yet with tourists and cruise-ship passengers. I wanted to explore further the Antilles and their music, and then head down to the continent to conclude my journey up the Andes of eight years earlier.

My stay on Trinidad was legal for only one more day. I went to the docks, where three likely-looking boats were in: two beaten-up coastal steamers that were going to Guyana, the wrong way, and a schooner worked by a rasta family who lived in the stern and were heading for St Vincent, but not until after the weekend, too late for me.

So the following afternoon I caught a plane to Grenada, the island to the north of Trinidad. We landed just as a storm of warm rain broke and I was given a tepid shower as I walked down the steps of the plane onto the airport ramp. It was a grey, windy, swirling dusk. I shared a taxi into town with an American who had hoped to sail from Trinidad to Antigua. He had spent a month on a yacht waiting for it to leave, and finally lost patience.

The taxi driver saw my trombone over my shoulder and told me he played trumpet in a gospel band. Under cover of the airport rank he opened his car boot to prove his claim, taking his trumpet out of its case and showing me his portfolio of hymns and gospel songs. He propped a sheet of music on the case in the boot and jammed the trumpet into his face, puffing out his cheeks, and blasted out two lines.

'I learnt to read two years ago,' he said. 'A lot of fellers here don't read. They play by ear.' He pointed to his ear. The Police Band could all read, he told me. They were the island's best band.

That night I strolled around the harbour of St George's, the capital. It was like a black basin, encircled with a bowl of old clay-roofed houses. A floodlit cargo ship's engine hummed at the quay out by the harbour mouth. A floating rum shop crossed from side to side of the expanse of water, invisible, but traceable by the gap its wake made in the quilt of stars that danced in the water, and out of which void came the thump and tinkle of seaborne music. A three-masted luxury yacht glistened beside a row of four rusty coasters flying a green flag scrawled with several lines of Arabic in white. A few people sat on benches under awnings around the waterfront. It was a quiet harbour kept tidy for the cruise ships that called.

The roads that cut among the houses of the port were interwoven with alleyways winding between iron fences, turning around the corners of houses, climbing steeply. I laboured up one, my face in bright light from a backdoor lamp, my legs wading blindly in pitch blackness. I was looking for a peaceful bar.

I emerged at a junction of two roads. There was a red and white striped traffic policeman's shelter over on the far side, next to which was a yard. At the back of the yard there was a shaft of light emanating from an open door and out of which came laughter and shouts: a rum shop.

Inside, an old man was talking loudly into a telephone. He was boasting in explicit terms about the effects of under-the-counter rum on his virility. Three overweight ladies were shouting at him and each other. The life of the place was going on behind the counter. Two of the women and the old man stood between the counter and a set of open shelves, among crates and boxes of vitamins, cigarettes, beer and rum. Beyond the shelves was an enormous table, one end of which was covered with huge saucepans and plastic bowls, and the rest filled with dirty plates, and around which sat a group of people, on benches, drinking and eating and talking. They spanned at least three generations. Beside the table was a sink and a large set of black catering gas rings which roared beneath more giant pots. Now and then a girl or young man or an old woman came in to buy a sweet or a cigarette, but it seemed to be more of a meeting place than a business.

Sitting at a small table the near side of the counter with my back to the action I was able to write a page or two of my diary in peace. But there was no shortage of distractions. A scrap of paper taped onto the wall in front of me, near the door, caught my eye more than once. It read: 'Absolutely no credit, you are being inhuman asking, still, this notice include everyone, if you don't pay how we to buy more goods?'

And on the radio a woman was giving a speech. She sounded like a politician: 'Mr Speaker, our hospitals are guaranteed to make you ill. So, Mr Speaker, why don't we ask the business community to make contributions to our hospitals in return for a moratorium on their delinquency?'

A cellar door of heavy wood fitted an arch in the stone wall beside me. The building was at least two hundred years old. Slaves had probably been locked behind the door. The thought of it distracted me.

I felt someone standing over me. 'Oh boy, lemme see you writin,' he said. I glanced up at him, laughed, and carried on. He was an old man with grey hair and shiny, rheumy eyes. 'OK, OK,' he said. 'You writing OK.'

He stood there a while longer. 'Research?' he asked.

It wasn't, but I nodded.

'From the way you write it I realize research.' He walked back to the kitchen area and shouted out, 'He writin research.'

Then a young man came out from behind the shelving and approached me. He introduced himself, announcing that he often looked after tourists, and sat down at my table. I closed my book. He was the son of a diplomat, he told me, and had lived all over the world. He had a transatlantic accent and smelt strongly of aftershave. He was well shaven and had a chubby face. But his eyes faintly showed nervousness.

The women behind the counter invited me over for a plate of chicken and fish, peas and rice, plantains and watercress, and plenty more beer. Two of them were sisters called Silvia and Celia, both of whom were large and had short curled hair and puffy faces. Their cheeks shone with a film of sweat and grease from all the cooking. They watched me eat and kept piling more on my plate. They were the owners of the rum shop.

They told me it was the eve of St Patrick's Day. Grenada has seven parishes, and the parish of St Patrick was hosting a carnival the next day at its chief town. The ladies were hiring their own bus to go up there the next day. They invited me along.

When the sisters closed up they directed me to Tasties, which I understood to be a nearby bar. In fact it was a barbecue chicken stall a half-hour amble out of town. On my way there I ran into a lone woman easing her man trouble with a midnight stroll. She told me about her boyfriend's girlfriend, who came from St Vincent and worked in the petrol station and should never have left her island.

Tasties was a tantalizing goal, always seemingly just round the next bend, or at the lights ahead, so I kept going. Its music came clearly across the flat, black bay. When I finally saw it, a kiosk with an oildrum barbecue outside and a huge sound system blasting ragamuffin, a brand of reggae I had yet to come to terms with, I was so surprised, having expected to be able to sit and drink and work, that for a long time I kept my distance, watching the shifting clientele from the shadows in a state of bewilderment. I didn't know what to do – drink, even though I was drinking for strictly professional reasons, namely to lubricate my pen, or go back to my clean guest house and let the fan cool me to sleep, or have a leg of chicken. While puzzling it out I watched the drinkers drift up to the counter, receive a plastic cup, knock it back and then hold it under the tap of an urn of iced water to wash it down. I soon found myself drawn into their midst.

The next day, after a morning of coffee and further attempts at unclogging the pen, I was driven by Silvia up to her home in the hills above St George's. It was a comfortable modern house with one old fort, now a hospital, rising up behind, and another, now a prison, squatting on a crest in front. In the garden, which swooped away from the veranda, were lime, banana and papaya trees, three pigs, some sheep and a long pile of old pieces of wood. Her son, in shorts, was sweeping the sitting room to a tape of ragamuffin. There was a box of empty bottles by the French windows.

When the minibus arrived an hour late it was already filled with the two sisters' friends, but as yet none of their laps were occupied and everyone was sitting in reasonable comfort, so there was no question of the bus really being described as near full. The three of us, Silvia, Celia and I, clambered aboard.

It was Sunday. Children were swimming on all the beaches, boys hurdling waves, girls wallowing in the shallows. The jungle sprawled all the way down from the mountain peaks to the beaches and rocks. It took an hour to drive the twenty miles from the south to the north coast.

The capital of St Patrick parish is Sauteurs which is perched at the top of a small cliff. It was named after the last of the island's Carib Indians, who leapt off the cliff when cornered by the French in the eighteenth century. They chose suicide over defeat. The celebrations were dubbed a 'fiesta'. It was an emphatically Caribbean event: a population of African descent on a British island celebrating an Irish saint's day with a Spanish party in a town named in French after the heroic suicide of some Amerindians.

Parked cars crammed the outer streets of Sauteurs. On the one main street that rose from the fishing beach up to the church and the cliff, bands and disco sound systems had been set up. Flags and streamers fluttered on ropes above the crowds. Every rum shop was open and many independent drink vendors had slogged up the street with a pair of filled iceboxes and a stack of paper cups. Everyone was drinking rum. Barmen would decant from large bottles into old Coke or Lucozade bottles, and into diminutive bottles half the height of Coke and half as slender. The drinkers poured out their shots from these, into tiny paper

cups. On every bar there would also be a bottle of cold water.
They knocked back shots of rum and swilled them down with
water, as I had done the night before.

I laboured on alone in the back room of a rum shop on
Sauteurs beach for the remainder of the afternoon. It was a
very small room. Landlords create the tiniest spaces for people
to drink in: minute cubicles with tables the size of a chair seat
and stools the size of a book. Even a small rum shop may give
up space for a tiny room or two, because if drinkers take over
a room the price of the drinks goes up. My room had a stable
door overlooking the sea. I gave up working at sunset and sat
for a while looking out over the smooth purple sea and smoking
a cigarette. The smoke corkscrewed lazily out the door.

In the thronged street I found the driver of the minibus and
one of the sisters jamming up together in front of the Police Band,
who were not playing well. Their brass were out of tune, the
vocalist was singing staccato to hide his own intonation problems
and the tempo was dragging. There were twelve or fifteen of
them on a wide shallow stage. They had a uniform of tie-dye
shirts and glum faces. They didn't even look like they might be
playing well. There was also a five-piece steel band further up the
street, and another soca band that was playing mainly reggae and
some zouk, the music of the French Caribbean.

I had been hoping to enjoy hearing the songs I had been
playing from the other side of the speakers, but the systems put
out reggae. I paced the length of the street hopping from bank to
bank of the yard-deep ditches that flanked it, between the crowd
on the pavement and the crowd on the road, in search of soca. I
caught the tail end of the odd song. Finally I found a weak system
playing a tape of Mighty Sparrow hits in a shop beyond the main
action. A few shy or weary souls were dancing in the dim light the
shop cast across the road. A man was selling drinks from the back
of a pick-up truck outside. His wife was selling fish sandwiches.

Silvia and Celia were still wining in the street, drinks in hand,
with the bus driver. They had him sandwiched between their two
behinds and were rolling him around. He was grinning wildly.
We didn't leave till late.

The next day I went along to the police station and introduced
myself to the Police Band. There were two constables in the band
room. The rest of the band were in the courtyard outside playing
basketball. They both showed me their music parts and their
instruments. They played everything: Bach, jazz, calypso, zouk,
swing, salsa.

One of the men was a trombonist and he handed me his
instrument. It was an old silver trombone from France, made
in the thirties. It had a very small bell and a neglected slide that
nevertheless glided exactly as you wanted. I played on it. It had
a bright and full sound, and I found I could play things on it
with great ease that I could hardly play at all on mine. With it
in my hands I suddenly became a far better trombonist, far more
agile and delicate, than I had ever been before. It was the best
trombone I ever played.

The other was a saxophonist called Brian. He was a very good
musician and had his own jazz band, but he was deliberating
whether or not to leave Grenada for the United States. He asked
me to play a duet with him, and put a version of 'Raindrops
Keep Falling on my Head' on a music stand. We swung through
it sympathetically.

In the afternoon I went down to the airline office by the
harbour. I wanted to arrange my transport up the islands.
I intended to look into the flights and then investigate the
maritime possibilities. But after spending the whole afternoon
and the following morning in the airline office mainly waiting
in line but also trying to figure out a way of dodging the
return-ticket laws of the region – which turned friendly looking
thirty-dollar hops into two thousand-dollar monsters, with one
quick pout of the assistant's over-lipsticked lips – I decided to
stride down to the docks, bag on shoulder, or rather, after a few
of those downhill strides, in shoulder, and go to sea.

And sure enough there was a tramp steamer waiting at the
quay, about to set sail for Carriacou.

TWENTY-ONE

'You the sax feller who was on the BBC talk show?' a rasta asked me as I rounded the deck structure at the stern of the MV *Winifred*. He spoke quickly, excitedly, with a grin, so briskly in fact that I only arrived at his question after a few repetitions.

'Trombone,' I said, hoping it was some kind of answer.

'Yeah, yeah. Trombone,' he agreed. 'Yeah, Anne Marie Grey was talking to you all about you travelling with your saxophone in the Caribbean.' He was smiling at me intently, as if waiting for some sign of recognition.

I suddenly realized what he meant. So it had been broadcast. I had given an interview on a World Service programme, the 'Caribbean Magazine', a month or so before leaving England, with the presenter Anne Marie Grey. She had told me they would broadcast it later.

I asked him his name.

'Algie,' he said. I thought he said IG.

'IG?'

'Yeah. Algie.'

He was a slim, fit man in his early thirties. He had a short goatee beard that curled under his chin and small, rounded cheeks. He looked friendly. There was a certain childlike vulnerability in his face, as if he were afraid of being hurt or scolded.

But he promptly offered to be my official escort on this voyage to Carriacou and during my stay there, and told me that probably wherever I went I would meet people who had heard the radio show and would help me out.

He wore sunglasses, a yellow tee-shirt and carried a brown paper bag with three long white bread rolls in one hand and a 3D Superwoofer cassette deck in the other. He was playing a tape of reggae remakes of soul and Motown classics. We sat in the stern on a large piece of foam rubber. Beside us was a bundle of short mahogany planks tied together with string, which were what Algie had come to Grenada for. You couldn't get hard wood on Carriacou and he was a woodcarver.

He had had a hard time becoming an artist – when I asked him if he regarded his carving as artistic expression, he said, 'Yes, yes. It is in Arts and Crafts' – because his family had wanted to keep him in the mainstream. Most of his close relatives were in London and they couldn't understand why he didn't join them. But even St George's was too much for him. 'You gotta keep out of the system. Too much hustle, too much worry. My soul was never at peace in the system.'

He had gone up into the mountains of Grenada for a year and lived there with another rasta, in a pair of shacks in the bush. He had grown some marijuana, as well as a full garden of fruits and vegetables cultivated from wild cuttings and seeds. He had slept on a bamboo bunk under a tarpaulin. When the mosquitoes were bad he burnt coils. The cover kept the rain off.

During that year his soul had found peace, escaped its restlessness, so that he could concentrate on his carving and painting. His friend there taught him some woodworking techniques. He would meditate and carve and watch the insect life, which was full of wisdom. There was wisdom wherever you looked. For example, the ant: no matter how fast they are going they always stop to greet one another. Now he was at peace. He lived on Carriacou, a Grenadine whose capital had a population of under one thousand, in a house on the far side of the island where he had a garden and his tools. A friend sold his pieces at the market and another fellow had a few in St George's. He had no wife or kids. He didn't believe he could find a woman who wanted to live the way he did. Maybe he would one day. Meanwhile he was living in peace.

The *Winifred* was a small white coastal steamer with a large deckhouse that plied its trade sailing up and down the Windward Islands. There were two chairs aboard the vessel, one a wicker sofa in the stern, the other an old armchair on the roof. The roof was used as an open-aired floor with a metal deck that ran the length of the boat, interrupted only by the wheelhouse and a pair of ventilator hoods, between which was wound a long silver wire for fishing. Once we were plunging and rearing up the coast of Grenada a man put out the line with a silver spinner the size of a mackerel that bounced on the white wake. As he let out more and more line it was able to take in the flesh of the water and lay there wriggling to lure tuna or marlin.

The sun slipped beneath the rim of the sea. The green of Grenada's hills, which had been growing deeper and stronger by the second, gave up its intensity, relaxed into smokiness and gradually faded, merged with the weakening sky.

Pick-up trucks and men were waiting on the jetty. Algie struggled to the road with his package of wood, all the weight concentrated in that string knot at the top. He left it in the back of a pick-up that he and another passenger were sharing as a taxi and rushed me to a guesthouse a couple of doors along. He didn't want to keep the taxi waiting. He told me he would see me tomorrow.

The guesthouse was a clean place, the second floor of a new store called Ade's Dream, owned by the same family that ran the small supermarket across the street. It was in fact so new that a brother who had flown down from America to help fix it up was still hammering in one of the rooms. He was leaving next day but not before all the work demanded of him was completed.

I lay on my bed listening to the hammer blows for a while, still basking in the glow that follows a sea crossing. As I lay there a man I had met seven years earlier rose up from my restfulness. I had sat next to him on a four-day Magic Bus ride from Athens to London. He was nearly thirty, which then was still unimaginably old to me, and had been living on a Greek island for two years in a separatist community under the leadership of a wise old man. He had been staying there in order to stop being unhappy, which was what the old man claimed to have a cure for. It was something to do with having a naughty child inside you. The man on the Magic Bus was both a writer and a musician and he told me about his life, in particular about a year he had spent travelling in Italy and Greece. He had taken his flute with him and busked his way around. At the time, sitting in the bus, it sounded idyllic to me. What a way to spend a year, I said. Why not longer? And then he told me it had been one long nightmare. Why? He said he didn't really know, he just hadn't seemed to want to do it and had made himself do it in the first place simply because he couldn't think of anything else to do. I had thought to myself: I'm lucky that I'll never be screwed up like this man.

But now here I was, twenty-seven, travelling in the Caribbean with my trombone over my shoulder. Was I doing it because I didn't know what else to do? A shiver went through me. Had that man jinxed me? Was I travelling because I didn't know what I wanted to do more? Was I meandering as aimlessly as he had seemed to be?

I finally gave up trying to sleep and went out to find myself some dinner. A nearby rum shop had a little extra room for a restaurant, furnished with white plastic tables and chairs, a murky aquarium, a strip light and patches of different wallpapers, and was owned by a gruff woman who sat outside shelling a huge mound of peas. The girl who served in the restaurant when there was a customer, and otherwise helped shell peas, said quietly: 'She ignorant.'

At first I recoiled in horror from the little restaurant, a repellent cell of pseudo modernity, of Western consumerism, especially since there was an open rum shop next door. But if I wanted to eat, even just a roti, it had to be in there, and with a place mat and a napkin and cutlery – it was the first time I hadn't eaten a roti by hand – and the bizarreness of it finally won me.

The fat woman was playing reggae next door. The electricity supply was inconstant. The music whined gently up and down like some specially innocuous siren. 'Whatsa matter you,' went the song, 'Ah shut up you face.' It seemed a song that suited the woman, as she laboured her bulk from the bar to the heap of pea husks. She scowled at the peas. She scowled at everything.

At eight in the morning Algie was calling for me. He wanted to show me Carriacou, and the best way of doing that was to walk up the hill to the hospital from where you could see not only the whole island but also the chain of the Grenadines reaching up to St Vincent.

It was a long hot climb up a potholed lane. The vegetation was

sparse and parched. Carriacou was short of rain. It had no rivers.
The hospital had been built high on the hill for the relative cool
up here, out of the worst of the fiery breath of the wind.

The island was a crescent ridge falling gently down through
fields and scrublands on either side to a sea of an unnatural
sapphire. It looked like a treated photograph. It was a sickly
turquoise. Further offshore there were large stains of dark blue,
coral reefs, to relieve the stomach. Here and there a spit of sand
rose out of the sea, disembodied and barren, surreal.

Algie and I sat on an old wooden cable drum that lay on its
side to serve as a table, under a tree. There was a shop opposite.
We drank Cokes. One day he wanted to go to London just to see
it, but he would never go back into the system. It wouldn't be fair
on his soul. If I ever wanted to go up into the mountains with him
– because 'The mountain has it, the mountain is a sacred place,
on the mountain you find enlightenment, it is there, where did
Moses go to get the Ten Commandments, Moses take off your
shoes, the Lord said, you are in a sacred place' – Algie would
take me. A month, a week, a year, whatever I needed to find my
peace and practise my art. Algie would take me up and show me
how to live there.

TWENTY-TWO

I caught a dawn flight from Carriacou up to Guadeloupe,
from where I could easily get to Dominica. Guadeloupe
was one of the French islands, a department of France. I
knew it was more developed than most of the Caribbean,
but I did not know how much more.

The flight, which called at several islands on the way, was like
dive-bomber training. We swooped over mountains and plunged
to airstrips the length of tennis courts and the width of mule
tracks. The aircraft was a STOL (Short Take-Off and Landing)

plane, and it certainly lived up to its name. It was half-way to a helicopter. The pilots were not shy of their skill or nerves. They left the cockpit door wide open so we could scan the diminutive landscapes ahead for the back gardens in which we were to land. Invariably they appeared only an instant before the wheels found them.

We flew from one paradise island to the next, past huge ancient tree-clad peaks looming over still bays, past snow-white beaches lapped by mint-green water, past little towns tumbled by steep slopes to the water's edge, past awesome black and khaki volcanoes smouldering beneath their own grey cumuli. At last we flew into cloud. When we dropped out of it, as if from some magician's cloak, we were plucked into another world. It was a familiar world. Below sprawled a grey metropolis. Factory chimneys smoked, gantries rested beside container ships, tankers lay beside constellations of round petrol tanks, and a city of pallid high-rise blocks erected on a grid, accommodation for the operators of the industry, spread over the plain. It was Pointe-à-Pitre, the capital of Guadeloupe.

The airports we had been visiting had terminal buildings like garden sheds. Here there was an enormous concrete complex. The letters saying 'Bienvenue à Pointe-à-Pitre' running half the length of the structure were several feet apart. Inside there were baggage carousels, flags, enormous colourful maps of the island painted on the walls, ranks of passport desks. Jumbo jets called several times a day to deliver and collect holidaymakers.

But I didn't lose heart. Guadeloupe has two halves, Grande Terre, which is flat, developed and has the chief city and airport, and Basse Terre, which is mountainous and less developed.

I had met a Swiss man on the plane who also wanted to go straight to Basse Terre city. He was called Peter. He had tidy blond hair swept back from his face, and a ruddy suntan. On the bus we discussed motives for travelling. Peter believed that people travelled either to prove something to themselves or to escape home. You had these young people with lists in their heads of exotic places that it would change them to have visited. The mentality was akin to the mountaineer's or the

single-handed yachtsman's. Seeing life meant seeing the world.
Solitary experience outvalued love, even though it never satisfied
because there were always more mountains waiting. Nevertheless,
he added, there were a lot of interesting places to see. It made
sense to go and see them. Which was why he was travelling.

Zouk and merengue played over the radio on the bus the whole
way. Zouk, which comes from Martinique and Guadeloupe, is
fast slick music with a heavy bass beat. The lyrics are in Patois,
and zouk itself is a Patois word, meaning 'party'. Zouk grew out
of cadass (cadence), a style that became popular in the seventies.
The biggest zouk band is Kassav and they play all over the world.
They are a huge team, as many as forty or fifty people on stage,
but they are run by a core of three: Georges Decimus, Jacob F.
Desvarieux and Jocelyne Beroard. Jocelyne Beroard sings and
writes. She has the finest voice in the French Caribbean, clear
and soft and pure like a choirboy's, but rasping too when she
wants it to be.

Every other song on the radio was by Kassav. I enjoyed
hearing snatches of their vocals and trying to work them out.
Take for example, 'Siwo, om dous kom siwo,' which translates
in French roughly to 'Sirop, homme doux comme sirop,' and so
into English as 'Syrup, a man sweet like syrup.' Or 'Pale mwen
dous,' meaning 'Talk sweetly to me.' Or 'Zot vini pou zouk'
approximating to 'The others (*les autres*) come for the party.'
Or 'Zouk la se sel medikaman nou ni' which becomes 'Zouk is
the only medicine we have.'

Merengue comes from the Dominican Republic. It is an
old musical style, as old as Cuban son, which emerged from
rural obscurity into the dance halls of Havana in the twenties.
Merengue has the fastest beat of any Caribbean music. Originally
accordion and saxophone were its characteristic instruments, but
now all the usual electric instruments and full brass have found
their place. All the Caribbean styles are closely related and
merengue has almost exactly the same beat as soca, only faster.
And merengue and zouk have the same frenetic feel, blended with
the same slick style.

The road across Guadeloupe was smooth and with the centre

lines freshly painted. The cars were shining Renaults and Citroëns, the villages clean and their buildings modern. Only beheaded palms gave notice of Caribbean hurricanes, and the odd wooden house with ornate eaves and rich primary colours painted on its shutters and shingle walls unsettled the familiarity.

Basse Terre is a great blue and grey volcano with its peak always wrapped in cloud. And Basse Terre city is a port, strung along the shore at the foot of the mountain. We arrived in the early afternoon. Every shop was closed and the town was deserted. On the main square, overlooking the empty concrete dockside, the doors of an ancient café stood open. Inside iron pillars held up the ceiling. An old woman sat by the door fanning herself with a newspaper and puffing and crying out now and then, 'Chaleur.' She had few customers, a shot or two and a soda to chase, in the hour we were there. Finally she summoned the energy to trudge over to the switch for the ceiling fan. This was the only oasis of shade. We fortified ourselves with a few litres of Coca-Cola and set off to find a hotel. The tingle of caffeine in the fingers wore off after a few paces in the afternoon sun. Our brisk strides slackened. We were soon pausing between every step of the climb up to the Hotel de Basse Terre, a modern building that we could see rising clear of all neighbours.

It was a simple place: an open stairwell, a long balcony and five rooms on each floor, windowless, unless you arrived early enough to get a room with a balcony. It had evidently had good write-ups in the guide books because the clientele consisted of pairs of holidaying French women, who left the showers with only handtowels for modesty and lingered on the way to their cells.

The man who ran the hotel had one enormous buck tooth and a ball of frizzy hair. He was skinny and wore purple flared trousers and an unbuttoned shirt. He was polite but inflexible about immediate payment. He was doing a roaring trade, even on a day like this when the town lay in coma.

We joined the stupor for what remained of the afternoon, in one of his ovens. It had a fan but it merely made the room function like a convection oven: you put the person in, closed the door, and switched on the fan. The person lay on one of the two beds, which sagged like hammocks and had mattresses of foam that heated on contact with human flesh and moulded to it. The hot air swirled round and round basting them evenly until they passed out. An hour or two later, when they were glistening from head to toe with succulent melted fat and had had most of the moisture burnt out of them, you could take them out and prod them for signs of life.

I awoke with a start. The door was open and had allowed in an impertinent breath of fresh air which immediately filled my head with a dull ache and parched my throat. Like one lost in the desert I staggered around the room searching for water, for a basin and a tap, and banged my shin on a bidet. For a terrible moment I eyed this as perhaps my only available source of life-giving water. But even this was of no use to me. It was the rim-outlet kind, and had no plug even if I had been desperate enough to fill it and drink from it. I was furthering my quest outside the room on the landing, which was open to the sky through a large hole in the roof and to the breeze at either end, when a sound on the wind stopped me in my tracks. It was drumming, unmistakably, a fast beat composed of several percussion instruments. Something in the resonance, or in the variability of the rhythmic composition, told my finely tuned ear that it was live music.

A voice said, 'I thought so. Today is a holiday. Mi-Carême. It's a carnival.' It was Peter, calling from the balcony which overlooked the town. Lent was too long for people with carnival in their bones. They gave themselves a half-way reward.

I found the shower and slumped against its cool, concrete wall.

TWENTY-THREE

It was a small carnival: seven or eight masquerade bands that worked their way around the town in the late afternoon and over sunset, and then disbanded. There were no big crowds. Along the main street spectators lined the pavements loosely. The kiosks selling cigarettes and sweets and newspapers didn't open up for it. It was just a light Lent relief.

The bands moved fast. They danced mainly to drums. Each band had around twenty drummers, and some had a handful of melodic instruments: either a trombone and trumpet or two, or, in the case of two bands, a pair of keyboards on the open tailgate of a pick-up truck that crawled along in front.

They had normal drums but they also used big blue plastic bins tied round their necks with scarves, and plastic buckets and pots of all sizes. They played fast carnival music, a rhythm close to merengue. The other instruments played no melodies, just chords and arpeggios.

The masquerade bands were also small, with no more than thirty in each. You had to walk fast to keep up with them. One wore red and black, the girls in black trousers and red bikini tops of satin, the boys in black hats and red shirts. Another band wore tall straw hats and tunics made out of old sacks. They ran through the streets beating their drums and crying out a fierce song that was more like a war chant. One of them blew a conch shell. There was a band of children in red, with teachers fussing over them and spoiling their fun, causing them to walk quietly and shyly, without smiling.

The thin crowd on the main street had to wait a long time between bands. Rum drinkers in the old woman's shop would get up from their tables and stand watching in the doorway when they heard a band coming. Half an hour's heavy rain came down and by the time it stopped it was night. Only one more band came by, followed by a car. The masqueraders' feet and their shadows flashed across the yellow glare of the headlights on the wet street. After this last band the woman closed up shop.

I found peace on the hotel balcony. The carnival was evaporating, with the last vapours of music drifting up from the plain of rooftops below. The sea beyond was dark blue, and rich grey clouds floated in the luminous sky.

The next evening, another sunset. In the one corner of Pointe-à-Pitre where I felt safe, beside a collapsed fishing shed, on a wharf warped by the last hurricane, I contemplated my day in Guadeloupe and calculated my fading chances of ever getting off the island. Pointe-à-Pitre is a sprawling modern city, and nothing comes easy here. I queued for two hours this afternoon to make a phone call in the Post Office, which had taken me some time to locate, only to find that without a passport to hand over I wouldn't be allowed near a cubicle. All the public telephones on the street used special cards which you could buy only at one telephone office. Queues snaked all around the inside of banks. I spent the morning in one only to be told that my particular brand of traveller's cheques was unacceptable. It was an expensive city too, more expensive than Paris.

Even the market, in a central square, was expensive. The stalls sold fruit and vegetables and clothing, and many had arrays of aerosols and soaps and perfumes spread out on their counters. But these were not cosmetics for the body. There were 'eaux pour être aimée', there were aerosols that generated 'Répugnance' or 'Triomphe'. You would spray yourself with the appropriate fragrance before a visit from a wanted or an unwanted lover. There was soap that made you 'irrésistible'. 'Money-drawing Room Spray,' one can boasted. 'Amour Éternel,' claimed another. 'Success Spray,' bragged a third. But on each of them, in small print around the base, the government had stamped, 'This aerosol does not contain supernatural powers.'

Peter had confirmed that the neighbouring Antille, Dominica, was the most beautiful and least spoilt in the West Indies, which was welcome news since I had been trying to arrange the speediest possible escape there all morning. I discovered there was an express catamaran service to Dominica the next day. But having undertaken an arduous round of travel agents, with long waits in each during which I strove to muster interest in cruise ship brochures and wound my nerves so tight that I almost came to believe I would like to go on a cruise, in fact wished I were on a cruise, the vacation option that figures showed has the most re-bookings, and having been told repeatedly that I couldn't make a reservation because I had credit cards, travellers' cheques, dollars, everything in fact except a wad of colonial cash, francs, and because I didn't have my passport on me, I ultimately got nowhere. At one agency the possibility of a citizen's arrest for not having it suddenly became very real. I had to back out fast under cover of a sudden lapse in my French.

Sitting on the dock waiting for nightfall, mangled rods of iron protruding from the concrete beside me, I watched a group of fishermen standing around a boat on a trailer beside the wharf. A large woman, probably the wife of one of them, had been sitting in the front seat of a car with one leg out for the last two hours. She hadn't moved, she hadn't said or done anything. A field of iron shacks and disused yards spread one way, the other the sea was the deep blue of sunset, very calm. Across the water were the big docks, and above them the grey hills of Basse Terre which lifted their heads into cloud.

I had hardly eaten for two days. Either the heat or the prices had killed my appetite.

I ate a slow lunch the next day and then slept for an hour in the bandstand on the main square, which offered the only shade around. I had checked out of my hotel. I was leaving for Dominica. Or I hoped I was, having secured enough cash for the catamaran ticket.

I woke up and walked to the port, to the warehouse where the catamaran's office was supposed to be. There was no sign of anyone. There was no office, no counter, it was just a warehouse, although it did have a curious roped-off area like a dance-floor in the middle with a loud-speaker in each corner and flowers arranged in tall pots and strings of carnival banners hanging from girders in the roof. It was either the relics of a party or a permanent welcome-station set up for passengers disembarking from cruise ships.

After two hours a lady in a jacket and skirt arrived with a briefcase in hand. She walked into the warehouse, looked around and called out, 'Anyone for Martinique?'

I was alone in the building. 'Dominica?' I answered.

She took my money, wrote the ticket, which of course had to be a return, what with the one-way ban, but she had no change, and not until they were casting off the lines did she reach across with the sixty francs she owed me.

I stood on a small deck in the stern feeling the warm breeze stiffen and, with the murky dusk thickening, I watched short strings of lights appear out of the gloom. The boat, white and new, was lurching and pitching on the sea. It threw out huge plumes of water ten yards into the air behind us. It was a jet boat, a brand-new catamaran, and extremely fast. The stars were out in force, thick like a froth. Sometimes clouds erased them. Two men were out on the deck too. One sat on the railings at the back holding on tight, the other stood by the door, put off by the rolling and the speed. I ate a sandwich and a packet of crisps, in exchange for fifty francs.

Soon the mountains of Dominica wiped the sky clean black. The town of Roseau, the capital, appeared, small and friendly and built of tin and wood and studded with crowns of tropical fronds. The air became hot and fragrant again as we slowed down. Men unloaded the luggage onto a fork-lift truck at the dock.

A taxi, a large, quiet Nissan, took me to the historic Cherry Lodge Hotel, established in 1892, a huge, wooden edifice where all the inner walls were partitions topped by lattice-work. When you turned off the light the room filled with dim illumination from other rooms and you heard conversations across the hall and laughter. It was like staying in an Amerindian longhouse.

You had partial privacy and you felt not alone, not an isolated nucleus but part of a community. I slept soundly.

TWENTY-FOUR

Dominica is the most mountainous of the Antilles. It is a clump of old volcanoes rising out of the ocean and draped in thick rainforest. It was never developed like the other islands. In the seventeenth and eighteenth centuries it was not suited for the sugar industry since its terrain was too steep for large plantations, and today it has too few beaches for the holiday business. Most of its beaches are black.

The Carib Indians survived longest on Dominica, sheltered by the geography. They are still there today. In the early years of this century their great chief Jolly John fought for the creation of a Carib Reserve, which he won. The wild north-east coast of the island is now the Carib Territory. The hills and forests also used to protect camps of maroons, run-away slaves, who sometimes fought side by side with the Caribs against colonial militias.

For a long time Dominica was just an island where slave ships called to stock up on provisions and water. It is the lushest of the Antilles with its mountains full of streams and pools and falls, and hardly a day goes by when the trade winds do not unload a shower gathered over the Atlantic.

The island lies between Guadeloupe and Martinique. The French and English fought over it for three centuries, and it changed hands many times. The official language is English – it was a British colony up until 1978 – but everybody also speaks Patois, and the culture is predominantly French, or Creole. It was in Dominica that cadass first emerged, the music that later became zouk. A band called Exile One developed the style, exported it to Martinique and then emigrated to Brooklyn.

Dominica's population is only 80,000, not enough to support ten professional musicians.

Today zouk and reggae blare all over the island, from the bars and shops and in the Toyota mini-buses that serve as public transport. Dominica is full of rum shops, little wooden houses that people turn into stores and bars beside their homes.

Roseau is a ramshackle town of old and new houses arranged on a grid. It lies in the middle of the west coast of the island, on the Caribbean side.

The highest waterfall on Dominica is Trafalgar Falls. To reach it you have to climb up a gully between black boulders and shining forest, but even from far off the roar smothers all other sounds. You catch glimpses of the falls now and then, a plume of white like a bird's tail cleaving the green of the foliage, feathers ruffling in layer upon layer like many veils, floating, bright silk over faded gauze. There is a trail of a kind – here and there a log leaning against a rock provides a surreptitious step, and sometimes a shoe print shows in the black mud – but the barefoot guides who accost you at the entrance to the forest have kept it barely traceable. Every natural feature may lead to the Falls, but as long as there is no actual way-marked path they can honestly ply their trade. What they take you to is a surreal scene.

The falling water has either pounded bare an ore in the rock or coated the rock with some mineral of its own. A set of broad, bright orange steps leads down to a pool shivering under the fall of spray. Basking on the steps are bright, pink people. There is a sense of great peace here, the roar seeming quieter, creating the feeling of stillness, immobility, calm at the eye of the storm.

There is also a sense of abandon, the kind of eroticism generated in a sauna, of organized nudity. The fall and the pool in the woods, the majestic column of water roaring unseen among the foliage – even the search for the source of the noise has a prurient quality. You pick your way through the dark under-growth shielded from the sky by the forest canopy, wondering when you will actually see what you can already hear. This is the sylvan grotto of pastoral convention. But here it bursts the flies of poetry and emerges as real, an instinct predating poetry.

At the Emerald pool, a small fall and cave in the heart of the island's mountain forest, I rounded a corner of rock and stumbled upon a couple overcome by the instinct. At first the little shock the nudity gave confused me. There was a man with his back to me standing on tiptoes with his legs bent and spread wide. His buttocks kept changing shape, from convex to concave and back. He had the purposeful concentration of a carpenter at a bench, as if he were performing some intricate craft. Then I realized that he was, and between his legs were the hams of a woman kneeling in front. They were both looking into the darkness of the grotto, in which her brief cries echoed.

A small party had collected at the last bend before the pool before me. A middle-aged French woman in a white baseball cap that held a Foreign Legionnaire's headshawl in place, and otherwise draped in long, white clothes like someone who could not bear the smallest touch of sunlight, turned around beaming and said to all of us, 'Ah. They are enjoying life.' She watched openly, eyes bright. The tall, slim Adonis with her, with olive skin and short black curls, lit a cigarette nervously and walked a couple of steps back, enough to draw the curtain of rock across. He glanced at me and puffed hard.

After several minutes the man with the mesmerizing buttocks looked over his shoulder and, with his partner, splashed into the pool laughing. They hugged each other in a mixture of embarrassment and pride. We took our cue and walked on down to the tiny beach of pebbles, where the French woman at once shed her garments to reveal a body tanned all over. Her boyfriend, or gigolo, or son, whatever, slowly undid his belt, pulled it out of his jeans, rolled it up and placed it on a stone, while she waded into the water towards the performers, who were still laughing in each other's arms near the churning water at the head of the pool. She laughed loudly.

One afternoon I caught a bus to the village of Soufrière in the south, and walked up to the sulphur springs above the town.

Several children from Soufrière came with me, showing me the way, a long lane leading up between banana groves. Forested valley sides rose up either way. There was a sulphur spring and a hot spring, which had been dammed to form a pool of clay-red water. The local lore about unusual heat pertained: if you bathed in the hot water, I was told, the merest drop of cold water touching you afterwards would make you feverish for weeks. You had to be certain that it wouldn't rain on your way home. Above all, if you wanted to swim in the sulphur stream, which was cold, as well as the hot one, you had to do that first. It was far safer to go from the cold to the hot than from the hot to the cold.

One of the children, a ten-year-old boy who had been explaining the perils of the hot water to me excitedly on the way up, didn't risk the sulphur at all. He only went into the hot. A radiant smile illuminated his face as his body disappeared into the warm, red fluid, and glowed until long after he climbed out again. As soon as he did he pulled on his shirt and shorts and shoes and could not walk back down to the village fast enough.

When we reached the town of Soufrière again music was blaring from a bar. The sun was about to go down. I felt refreshed and clean and faintly exhausted: just in the mood for a rum and some music. I went into the bar, a small concrete hall. It was full of children. There were infants in children's arms, toddlers being held out at arm's length as they stood or waddled about on the floor and children of every other age. Anyone who could walk was dancing. Some danced fluently and beautifully, some energetically and rhythmically, some energetically and out of time. But they all moved, however they could.

The weak rays of the dying sun glowed through windows in the far wall. Some faces were deep, rich orange. I drank rum and Coke and danced. All of the music was zouk. I wined away confidently until a woman came up and showed me the correct movements. Two beats to the left, two to the right. It was loud and the brass parts were wonderful long lines that skipped around over the beat. They owed more to salsa than to soca. The musicians even performed solos.

I went out to pee in the dark. There were a few young men in the road. I asked them where you could go to take a leak. One of them said, 'Right here,' pointing to a hedge next to a house. I thanked him and got to it.

'Eh,' I heard someone call. I knew it was directed at me but there was nothing I could do about it and so I carried on. It had to be over soon, although it was taking longer than I had expected. 'Eh,' the man called again. 'Pick it up. Pick it up.' He was right next to me so I had to look around. He was glaring at me.

'I'm sorry,' I said, still at it. 'The guy told me here.'

'Who said—' And then an argument got going between three of them which cut me out. Under cover of it I made my escape back into the throng inside.

TWENTY-FIVE

I went up into the mountains next day. I walked into the woods, up to a clearing with a view over the whole mountainous interior of the island. It was late afternoon, not long before sunset, when the light was still stern and uncompromising. The forest swept down from my feet.

I was feeling happy. Deep down inside I had discovered a breadth of optimism about the future. I had stores of good things to look forward to and that feeling I used to get as a child at the end of term: a mild nostalgia, underpinned with a bursting, delirious joy. I was enjoying my life more and more and soon I would be going back to South America.

Twilight arrives. The sun has flattened a long crest of the Morne Diablotin, the highest mountain of Dominica, and it now looks like a single sheet of torn paper. The paper is mauve. Above its ragged edge is a sky like a glass of citrus juice that has stood a long time and thickened at the bottom. The mountain rises up into the sky beyond a smoky breadth of jungle. The near leaves still catch a brightness from the departed sun. They look wet. They will never get dry. It is a couple of nights before full moon and the moon is already up, a yellow face peering through the fringes of a hill.

The sky above glistens like satin. Across it travel rags of Atlantic cloud blown by the trade winds. Here in the middle of the island they have already shed their load. They drift aimlessly, bodiless, dying into the Caribbean sky.

That far mountain becomes bleaker, calmer, shorn of its forest. It rises like a moorland into a pure sky. Suddenly the air is cool. A wind gets up, the wind of night's arrival. The banana trees clap ragged hands in welcome.

Up there on the mountainside there are no banana trees. Now there is nothing save a mineral shape, the sanctity of the peak. As the sky's radiance fades to a moonlit sheen the mountain becomes a dull blue, restful to the eye. Beside it, among its foothills where they reach down into palm-covered bays, the last of the Carib Indians will be turning in now, in the hamlets of the Carib Territory.

Two thousand Caribs of varying racial purity live here. They weave baskets in their doorways, they grow acres and acres of bananas, which they box and sell to the Geest Line of Glamorgan, they keep pigs to tidy the small gardens around their houses. They cut steps into the paths of red mud that climb into the banana groves, and remould them after rains. Their children stare at you and grin. They speak Patois and English. Some of the oldest generation still exchange the odd phrase of Carib. With the help of the Peace Corps they have built a carbet, a traditional Carib longhouse, for tourists to see. Sometimes their traditional dance group, the Waitakubuli Karifuna group, or Dominica Carib group, performs inside, to drums and flutes. The men and women wear cloth flaps over their loins and buttocks, and otherwise only an armband and a necklace of beads to keep away spirits. They still call the island Waitakubuli, which means 'the high one'. But mainly the Caribs live like the rest of Dominica.

Yet the Carib Territory is different. There is a peace in the air, a sense of harmony, that you feel nowhere else on the island. Everything is neater, the gardens, the plantations, the houses, no matter how small and how patchy their construction. Everything is well tended. And everyone is friendly. They stop whatever they are doing and ask your name and talk. Then you sit together a while talking little, or not at all, wondering if this is your cue to leave, when silence is in fact a vestigial Amerindian tradition, whereby two strangers should sit in one another's company a decent length of time before venturing to speak.

I caught a ride up to the Carib Territory in the back of a pick-up truck. It was a two-hour drive from Roseau. We drove through a rainstorm on the way. The two other passengers in the back banged on the roof of the cab when the drops first started and were handed a plastic sheet which we all spread out over our heads and clung onto so it didn't blow away. It was stiff plastic and the rain drummed on it furiously.

Roseau is on the west of the island, the Carib Territory is in the north-east, the opposite side, the Atlantic side. When we reached the other coast the rain stopped. Around the bays that we passed the palm trees were swaying in a strong wind.

I stayed with a local businessman, Charles. He was a small sinuous man known throughout the Territory. He had wiry hair that fell to his shoulders and a gaunt face. His lips were thin and wide and he spoke with a faint lisp for which he compensated with exaggerated enunciation. He had built a big concrete bar which had a sign up saying Melodie Enterprises. Inside there was a sparsely stocked craft shop, two bedrooms and a lot of space. As yet he hadn't got as far as stocking up the bar, though his wife Margaret, who was a rotund business-minded woman with cold, suspicious eyes, cooked meals for anyone who wanted, which she served on the balcony at the back, overlooking the Atlantic. Up in the beams above the balcony Charles had hung a hammock. It was so high up that the only way to get into it was to open the window and climb up on the window frame, grab hold of the hammock and jump into it, and then cautiously open it out. Once you were safely installed it was the most peaceful place in the world. You could watch cloud shadows flow in over the glossy sea, you could smell the rough, hempy weave of the hammock, you were up under the roof, way up. It was like being in a tree house. You could balance things, a glass, a book, a bottle, on the beams beside you.

Charles showed me his craft shop and talked about the demise of Carib culture. It was inevitable, he thought. But he was proud of his heritage. He showed me baskets and plates and the 'wife-pullers' that Carib men had once used: a long sock of woven wicker with a ring at one end. The wives would wear them on their little fingers. When you pull on the ring the sock tightens its grip. It quickly hurts. A man with several wives would thread all the rings of his wives' wife-pullers onto a rope when he went out, and lead them after him like goats or donkeys.

Charles told me that the Caribs had once been immensely powerful. For example, in the old days a Carib with knowledge could immerse himself in a basin of water and disappear in it and emerge in another land, somewhere else in the world.

On my second day I undertook a tour of the Carib Territory. There were six or seven hamlets strung along the road, with both Carib and European names like Salibia and Saint Cyr. There were several calls I wanted to make. The first was to Mona, a woman I had met the day before who had offered to turn up some trousers for me. When I had gone to her house later on it had been closed up. I had shouted her name, but no one had appeared. A pair of white ladies' sandals had stood at the step into the house.

Today she was there at her sewing-machine. The door of the main room was flung open to the sea breeze coming over the coconut trees, and I walked straight in. The crop-spraying plane, like a small World War Two fighter but bright yellow, was swooping back and forth across the valley raking out trails of smoke in the air. Mona had turned up her radio to cover the roar, while her feet rocked on the wide, iron Singer pedal. She looked over her shoulder when I came in, smiled at me calmly, and told me to call back for the trousers later.

Further down the road I stopped at a rum shop for a Coke. I took a seat and soon a whole classful of children surrounded my table. They said nothing. They would not even tell me their names. They were wearing either shirts or shorts, depending on their age. The younger wore the shirts.

They stared up at me silently from the table's edge, their eyes wide and bright.

Meanwhile an old man appeared in the window. He had high cheekbones and his skin was creased around his eyes. He growled, 'Get me a drink? A brandy?' The girl who served was outside sitting under a tree. The children called her. She came in and looked through the bottles. They had no brandy. 'A beer,' the man said. He walked around inside to drink it in one long series of gulps. Then he complimented me on my hair. 'Cheveux fins,' he said. It was the only patois I heard in the Carib Territory.

He promptly walked out, leaving me somewhat bewildered.

I finished my Coke and strolled down to the road again to catch a ride on to the Caribs' most sacred site, the Escalier Tête-Chien, a rock formation jutting out into the ocean. It was a few miles away, at the southern end of the Territory.

An old Cable and Wireless truck, yellow like the British Telecom ones used to be, gave me a ride a mile or two along the road to Saint Cyr. Arthur, a friendly worker in the back seat, offered me a bowl of his breakfast: chopped salad and fried fish. His wife had left for two months' holiday in St Thomas and he had fixed the meal himself, as well as a flask of 'chocolate tea', he told me with a proud smile.

They stopped by a street water tap in Saint Cyr, where children were splashing bowls of water over themselves. I sat down to wait for another ride.

A little girl, aged about three, walked past a man seated on a stone and tipped a cupful of water at him. It wetted one leg of his shorts. He stood up. She ran. He whipped her with a dried reed. She started crying loudly. Her grandmother came out of the house and shouted at her, then went back in to fetch a big bucket of water which she put down by the side of the road telling the girl to wash. The girl was still bawling. The woman came up and spanked her three times. A posse of children approached. One girl, with plaits and nipples just beginning to peg out her dress, stripped the little girl and poured mug after mug of water over her, into her hair and onto her shoulders. She stopped crying.

Eventually I gave up waiting for a lift and walked.

Atlantic waves, glistening and clean and jubilant, send up giant hands of froth that fall on a flat rock, and spread white into two broad rock pools, fizzing, dissolving like heads of beer, mingling into the clarity of the pools after their ripples have beached on the far barnacles. Here at Jenny Point the land has been beaten bare by ocean and rain, worn down to a sandy rock embedded with hard black pebbles. Over them, rising from the waves up into the hill of the headland, slumps the Escalier Tête-Chien.

The ladder of the boa-constrictor, the dog-head snake, is a rugged lava flow, grey, black, eroded into designs of wrinkles and pockmarks. The breakers smother its tail in white, and then rebound from wall to wall in the gullies either side before flinging themselves up onto the shelf of rock where their fight ends. The snake climbs up, rectilinear and stepped, sinking its head in the body of the island.

The Caribs believe that this long rock was the staircase on which the snake god rose out of the water at the beginning of time. It climbed on up the mountain and disappeared into a cave at the summit, sinking down into the belly of the earth and so engendering time. The trail left by its scales on the Escalier is still clear to see.

I sat watching the waves for a while. To the south a few roofs shone like stars among the green of the headlands, outlying farmsteads of Castle Bruce, the next village outside the Carib Reserve.

On a sudden impulse I stripped and plunged into the deepest rock pool. It was a big tub. I sat in the cool ocean water, rubbed myself, and sprang out again. I pulled my clothes on without drying and left.

On my way back to the road I passed through a banana plantation. Iguanas, their feet crunching on dry leaves, scuttled out of my path. The banana trees looked like giant clover, or cress. Under the solid canopy of their leaves the windless air was hot and wet like a greenhouse.

A big old truck heaved me back to Salibia. I wanted to see the Catholic church there which was said to have a canoe for an altar. I followed a track down to the church, a small white building with a rotten door propped open by a rock. A half-completed Carib dugout canoe stood on the ground outside. It was undergoing the most time-consuming phase of its construction: after being hollowed out with fire and chisels the tree trunk has to stand a long time filled with rocks and water, which together make it spread wide without splitting. This one had months to go before its cargo could be offloaded.

Inside the church was dusty and untidy. Here and there a rock lay on the floor. The pews were unevenly ranked. Up at the end stood a large block of varnished wood. It was solid, but shaped like a canoe. A crucifix stood on top.

The wall behind it was covered with large paintings by a local artist. The largest depicted three Caribs in native dress, one crouching, two standing, and all of them making strange gestures whose significance was not apparent. They were in a swirling Garden of Eden where some of the Reserve's vegetation grew. Beside it were a few unfinished murals of biblical figures. One was a man in a white cassock. He was dark, had a beard and wore a pair of glasses. He looked like Peter Sellers in one of his disguises. A man came into the church who had just tethered his two cows outside and I asked him who it was meant to be. He merely laughed a short, hard laugh in reply.

Later I passed Leonard the Swede. He had been living in the Territory for twelve years, long enough to gain right of residence. He had a bushy, silver beard and straggly hair and had teased out the ends of his moustache. What you could see of his face was bright red.

He spent the day in his workshop on the road. It stood in an iron frame on old gearboxes, its floor made of rusty iron sheets and its roof of blue plastic. Leonard was a handyman. He had several old truck engines geared up via a series of pulleys and old fan belts to turn a pair of lathes. They ran without silencers, so when he explained what he was doing in his heavily accented English all you heard were the Scandinavian vowel sounds, the long ö's and er's. He seemed to have two projects in hand: one was his plan to mass-produce railings and bannisters on his wood lathe and the other was the manufacturing of artificial legs. Leonard showed me the fibre-glass prototype he had nearly finished. He explained how the revolutionary spring in the joint worked, and that the thing would probably fetch $30,000 in the United States. He asked me to send him a note verifying this fact, if I ever got there. As he showed me the design I noticed that he was missing the tops of not one but three fingers of his left hand.

Beside his workshop stood a gutted tractor. Its chassis, engine cover and one wheel remained.

Leonard's wife lived a mile away. She owned some banana land.

There were still three days to go but already everyone was talking about the cricket. Both men and women asked me if I wasn't involved in it, as some forerunner or scout of the touring team. It was a British team, the Rum Runners of West London.

On the day of the match itself, preceded by a day of rain which had come in from the Atlantic in one grim shadow after another and which had occasioned much contradictory prognostication about the state of the wicket, radios in every house hissed out the match commentary through doors and windows opened wide. Everyone said they were going down to watch the match later.

The match was being played at the Jolly John Memorial Park. The pitch was of red earth with one patch of brilliant turf, like a fungus on the baldness. On one side was a banana grove, on the other a steep hill of bare earth that rose in steps. It would have served as a natural grandstand had not the boundary swung up onto it. The crowd was to be found above this edge of the pitch, among the trees higher up. A good two thousand had turned out. There were pick-up trucks parked all around. Three bamboo stalls were selling drinks. In one a couple were frying chicken and bakes, dough balls to go with the flesh. By lunchtime all the soft drinks and rum on the ground had been sold. Only brandy, whisky and stout were left.

The English batted in the afternoon. The Carib pace bowlers

took three wickets before the innings reached double figures. At this point a batsman in a red cap emerged. He won respect from knowing members of the crowd and earned him the soubriquet Red Cap. He held the innings together, carrying the side to a defeat by fifty runs, which was at least not laughable.

After the match, when the ground was submerged in the shade of the mountain and only the far palms of the next headland still glowed, there were speeches and presentations, delivered with ceremony, for the benefit of the team members. A man in a yellow satin string singlet and beard who described himself as a sports sponsor walked around the group blowing loud notes on a conch shell. No one asked him to stop.

I walked back up to Melodie Enterprises and swung in the hammock as the sun set. Suddenly I found a pining for South America stirring up inside me. Something about the Carib Territory, the peace here, took me back there. I remembered again the cool purity of the Andes at dusk, the chill air, the fiery sky, the streets below filled with Indian marketers. That was where I wanted to be, and now it came to me how badly.

That night when Charles and Margaret went for their evening 'stroll down the road' in his pick-up they took me along. At every stop he got into discussions of absurd lengths with passers-by about the day's umpiring decisions and team selection.

'Stop talking about cricket,' Margaret would mutter in quiet exasperation, which only made him raise his voice.

He offered me a beer when we were back at Melodie Enterprises. It was a Sisserou beer, a Dominican beer which I hadn't heard of before. I asked him, 'Why is the beer called Sisserou? Where's Sisserou?'

'Sisserou is a pirate,' I thought he said.

'A pirate?'

'Yes. A pirate.'

There was a picture of a Sisserou parrot on the label to prove it.

The next morning I decided to move on from Roseau and catch
a lift round the north coast to the town of Portsmouth in the
north-west. Portsmouth was the second town of Dominica. I lay
in the hammock overlooking the ocean reading a novel, a sketch
of troubled tropical Colombia, for which a hammock was the
ideal reading station. I planned to finish my book, then pack
up and go. But my belly started distracting me. It hurt more
and more until I had to leave the gentle swing for my bed. I
slipped through the mesh of pain into sleep and woke at four in
the afternoon with a thirst so severe it had given me a headache.
I drank five bottles of Coke, for rehydration, revitalization, and
as a test of my stomach's recovery, and then sat on the road with
my bag.

It sounds so easy, getting out of the hotel and slumping down
in a heap in the street outside, but it wasn't. It seemed to take
all the willpower and strength I could summon. My stomach
was feeling better but my mind, no doubt debilitated from
the intestinal battle that had been raging, had suddenly been
stricken with an attack of anxiety. Should I or should I not
leave the Carib Territory, this settlement where I had been so
comfortable? The Easter weekend was starting the next day.
The Carib Territory was having a procession on Sunday, and
on Saturday night Charles and Margaret were hosting a big 'pot
luck' party. However, Portsmouth, the biggest town in the north,
where I was headed, would have all kinds of Easter events, maybe
some of them musical.

In the end my first lift was with Charles. He had a truckload
of hairy, dehusked coconuts for the bakery in the next village,
where we stopped to unload them by hand, throwing them onto
the ground. An old man, the baker, came out to help us.

We wound in and out of small bays to Marigot where Charles
hoped to buy fish and return home. Boats had been pulled up
on the pebbles. They were different from the Carib boats, built
as they were only of planks. The Marigot fishermen were going
out daily but the Carib boats had not fished for six months. The
sea had been keeping strong, one skipper told me, too strong
for them.

Lifts from two pick-up trucks carried me along the rugged bays of the north coast to a village called Dos D'Ane. 'Do you know Mr Tambourlain, that man from Charlotte Vail? He jump on a jackass back, put over he left foot, put over he right foot, he shake a leg, he shake a leg' – a Trinidad folksong.

In the last mini-bus of the day into Portsmouth a lady called Vera put her hand on my thigh while explaining the pleasure of a hot and a cold spring on the other side of the mountains. She offered to take me there, to the other side. We made an open arrangement for the excursion.

I checked into the Portsmouth guesthouse. It was a plain modern building on the main street, owned by Mac Douglas, the chief local businessman. He was a tall man with a pot belly. He had a stern, serious face, and was bald at the front of his scalp. His hair rose up in a fan at the back of his head. He had several business interests, in shipping and catering and retail.

I inevitably succumbed to a brief onslaught of remorse. I was back in the normal world, having abandoned the idyllic remoteness that suited me so well. Here I was again in a dreary small town. The houses announced the influence of Britain and France. On my journey around the island I had passed a small guesthouse in its own abundant garden just outside the Carib Territory: I should have stayed there. I still wasn't well. I couldn't hold a conversation of more than five words without yawning. My head ached. I needed to recuperate in some remote place. I went to bed early, to smother my futile thoughts with sleep.

TWENTY-SIX

It is Good Friday morning. Portsmouth is sleepy. I stroll around the town with no clear idea what to do. I feel restless. The town is small and rundown. Its centre, which is no real centre at all, is a tiny square, just an open space, a yard, opposite the guesthouse where I am staying. Along the streets most of the houses are built of concrete, though there are some old wooden Creole houses. The town is pervaded by inertia, by a sense of listlessness. The Geest Line stopped using their depot outside Portsmouth after Hurricane Hugo devastated the northern banana plantations in 1989. Half the town's men found themselves suddenly without jobs. Many left, for Roseau or other richer islands, St Kitts, St Martin.

Reluctantly, I am coming to recognize that I will probably have to spend the Easter weekend here. It won't be before Tuesday that the transport starts flowing again, at which time I can head to Roseau and start checking out the bands of Dominica, and arranging my travel to the continent.

There were other travellers hanging around in the guesthouse. There was a Swede, Kjel (pronounced 'Shell'), a technician who had worked for two years in Saudi Arabia and had travelled all over the world. He said he had no curiosity left at all. He wore small round glasses behind which his eyes were completely expressionless. He had a short, blond moustache and his lower lip sagged slightly, so his mouth never quite closed. He worked nine months and travelled for three each year. He spoke little, although his English was good. He said he did not enjoy his life at home, but then his travels didn't seem to please him took much either.

There was Nigel, an English teacher wandering in early retirement for six months. He was a short, thin strong man with curly, black hair and a rugged tan. He wore shorts and open denim shirts and kept a flask of rum with him at all times. He told me that the poverty of Portsmouth made him feel guilty.

He wanted to go local, hang out in the roughest hotels and bars, but then felt bad when he did because he had so much more money than the rest of the clientele. As soon as he expressed any opinion he would snarl: 'Nah. It's the same old story.' He was living in permanent indecision, not yet having fulfilled his original intention, after five expensive months of travel, of going to Rio. He drank rum from sunset onwards.

At the square a small pier reaches out into the bay, Prince Rupert Bay. I stand watching the coming and going of boats. A boy takes the cover off an outboard, reaches a hand into it and pulls the cord to start it up. He swings the boat round and whines off to the other side of the bay in a wide arc, curving round the bow of another boat that comes into view from behind a tree, a long, slow-moving canoe carrying three men, two of them still huddled in capes from a recent shower. A few men gather at the pier when the canoe puts in. A lone frigate bird plies the shore, gliding with its chest puffed out as a brake.

An almond tree stands by the pier with a giant cog lying on the ground at its base. Beside that is a rusting trawler, a great old boat that climbed half-way up onto land during a hurricane some years ago. Out in the bay a pair of old coasters drift together around their anchors, like the slowly turning hands of a clock. Listless shower clouds blow across from the mountains and travel out to sea as shadows on the bright surface, until the morning sun sets in in earnest.

A gang of men collects by the pier. They are there every day. People call them the Jetty Boys. When a car or bus of tourists pulls up or a boat puts in they offer themselves as guides to the Indian river, trying to keep up their friendly front to the foreigners while fighting each other off with fierce bursts of Patois and broken English. Mostly they sit under the tree and shout jokes at one another.

The Indian river is the largest river on Dominica. It slumps into the sea just beside Portsmouth, after its wearying descent from the hills. In fact it slumps to a halt, powerless to resist the tides. It loses its brown water little by little, with each ebb.

The Jetty Boys share two rowing boats to take tourists up

the river. A rasta called Yellow, after his pale skin, pressed me to go on a trip with him. I had time to kill. He didn't have to press hard.

It was quiet on the river. Along the banks, among the black roots of bushes, big crabs lurked. They stood watching the current, holding their claws on the ground with all their armour stacked up beneath their protruding eyes looking like ice-hockey goalkeepers squaring up to save a penalty flick. Mangrove trees, with gnarled fans of roots and roots lying in heaps like old cables, made the river's passage a long Gothic nave: the trees were the colour of stone and fluted like columns, its floor was green marble strewn with leaves of sunlight. Where the light fell it illuminated the interior beneath the surface, pockets of crystal in the rock.

Flags appeared among the foliage ahead, emanating from the roof of a bamboo shack. This was our destination: a bar that marked the furthest point that the boats could travel up the river. The Jetty Boys had built it to take tourists to and they took it in turns to man it. Yellow stripped naked and jumped into a pool in the river bottom. He bent over to rub his locks together in the water, then stood showing off his manhood.

'I only need ten minutes,' he called out to me, with a proud grin. 'Ten minutes of talk with a white girl and I take she away from she boyfriend.'

I asked him what he talked about, out of purely idle curiosity.

'Roots culture and reality.'

The man in the shack named the impressive range of punches in the bottles on his counter. Soursop, coconut, passion fruit, mango, liquids the colours of old-fashioned medicine, creamy pink, mauve, dirty orange. Small black crabs like spiders stole up the stilts of the shack.

On the way back down we passed two boys in a dinghy, one rowing, one standing in the prow with a harpoon gun. They were out fishing for mullet, which streaked from bank to bank in small parties. When we moored again a man in sunglasses jumped into the boat, took the rope from Yellow's hands and rowed fast up the river. The two boys were in his boat and he had tourists waiting.

I strolled around the Cabrits, the peninsula that made the bay at Portsmouth. It was a big hill. The British and the French, in a series of reciprocal seizures, had between them constructed Fort Shirley on the side of the hill overlooking the bay. Alternately they used it to cannon one another's ships whilst, conversely, they both at times found themselves bombarded by defences they had built. Their garrisons protected the bay at which the slavers called for water and provision. The fort was abandoned in 1845. Old cannon barrels now lie all over a lawn amid the battlements.

As I was walking back into town I heard music. I knew it was live because the quality was not good. Two keyboards were trying to pick out the tune of the William Tell Overture over a zouk beat. Some guys were hanging around a street corner opposite a disused bar. The musicians were inside. I stood listening until someone waved me up the steps.

In a back room four young men were playing electronic equipment. One was hitting drum pads intermittently, another sat on an old wooden speaker playing a simple keyboard, someone else stood in front of a window at an even simpler one, and a drum machine was putting out the beat. Both the keyboard players were searching for the tune, in different keys. One of them nodded at me and smiled, so I stayed.

After ten minutes they gave up and asked me if I knew how it went. I showed them. They asked if I was a musician and we got talking. They were called Hi-Voltage and were Portsmouth's only band. They sometimes backed the best band on the island, Roots, Stems and Branches, or RSB. The bassist, tall with two conspicuous gold teeth, who had been playing around on a keyboard, was called Derrick but known as Sandy. Another man, a small man in a yellow wool cap, was called Minchingham, or Minchy, and played drum pads. The following night they were going to be supporting RSB, who were coming to play a show in Portsmouth. It was going to be held in the downstairs hall of the very guesthouse where I was staying. They asked me to play with them. Without even looking for it I had stumbled into the music scene.

That night I saw a moonbow. I was at the pier looking out

over the bay. The moonbow rose from the Caribbean and disappeared in an inflamed cloud above the Cabrits. It was composed of a faint silver dust in a long, fine curve. I had never seen one before.

TWENTY-SEVEN

Mac Douglas of the guesthouse heard me whistling a calypso the next morning.

'Nani Wine,' he called out. It was the name of the song.

'Yes.' I smiled back.

'We had Crazy to stay here one time.' Crazy was the singer of the song.

There followed a long session in which we exchanged choruses of calypsos, which were his chief love, while I helped him stack boxes of beer behind the makeshift bar for the dance that night. He had attended every Notting Hill Carnival for a decade up until 1988. Just as he was telling me about Jing Ping, the local traditional music, and that he would put me in touch with a Jing Ping band, Minchy appeared at the door. A torrential downpour was starting. The eaves above Minchy immediately began to gush in thick streams onto the street. He came in and told me Hi-Voltage were rehearsing at noon and expecting me. His face looked bright and eager, as if he was happy to be playing a show later.

I was certainly pleased to have a flow to go with. I went along to the band room before noon. The storm had long since passed. The band was standing around on the street corner. Minchy was eating a piece of chocolate sponge cake and stooping now and then to drink from a bronze handleless tap on the pavement. The sponge wasn't fully cooked. It had a layer of icing-like moistness in the middle.

We worked out three numbers. The band enjoyed hearing brass in the sound. They asked me to play with them that night.

I had never seen equipment like it. One of the bass guitar's pick-ups had a short circuit that sounded like a fuzzbox. Minchy, while hitting the drum pads, also wore a pair of Walkman headphones twisted round so one of the ear pieces was over his mouth. They had rewired it to act as a microphone for him to sing backing vocals. The lead vocalist had another pair of headphones with the arm of an old turntable attached so the cartridge hung in front of his mouth, like a pilot's headset. Where the needle had been a small mike was taped in place. The keyboards sounded like the kind of toy Casio synths children might get for Christmas in Europe or America.

Most of them were under twenty. They had written several of their own zouk numbers, simple but effective party songs. They all shouted out different lines for me to play, and grinned with pleasure when they heard them. Brass was what the songs needed, they told me afterwards.

On my way back to the hotel I saw two wooden No Entry signs standing in the middle of the road, closing off a block of the main street. The Magistrate's Court was in session. Friends, lawyers, witnesses, stood on the opposite pavement. A man with a clipboard called out names from the doorway of the court. The proceedings inside were open for all the street to see.

While I was trying to fall asleep in the afternoon someone knocked on my door. It was a thin man who introduced himself as Glen. He had a David Niven moustache and sharp eyes. His face was thin but open and friendly. He told me that Mac had been in touch with him about Jing Ping. He ran a Jing Ping group that he wanted me to hear.

'Whenever I call on my band they give me a number,' Glen assured me with a smile. 'The onliest ting is you might have to buy them a drink.' I could hear them whenever I liked.

Everything was going my way. I would leave the island having heard all sides of its musical life without even searching it out. Glen was even going to show me how to play some of the instruments.

In the late afternoon when the streets were in shade I went out
to a supermarket to buy water. A notice on the wall behind the
counter said: 'Get your fresh pig tail,' the word tail underlined.
Another notice higher up said: 'Credit is dead, don't ask for him.
Who kill him bad pay.' I strolled back down the road.

As I reached Mac's guesthouse an old wooden Bedford truck
rolled slowly into the square and stopped outside the hotel.
Several men were sitting high up in the back on a load of
speakers and music equipment. One of them, in a blue shirt
and with a pair of shades perched on his hairline, caught my
eye. He saw the trombone case over my shoulder. He jumped
down from the truck and introduced himself as Tony.

'You play?' he asked me. He had big eyes and smooth, oiled
skin. He smelt faintly of cologne.

'Trombone,' I told him.

'What kind of music?'

'Any kind,' I said.

He was the keyboard player and the arranger of RSB. Within
a minute he had asked me to play with them tonight and told
me three soca songs they did that I knew already. I just had to
wait for them to set up the stage and then we would run through
them as well as some zouk numbers.

While we were talking under the eaves of the guesthouse for
shelter from a light dusk shower Minchy and Glen both walked
up to me within a few minutes of each other. Glen had fixed up
his Jing Ping band for the morning. Minchy wanted to check
that I was playing tonight. Then Tony told me that RSB were
heading down in their shaky truck to a village in the south-east
of the island tomorrow afternoon, and asked me along. I was
glutted with musical opportunities.

Tony had time to show me the brass parts of six numbers at
his deck of three keyboards before a large lady called out from
the door of the hall. There was a mass going on in the cinema
next door and could we please wait until the service was over.
(The Catholic church had lost its roof to Hurricane Hugo last
year, and they were using the cinema while it was being repaired.
The cinema also doubled as a hurricane shelter. A cannon stood

in the foyer pointing at the street.) We left it there. I had learnt my first zouk lines, long and intricate.

I lay on my bed trying to rest. From the church came hymn-singing. A man with a reedy voice kept singing high harmony lines. He must have been sitting near an open door because his voice rose clear of the congregation. Then he was reading the lesson. At least, I thought it was him, and then realized it was in fact a woman reading. Maybe he was a woman. But at the next hymn I was convinced that he wasn't, and decided he just had a feminine voice.

Reggae bass carried clearly from a nearby bar. Then the drumming of a brief downpour on the hotel's tin roof smothered all other sounds.

At ten o'clock when the jubilant crowd in white dresses and shirts spilled out from the mass in the cinema RSB did a soundcheck and then Mac expelled the crowd that had already formed in the hall so he could start taking door money. The lights went down. A few people came in. After an hour there might have been fifty people in the hall, which could have held three hundred. All night it never filled. Another businessman was doing a deal on Red Stripe the same night in his Club International Snackette nearby.

I played in the first two numbers, a zouk version of the corniest Mexican tune turned by the dazzling tempo and beat into an exhilarating song, and 'Soca High' – about how soca makes you feel 'high, high, high' like a bird in the sky. We did both songs around ten times each.

The band played without lights on a low stage. Tony used a small flashlight to check the settings on his three machines. I stood between him and the trumpet player Keith, a slim relaxed guy in a scanty grey tee-shirt. The LCD windows of Tony's synthesizer glowed through the gloom. They said things like: 'Tony brass 1, piano digi, flute 2.' There was something reassuring about them, like an illuminated dashboard on a lonely road at night.

We played until two in the morning. Of the hundred or so people who paid to come in off the street, where a much larger crowd was listening for free through louvre windows and not sweating in a spontaneous Turkish bath, ninety or more were men. They danced with the energy and stamina of champion athletes who had been overdosing on steroids. Some did fast scissor kicks, others hopped with one leg raised perpendicular all round the dance floor, spinning as they went, and miraculously not bumping into people though seeming to bounce off them like pinballs off the pins as they altered course. When the band started playing reggae a great cheer went up to the opening fanfare of an Aswad number. People bent double and sprang back up straight twice within a single bar of the music again and again. They raised their legs and went through the movements of stamping something down in slow motion, twisting a foot in the air back and forth and lowering it slowly to the ground, a dance inspired by a dub song called 'Stamp It Down'.

In one of my breaks I sat upstairs. RSB were hammering through some reggae numbers below. I tried resting my elbows on the table but at the end of every bar the bass played some quavers which made the table tremble violently enough to trigger my funny-bones.

Around two o'clock RSB stopped and the lights went up. The crowd immediately gathered around the stage. They wanted more, but didn't ask for it in the usual way. They shouted and pointed accusingly at the band. 'Five dollars,' I heard a few times.

It was Hi-Voltage's turn. RSB ignored the crowd and explained their instruments to the young musicians, who had to run through a number for soundchecking several times under the watchful eyes of an unhappy and insufficiently drunk mob of their friends, and under stark striplighting. A lot of people left.

Minchy raised his eyebrows at me as he played, signalling me to come up and blow. They were about to launch into one of their own zouk numbers, in which they wanted not only a lot of trombone but also a solo, which I gave them. Even though I held the bell well back from the mike I still heard the horn flooding out of the speakers and filling the hall. It was exciting. I realized in an instant that I was up there free to do what I wanted, so I took the opportunity to run through a repertoire of lines that I had found floating through my mind over the past weeks, mainly mutations of riffs I had heard and semi-consciously worked out slide positions for. They were what had filled many a dull moment. Now at last I was blasting them out into a resonant hall until the hall was full of them as with a brilliant liquid. They filled it like warm honey and my head emptied.

Outside, leaving Hi-Voltage to perform the rest of their set, I went into the square to join the members of RSB who leant against the bonnets of pick-ups or sat on the bench beside the memorial to Lord Cathcart, 'who died of the bloody flux off Portsmouth in 1741 while sailing with Admiral Holborn to the sack of Cartagena'. Tony called them all together to arrange rehearsal times. They were cutting an album and needed more brass. They asked me to play on it, and next day in the south-east. I said fine to everything and went to bed.

I lay waiting for Hi-Voltage to finish, then for the packing up of the equipment, a job which was lightened for them by a stream of loud jokes and explosions of laughter. Dawn was not far off when things fell quiet downstairs. The moon had already set. I could tell because there was no longer any glow between the hem of the curtain and the window frame.

TWENTY-EIGHT

Sunday was a bad day. I got up before noon but failed to catch a lift in time to reach the RSB band room an hour away, near Roseau, before they left in their lorry for the south-east. No cars came. I sat in the ever-shrinking shade of a tree until there were only twenty minutes left before they would be leaving, when there was unquestionably no hope of my making it, and I gave up, but indecisively. I still thought I might try to get all the way down to where they were playing under my own steam, even though it was a long way beyond Roseau, which was itself a long way away on a day like Easter Sunday.

I was lying on my hotel bed thinking that any minute now I would go into the street and wait again when I remembered Glen and the Portsmouth Jing Ping. I lay there a while longer without deciding anything. It ought to have been easy to know what to do, and as time passed it should have become still more obvious. All I had to do was lie here and the music would happen.

The problem was Portsmouth. It was a restless place. It was the kind of place you might just be able to resign yourself to doing nothing in, but if you couldn't you had no choice but to leave. There were two beach bars that attracted a few yachts to the bay, as well as a minibus of tourists now and then. It had none of the remoteness of the east coast, but an uneasy quietness filled it. It was the kind of place I did not like to spend long in.

Nigel and Kjel were still around. The three of us kept reshuffling our company: I would walk out for a Coke and bump into Kjel on his way back from the beach where he had left Nigel; Nigel would stroll onto the hotel balcony half intending to go down to the street and find me slouching with my elbows on the rail. Any of these gentle collisions occasioned a few words, usually on the theme of highly inconsequential plans. 'I was just going out for a Coke' – 'Were you? I was thinking about a stroll' – 'Kjel is on his way to the beach' – 'Yes?' – 'But he said he wouldn't be there long' – 'Are you going to this thing tonight?'

When we deliberately hung around together conversation sank even lower. Once I even caught myself breaking a long silence by saying, 'I'm just going in there,' and pointing to the lavatory.

They were all puppet conversations mastered by the great unmentionable which pressed heavier and heavier on Kjel and Nigel: what were they going to do when the Easter weekend was over and transport flowed again? All three of us knew secretly that it was time to move on. The island's charm was wearing off. This happens. Nothing changes, you just don't look at it the same way. You think about elsewhere, about all the things you want to do before the year is over. If you don't leave then you overstay – which is what Nigel and Kjel had both done. Neither knew where they were going next.

Glen had not shown up in the morning. Later I walked up to his sister's house on a rise of land above the town to find him. He was out. His sister said he had left for Roseau and would be back around six. It was to be a long afternoon.

I took a siesta on my bed but my thoughts kept me awake. I couldn't reconcile myself to waiting in Portsmouth, though I had no choice but to. The plight of the town got me thinking about Europe again, and how the Caribbean has been part of the Atlantic economy for half a millennium. Although the place was so foreign somehow it was not exotic. Its problems have always been created by the system of which it is a part, like Britain, although unlike Britain it never played a controlling part. The islands could be egalitarian paradises. Instead they are still victims of the Atlantic economy – a company in Wales decides to send its ships to one port rather than another and a thousand people are out of work in Dominica.

All afternoon I wished I had taken a chance and got myself down to the RSB show independently. As the day wore on they became the ideal band for me. They were eager to have me, they had already invited me to give solos, they might even let me do some arranging of brass lines. They had asked me to play on their album. It was too bad to be missing out on all that.

At six o'clock I was out taking a sunset stroll along the beach. I was going out to the dock outside town, to check the boats there for a ride south. It was the main dock of Portsmouth, a single long quay where the Geest Line had their depot.

The beach, which skirted the town and then the road leading out to the dock, was littered with bottles, conch shells in various stages of sea bleaching, and the usual flotsam. The sand was a dark regal grey.

A line of shacks stood by the pier. All but one were closed up. A large young woman was sitting on a bench in its

door, with the folds of her long skirt bunched around her
ankles.

'All right,' she called to me.

'All right,' I replied.

'Why don't you stop to drink a beer?' she asked.

I did stop. She got up and ambled into her shack and fetched
me a beer from a freezer from behind the counter. She chatted
to me while I drank it, nodding her head knowingly when I
asked about the boats at the dock. She had a bob of black hair
hairsprayed into place that seemed too tidy and tended for the
rest of her appearance. Her dress and blouse were grimy and
smudged from wiping her hands on them.

She was called Nina and knew where all the boats were going.
They all went north, to St Kitts, St Martin, Antigua. There was
one, a large red one, which had been on its way south to St Lucia
but had had engine trouble. Another ship was coming next week
to take its cargo.

I went on down to the boats. A rasta was on board a
wooden schooner from Antigua called *Scentilla Scott*. He had neat
shoulder-length dreadlocks and muscly arms showing beneath the
sleeves of a red shirt. He called to me with a big smile and told
me, 'I from St Kitts, man.' He pronounced it with the stress on
the Saint.

He told me the boat he worked on was named after the owner's
daughter, who had been a girlfriend of Viv Richards. Then he
started talking about the Test Match, which was going on at
the time. In his accent there were distinct traces of British
west country. I felt a faint glimmer of fondness, even pride,
for Britain.

Then another sailor appeared on deck. He had curly, tangled
hair and his mouth was set in a permanent sneer. He was combing
his long, straggly beard as he came out and he butted straight into
the conversation, saying England had two West Indies players
on its side and still could not win. The rasta pounced on the
remark saying, 'What you mean? Eh? Them fellers, them Small
and Malcolm, them British or you would not see them play for
England.' A loud argument between them followed in which they

shouted their points not at each other but at me, as if I were a jury, or perhaps an umpire. I smiled dumbly trying not to be scared.

I returned to Nina's shack for another beer. She sat me down on a bench inside and pulled up a stool opposite to tell me the story of her business, how she had started out ten years ago here by the Geest wharf with a canvas umbrella and a box of drinks and had finally managed to buy this small wooden shack. Sometimes she slept out here. Normally she went back to her aunt's in town. She went to fetch us both more beer, then showed me the mattress rolled up behind the bar and the cardboard boxes to spread under it. The shack had a freezer, a cooker, a single light bulb and a small table. A shelf ran the length of the back wall. There was space for eight people to sit.

Once when Nina had been frying chicken legs under her umbrella in the old days a terrible heavy rain had started to fall. She kept on frying. 'You'll catch yerself sick,' the other women told her. She was risking the perilous mix of hot and cold, standing at her stove with the cold rain falling all around. She didn't get sick. Afterwards one of the women decided to let Nina use her shack from time to time.

'You is a brave woman,' she said to Nina.

Eventually when she herself got sick she sold it to Nina. This was it.

A man was sitting inside, hunched up in a corner. He never said a word. He had an infant in his arms, Nina's son. He was its father.

Night had long since fallen when I got back to the guesthouse. At the bar they told me Glen had come looking for me five times. That meant he had got his Jing Ping together. It was nine o'clock now. Probably they would have broken up again by now. But I wanted to make certain. Just as I was walking out to go to Glen's sister's, Nigel appeared with a mug in his hand.

'Do you want some rum?' he asked, with a half-hearted grin.

I thanked him and said later, I was in a hurry.

'Oh. Where are you off to?'

'Trying to find Glen.'

'Oh. Right. Maybe I'll—'

Nigel and I quickly got lost in the dark. Finally a man led us down a narrow path between some gardens and up to a back door. It had louvre panels. The man rapped on them. Glen's sister was inside along with four children who came to the door and peered up at us between the slats.

Glen was back from Roseau but he was at his girlfriend's place, in Lagoon, a district near the beach, pronounced Lago. We would recognize the house, we were told, because it was by a pipe, that is, a street tap, and 'had a lot of iron'.

In Lagoon we did recognize it. It was unmistakable: a long fence of sheets of iron enclosing what appeared to be an orchard run wild, a mass of foliage dense as a jungle. There was a wooden doorway in the fence, half open. In it sat an old man with a basket in his lap. Under a cloth in the basket he had coconut patties which he was selling.

I told him I was looking for Glen. He looked up at me, not understanding at first. Light from a bulb somewhere shone on one side of his face. Then he said, 'Wait a while.' He called back into the forest.

After a few minutes, during which Nigel ate a patty and drew out of the old man its recipe, an old woman in an apron appeared in the tunnel of boughs. She beckoned us. 'Vini, Vini.'

Along one side of the tunnel was a series of open rooms. Two children slept in one, a dog in another. They were partitioned with wooden latticing that caught the chiaroscuro projected by a bare bulb at the far end of the corridor, where the main house was. There was no sign of a band of any kind, but on a bench inside we found Glen pulling on his boots.

He shook his head for a while. He had had the band waiting an hour and a half just now. 'Some of them does get real vex,' he said.

'But Glen,' I said, 'I thought we said this morning.'

He was still shaking his head, but I could see that he was smiling faintly. 'My sister tell me six o'clock,' he said.

We walked up road to the house of the leader of the Jing Ping band. On the way Glen started chatting happily. He was a naturally cheerful man. He told me he was a mechanic in his brother-in-law's garage. He wanted to set up his own workshop.

He also wanted to travel with the Jing Ping group, of which he was the dance leader. The full group was four musicians and eight dancers. He led the dancers.

He walked with a slight spring in his step, and with his head held very erect, with the poise of a dancer. Many of his cousins and brothers had left Dominica for Canada or America. He had no wish to follow them at all. He loved life on the island.

The leader of the Jing Ping musicians, who lived nearby in one of three small houses built on stilts around a tamarind tree, was Edward, a quiet and solemn man in his sixties. When Glen called out to him from the yard he appeared in the doorway of his house. He had short, grey hair and a lean face, illuminated by a street lamp outside.

He invited us into the living room. Four chairs stood side by side. It was a small room. When you crossed your legs with your back to one wall your toes tapped the far wall. The four of us sat in silence for a while. Now and then he and Glen muttered about the wasted time earlier.

Nigel tried to hurry things along by saying, more than once, 'It's over now, it happened, so what are you going to do?'

Edward finally said, with a faint, wry smile, 'So you were looking for him at his house while he was looking for you at yours.'

That wasn't quite right, but it seemed to break the ice, to resolve the impasse. We all laughed, and arranged the session for five o'clock next day.

TWENTY-NINE

Easter Monday was beach day on Dominica. One after another, the pick-up trucks rolled through Portsmouth heading for the clean sand on the other side of town. Each one was crammed full of people who shouted at pedestrians on the street, who shouted back and made the truckfuls sway with laughter. There was a disco on the beach two miles away which you could hear from the square.

At five o'clock I went to Edward's house. He wasn't there.

At six o'clock not only was Edward there, accordion in his lap, but so was the whole band. They were sitting on chairs in the yard outside his house, already playing.

They stopped when they saw me. Edward got up to fetch me a chair from his house. I shook all four players' hands, and soon they launched off into their music again.

Jing Ping is archetypal Caribbean music: a European instrument, the accordion, playing nineteenth-century dance melodies of the planting aristocracy over African rhythms. The shiak, the boom-boom and the drum create the rhythm. The shiak is a tin shaker full of seeds. One hand shakes, the other scrapes a wire brush over its ribbed surface. Even maracas are much harder to play than they look, but becoming a good shiak player takes years.

The drum is a wide goatskin stretched over a wood hoop. It is less than a hand's width deep. You play it with a hand either side, the inner one beating and deadening the sound. It is like an Irish bodhran.

The boom-boom is a bamboo tube four feet long, with the joints knocked through. You play it like any brass instrument, by blowing at one end with your lips vibrating. You put it to one side of your mouth so part of the cheek vibrates too. That way you get a full sound. The whole tube vibrates and rings, tingles in your hands. It is like singing in the bath when you suddenly find a certain pitch that makes the whole room ring.

The shiak player, a fit middle-aged man, wore a tight black

tee-shirt and a black beret. He looked like a sailor. He sat clear of the back of his chair, his shoulders raised and his hands moving in a blur of speed. His music was crisp and dazzling, white water over the rock of the drum beside him.

The drummer was an old man with short white hair who smiled as he played. He never hit a downbeat. His rhythm kept modulating, one cross rhythm after another. Sometimes he would take a little time out, a pause to accent a coming tumble of triplets, after which he would break back into changing patterns of offbeats.

The boom-boom player was a shy man. He sat for a while resting the bottom of the pipe on a crossbar between the legs of a small table in the yard. Then he stood holding the tube with both hands, one in the middle, one up near his mouth. He stared at the ground. Both his cheeks puffed out equally when he blew, even though one did more work than the other. He looked nervous, occasionally glancing towards Edward, but he played confidently, his vibrant notes coming in quick, short volleys right after the downbeats, looking down over their shoulder.

Edward played with his legs apart. He rested one side of the accordion on a knee and drew the other down between his legs. Sometimes he tugged vigorously or pushed up in jerks then pulled out with long smooth languorous ease. He shaped the music with his hands like a potter, and the shape he gave it had nothing to do with the original melody. The accents over which he made the tune hurdle popped up all over the place but never on a downbeat, which was where you might have expected them.

Edward led the band. He would announce the tune: 'Hillanto', meaning Heel and Toe Polka. Then he would play the melody through on his own. It would sound dull and predictable and flat, a piece of child's piano music. Then the three rhythm instruments would join him, and suddenly the music left the ground. It floated and danced. All the accents were off the beat, the melody became a syncopated flow rising and falling over brilliant drum beats that flashed through bar lines, beating down, eliminating the strict square patterns of the tune, which would go on and on, over and over through its different sections, itself transformed by the rhythm into part of the rhythm, fluid and syncopated and flexible, and the tune was dissolved by the beat, it became merely another facet of the single musical whole, which was a rhythm. The whole body of sound was African not only in its offbeats and crossplays, but also in its composite nature. The separate rhythmic strands that made it up were neither supporting each other nor playing together into the hands of a single beat. They were all following their own inner momentum and coinciding in one different way after another. The whole rhythmic body was a single unit, but like a cut jewel each facet faced its own way. Western classical rhythm was infantile beside it. The piece was an allegory, a parable.

They played a series of tunes, quadrilles, polkas, waltzes, 'mazookas'. In the surrounding houses the windows and doors opened up. People came out onto their steps to watch. On the road people walking back from the beach broke into dance steps as they went by. Old men and women came up to the table and danced a few turns, laughing when they finished. Glen got up and joined them, dancing with short dainty steps and twisting his hips to the rhythm. Two of Edward's ten granddaughters, aged eight and nine, demonstrated the steps of the Heel and Toe Polka. They turned hand in hand kicking out their feet to the back and in front in brisk but smooth movements.

'The people of yesterday teach the people of today who will teach the people of tomorrow,' Edward explained in a break, referring to himself, Glen, and the children. He spoke slowly and clearly. Glen added that the old people were always there to correct them.

I ran out to buy a bottle of whisky in a rum shop. I bought Johnny Walker and a bottle of Coke for myself, to drink right away. I was thirsty. After he had served me the boy sat down on the steps by the door. 'Yeah man,' he said quietly as I left, stammering a little. 'It going to refresh you. It cool, man.'

Edward's wife brought out a tray with four glasses and several plastic cups. She was wearing a long dress and an apron. She was smiling calmly to herself, pleased by the music. A young man came across the yard with a large tin mug of solid ice, a metal bowl, and a knife. He hacked the ice into lumps which he tipped out into the bowl and set on the table. He fetched a jar of chilled water. Edward led the drinking. He poured out the shots in breaks between numbers and raised his glass first. He would say, 'Cheers,' and knock his back, then wash it down with a finger of water.

Several times people explained that Jing Ping was culture. It awakened a dormant patriarchy into which everyone obediently stepped, even the women, who became meek servants and bashful dancers.

Edward had three boom-booms. One was an old exhaust pipe with a bend in the middle, another had been painted with strips of colour. Glen started blowing the exhaust and Edward handed me the striped one.

I followed the other player, which was not easy because he kept changing his rhythm. Eventually patterns in his part would emerge, usually not long before the number was over. Once I did lock on it became the most exhilarating playing I ever did. The top of the pipe had been cut off at an angle. I didn't notice at first. When I did, and placed the mouth the right way round, it began to ring loudly and easily and I got into the sequences quicker. Very soon you no longer had to think about when to play. It happened automatically. And then if you did think about it you were more likely to get it wrong. It was music you had to allow to take over. All you had to do was relax and submit and then it carried you along. You lost yourself in the music and when it finished you felt like you had been in a trance. You felt your mind readjusting to deal with the reality around you. Even a few minutes of playing like this were enough to make you deeply calm and happy. It was like having the aftermath of good sex and a project accomplished all at once. All you had to do was go with the music and it did the rest.

We played late into the night. I paid for a second bottle of whisky, which Edward sent one of his sons out to buy. Again I didn't sleep till dawn.

THIRTY

Finally the day arrived when I had to go down to the port of Roseau looking for a ride south. Dockers were unloading cement from a black Trinidadian ship. It came out in bags bundled together by thick plastic sheets and canvas cords. Cranes on the boat swung them to shore, where four stevedores unhooked them and then held up the four loops of the cords for a forklift truck to drive its prongs through. The truck then lifted the packs into the air and swung them around and drove alongside waiting lorries, where it swung again to lower the loads onto pallets in the back. When the empty trucks arrived the drivers leapt into the backs to arrange the pallets in two rows ready for the cement.

The captain of the cement ship was not on board. One of the dockers thought he would be back soon. I had been waiting over an hour. I waited some more.

The dockers wore gloves and masks because of the dust. Now and then a cloud of dust exploded beside the boat, white like smoke. One worker, a short man with a pot belly and wearing a white hat, mask and gloves, started dancing. He stepped to a remembered beat with his hands raised up by his shoulders, shuffling and swaying from side to side. He let out a series of yells that nobody showed any interest in. No one even turned to look. He was shouting out the brass tune of a recent soca hit.

Later on a gleaming new coast guard boat pulled in. It had six tall aerials, a radar, a new dinghy with a silver and blue outboard motor, and six searchlights. Work stopped on the cement boat and everyone lined up on the dock to look at it.

On the beach beside the port I watched a boy run into the water to kick a red football. He tripped over the ball deliberately and flew into the sea.

In the middle of the afternoon I gave up. I walked out of the dock gate and stopped to buy lunch at the fried fish store outside. While he was frying up my snapper the man told me how he caught flying fish. 'They very stupid. You set a trap with fresh, and they just dive in. But it hard. The fumes get into your head and ting. Working with all that fresh.'

I said, 'What's fresh?'

He glanced at me and looked down again at his frying pan behind the jars on his counter. There were lines of sweat running down his temples. He laughed. He might or might not have heard me. He said, 'Yeah, man, fresh is fresh.'

The snapper was good. It came on a little piece of paper transparent with oil.

I had been in Roseau two days. I was trying to get out any way, either by boat or plane. Either way I needed an air ticket, because I wouldn't be allowed to disembark on any island without an air ticket out of it. I didn't know where that would be until I got to talk to one of the captains, but I needed to get the cash ready anyway.

I went to the bank in town. It was a plush new Barclays Bank in the centre of Roseau. While I was waiting a man crawled in on his hands and knees. He was wearing thick gardening gloves and pads of foam tied to his knees. He slumped onto his side near the door and stayed there all the time I was in the bank.

The next day, before I knew it, I was on the cement boat steaming for Trinidad. The ship had finished offloading its cargo and was sailing back empty for more. Its voyage was along half the chain of the Caribbean islands.

The crew were mainly regulation tough guys. 'You sick? Just wait till we clear the point. Ha ha!' In the middle of the night I pulled a pair of trousers over my shorts. 'Cold? Ha ha!' Five of them came from Carriacou. They were from Windward, a village on the north-east coast. They say this is the Scottish part of the island, that up there they still build their fishing boats according to a Glaswegian design. It's true. Every boat moored in the bay is the same shape, distinctly different from the usual open canoes. Everyone there has a Scottish name. This is one of the good things about the Caribbean. Everything is the way you expect it to be. You are never disappointed.

Captain MacFarlane was a small, self-contained man laconic

almost to the point of dumbness. He had a pale, wrinkled face and a drooping moustache. When I had asked him for a ride he just beckoned me on board without a word. His eyebrows rose up just a little.

'Do I need to bring food?' I had asked.

'I expect Total can fix you up. Sleep in the mess. Not very comfortable.' These were more or less the last words I heard from him.

Total was the cook. He wore a red bobble hat all the time, and had wide eyes that seldom looked at you. He was shy, he spoke little, but he did everything very decisively and vigorously. When he opened a can with a knife, for example, he did it in four bold strokes. He put out the fishing line when we moved off from Roseau docks. He took a strip of frozen fish from a plastic bag on the galley sink, cut off a fin with a long knife, then shaved away a few leaves of skin. He washed the flesh under the outside tap to thaw it so he could get the big hook through, which he did, and then wrapped a length of thin hard string around the flesh to hold it against the shaft of the hook. He threw it off the stern. A moment later he was hauling the line back in. 'Too many fish pots,' he explained. 'When we clear the point.'

It was a shallow channel. Along the western side there was a long chain of breakers marking a reef.

Total sent me up to the bridge to take a look. The captain had set the autopilot to keep to the leeward side which gave him a more direct route south. The wheel, polished wood, with customary spokes and a chrome hub, twitched now and then. He rested his elbow on the sill of an open window watching his prow rise above and fall below the horizon. Now and then he peered into the radar unit. Voices crackled on the radio from time to time. It was a sunny afternoon.

Cosmos, a short plump sailor who always wore a wool cap and a donkey jacket, was also a Carriacouan. Wally Alexis, a big burly man in his forties, was from Trinidad. He had a long moustache and his chin was never quite clean-shaven. He had been a seaman since his teens. He played cuatro, the four-string guitar used in parang. He showed me some tunes at the table in the mess, a little metal room with two benches and a table. He didn't sing but he hummed along to his strumming and became restful and contemplative. After three songs the other sailors told him to join them for cards. They all spent a lot of time playing cards in the mess.

When I was standing outside at night looking at an ink stain above the horizon which I guessed was the island of Martinique, Wally Alexis came up to me and said, 'Checking de island? That Mattnick.'

'Mattnick?'

'Yeah. Martinique. Dey is French.'

He rested his elbows on the side next to mine. 'I don't like Martinique,' he said.

'Why not?'

'De people is very stick to deyself.'

'Which island do you like?'

'Saint Lucy. Saint Lucy sweet, man.'

We stared at the darkness in silence. Then Wally said, 'When you ready to catch a res' jes' go in the mess.' The card playing was over.

We spent a night anchored off Carriacou. We arrived in the late afternoon and let the anchor fall into the clear, green water of the channel between Carriacou and Petit St Vincent, a small steep dry island. You could see the anchor all the way down on the sandy bottom once the water settled again. The whole place was very quiet.

I was excited. We were passing the night on shore. I was going to find Algie. He had told me to check him out if I ever got back to Carriacou.

We all climbed down a rope ladder, which Cosmos unrolled over the side, into the launch. The launch, which we barely fitted in, moved slowly, heavily against the water. The water was like corn syrup. It breasted up heavily against our prow, even though it was so immaculately clear. It was warm too. With the gentle breeze of our movement it became warm like a bath when your fingers touched it, a bath you would be happy to climb into.

The sun slipped behind Petit St Vincent. The island threw a

shadow over the wide shore at Windward on Carriacou, with its many white fishing boats littering the water and white houses here and there on the land. It was like the Hebrides. You expected to feel cold. You wanted to pull on a sweater for the evening.

I took a taxi, a mini-bus, to as near as I could get to Algie's place. By the time I had walked down a hill and through his garden of dry ploughed earth and was knocking on his door night had fallen.

There was no answer, and no light inside. I thought it was possible that paranoia might be keeping him from opening up, so I called out for him and said who I was. Right away the door opened. His face was there grinning in the light. He let out a long high laugh and grabbed my hand.

He was in his pyjamas, the shirt unbuttoned to the navel. The house was warm and bare. He invited me to stay in his spare room, but he had one big problem: he had run out of candles. Fortunately, however, I had half a candle in the bottom of the small bag I had with me, left over from the barrack at Tacarib.

Algie gave me a plate of food, 'a rice and peas'. He put the plate on the table and sat down opposite me. 'Does yer want hot sauce?' he asked – finger and thumb held up together – 'A touch?'

The candle didn't even last one hour.

In the morning Algie showed me a wood carving he had nearly finished. 'This is a rastaman,' he explained. It was a board of wood about eighteen inches square. Three quarters of it was a mop of dreadlocks. In one corner a small pretty nose and a pair of full blooming lips appeared in profile. They were the features of the little girls with huge tearful eyes who get sold along the Bayswater Road back in London. But it was neatly done, and there was something brave about that huge area of dreadlocks.

I only had till ten. Algie walked me to Hillsborough, the capital. On the way we passed an old man collecting firewood.

'Yeah, Daddy Daddy, mornin, mornin,' Algie sang out.

'Yeah,' the man answered.

We went to the Fatman Bar in Hillsborough for a Coke. It was a simple bar, run by a fat man. All over the pink walls messages had been scrawled in crayons and paints of all colours. 'He who like borrowing dislike paying.' 'My friends are welcome but please mind your own business.' Signed: 'One love.' 'Give and spend and God will send.' 'Some men are wise and some are otherwise.' But the commanding theme of the place, that greeted you on both doors and topped a list of *bons mots* above the bar, was: 'Give a fool rope enough and he will hang himself.'

I told Algie about the band I had played with on Dominica, and that I had turned down the chance to play on their album.

'Yeah man,' he said, 'sometimes you have to miss one ting to get a next ting. Like now you is here again.'

He urged me to go up into the mountains of Grenada for a year or two. 'Maybe you go up and you come again is a different person that comin again.'

I told him I was on my way to the Andes.

Outside another sign caught my eye. It was painted on glass above the door into the Morning Star Bakery: 'Trust is to burst, and burst is like hell, no trust, no burst, no hell.'

Mist hung in strands over the Gulf of Paria as I neared Trinidad once again. It was dawn. A small wooden fishing boat with an outboard came out over the smooth water to deliver the pilot. We drifted by a tall light buoy on which four pelicans perched in silhouette. One flapped into the air, almost dipping into the sea, as we glided by.

In the bow two sailors had ropes ready with their monkey-heads. They dropped one into the fishing boat when it pulled alongside beneath the great iron overhang. The boatman took it to shore, the line trailing out in the water like a fishing line behind him, then handed the rope up to a man on the wharf. 'That a long line, boy,' called one of the sailors. 'How we to pull all that in by hand? What kind of tying up is that?'

It worked out all right. 'Yeah boy,' Total the cook said to me. 'We just touch to go again.'

During the night oil had spilt over the deck. It had formed a sticky gravel with the dirt. Cosmos cursed it and then carried the swearing over onto the news that had just reached the boat that the wharf had been expecting the ship six hours later, at noon, so there were no dockers ready for loading. Someone had had to drive round to the foreman's house to get him up. It was lucky he lived nearby.

The mate and two sailors opened up the hatches. When you looked over into the great depth of the hold within you could hardly breathe. The air was thick with the smell of cement. A mangled ladder led from a half-way platform down to the floor of the hold. It was bent and twisted and diminutive. It looked like a hair grip, way down in the deep hold.

We docked at Claxton Bay. A morning haziness, a veil over the brightness of things, made the cement plant glow and shine as if with dew. Wally Alexis and I waited underneath it for a maxi-taxi to Chaguanas. It was good waiting. He was on his way to six hours, or twelve, with his wife. In that first hour of the day, with the taste of bacon and fried banana still on the tongue, having just now stepped onto land again, we were one with the morning bustle.

The Venetian light would have made anywhere beautiful, even the endless shabby suburbs along the Gulf of Paria. Trees with many small leaves, houses with iron balustrades, clumps of bamboo flag poles fenced in with rusty tin, the flags rags of red cotton frayed by the breeze and faded by the sea, family shrines to Hindu gods, it was all beautiful and exotic and welcoming.

I went into a bar in downtown Port of Spain for breakfast before checking into a hotel. Four Indian lawyers in white shirts and silver ties were breakfasting on beer. The bottles on the table were veiled with their own morning mist through which the dew ran in long lines.

THIRTY-ONE

Lent had finished a few days ago, and calypso fever was long gone. Nothing was happening in the music scene. In the bars where players hang out they talked about a new recording studio that was being built, about which groups were touring. Blue Ventures were going to Canada, Charlies Roots to Germany. Once or twice a week the odd band got a club show playing all kinds of music – soul, jazz, reggae, a little calypso. It was the season for talking not playing – which had really been the good calypsos of the year, which way soca was going if any, and that perennial question, why calypso didn't make it internationally.

There was a new sharpness to the question. Lambada was soca, and the Lambada dance was nothing on wining. Why all the fuss? Not only had the Brazilians stolen the style and given it the proper marketing calypso had never had, but they had even stolen a song. Koama's big hit was a flagrant plagiarization of Duke's song 'Thunder'. It was the same old story all over again. Harry Belafonte, who popularized calypso in the forties, was an American. The song 'Rum and Coca-Cola' had been stolen from Lord Pretender by the Andrews Sisters back then. By the time Lord Pretender won his lawsuit against them he had already overspent what finally came to him and lived destitute the rest of his life. 'Never Make a Pretty Woman Your Wife' was stolen by another American in the sixties from the Trinidad original 'Marry a Woman Much Uglier Than You' and turned into a big hit.

There was only one star of hope on the horizon, David Rudder. He was beginning to get some international attention. But was he doing calypso? Not to the purists.

I caught the last night of a stage show he was putting on, Down at the Shebeen. The songs I had heard him working out three months before were in it. It was good to hear the finished work. At the party afterwards I met many of the performers, friendly people who were scraping by off the arts.

'I'm a vibes man,' David told me. 'Call me next time you come through. Maybe we can do some work together.' I couldn't stay because I was on my way to South America now. In fact I had already bought my ticket. In two days I was flying to Quito.

But first there was one thing I wanted to see in Trinidad: a Shango ceremony. Shango is the Trinidad voodoo, and Shashu, a lady who had helped with the costumes of Rudder's show, knew of one starting the following night. It would run for five nights. All I had to do was get to her house at ten o'clock. She would take me along, provided I brought a bottle of puncheon rum, the strongest kind, or a bottle of olive oil.

The next afternoon, late, I went to an art gallery. I hoped the gallery would calm my nerves. I was tired and nervous at the prospect of the Shango: all night listening to that mad drumming.

Nine televisions had been stacked on top of each other in three rows of three in front of a big window in an air-conditioned concrete room. In the margin around them a sky of horizontal bands, a dusk sky, showed between dark walls of houses and a few silhouetted palm trees. The televisions were all playing a video of carnival. The soundtrack was Shango drums cut in now and then with weird electronics. They went straight to my head.

Everything is temporary in a modern tropical city. In the middle of a downtown dual carriageway stand rusted inverted triangles of cement. There are gaps between them. They are the central reserve, not replaced by a permanent parapet since dumped there as a temporary measure a decade ago. From the string of cars that pass by with their radios blaring your ear pieces together the snatches of music into a continuous song. They are all tuned to the same station. Beside a wire fence rests the giant camshaft of a ship's gearing. Rust stains have seeped into the tarmac beneath it. Wet patches appear on your tee-shirt as you walk. Your sweat smells fragrant like mangoes. Or maybe it is the air, mangoes cooking in a pot somewhere in the neighbourhood. Neon, concrete, yellow traffic lights, modern cars, all the paraphernalia of anxiety but no anxiety. The sensuality of the air forbids it because it is soft and warm for you alone. The odorous warmth caresses your skin, no one else's.

In the early night a tropical beer on a balcony. All things are relative and in a country with as much tropical sweetness in its atmosphere, in its tastes and smells, as Trinidad, Carib beer does its job. If you could think your palate back to a bleak northern climate it might strike you as sugary, even sickly, like a tropical fruit. Here it is good beer. I go out into the dusk city.

THIRTY-TWO

Shashu lived in a wooden hut on stilts beside her parents' house. It had one room, half of it occupied by the bed. There were two telephones, one mounted on the wall beside the stool on which she worked, the other by the bed on the floor. 'I lazy,' she explained. Her job was braiding people's hair. A head usually took her a day.

She herself had a mass of braids bundled up on top of her head and tumbling down her neck. They got tangled with her long necklaces, and fell into the copious necklines of her baggy dresses. She had a wide, strong face and a permanent faint smile. She was a self-assured woman.

We lay around waiting for our lift to the Shango. I had brought my bag with me. My flight left early the next morning, and the Shango was being held in a village close to the airport. Three of us were going: Shashu, her boyfriend Baal-Ogun, who was an initiate devoted to the god Ogun, and myself. We drank glasses of sorrel juice with big chunks of ice.

Baal-Ogun was an accountant in his early thirties. He had long, frizzy hair rising up from his head and his eyebrows were always raised, as if in surprise or amusement, or as if he

were continually inspired with divine bliss by his god. He and
Shashu disagreed over what liquor I should bring. Shashu was
recommending puncheon rum but Baal thought wine would be
better. The problem was they weren't sure which deity's night it
was tonight.

'Rum alway good,' Shashu asserted.

Baal finally agreed, so I went out to buy a bottle from a
nearby store.

Baal parried my questions about Shango. To whatever I asked
him he would answer that it was a matter of faith, like any other
religion, with his face set in its expression of cheerfulness and
mild curiosity. Either you believed or you didn't, he would say.
But slowly he revealed more. There were several deities each of
whom had different tastes in food and dance and colour. Shango
had been growing in popularity since independence. It had been
enjoying a revival as a suppressed part of the national heritage.

Shango is a possession cult of direct West African lineage. But
it has been highly syncretic, as syncretic as any psychic in the
classified ads. The chief source of extra ingredients has been
Christianity. But, Baal explained, if the deities have saints' names
too it is because they are one and the same phenomenon. The
goddess of the sea, Oshun, may also be called Saint Philomela. All
that proves is that certain early Christians with occult knowledge
recognized that particular force in the universe and gave it their
own name. Yoruba priests happened to give it another. But the
power exists as a spiritual force, to which its acknowledgement
by two distinct religions testifies.

The different deities possess in different ways. Each is summoned by its own particular drum beat, called as by a certain
peal of bells. When they arrive, when they come upon an
initiate, they have their own dance, their own actions, their own
purpose. Ogun spins and whirls and feeds the drummers rum;
while Oshun swims, with clumsy freestyle strokes, and feeds the
whole congregation water and honey. Shango himself, the god
of thunder, will touch only puncheon rum. He won't come near
a palais where weaker liquors are flowing.

From the outside the palais looks like a low-built church. It even sports a cross on the roof. The street is full of parked cars, new Mazdas and Nissans. Beside the building stands a row of tall bamboo flag poles with glimmers of light here and there beneath them, which come from diminutive altars on the ground. You hear drumming and over the drumming, again and again, a chorus of voices singing a simple two-part phrase: 'Kalambek – too . . . Kalambek – too . . . '

The palais is small and loosely crowded. People walk in and out freely. There is a long corridor. Half-way down a kind of pen opens on one side, a square room with waist-high walls and a tin roof. From the edge of the roof hangs a little fringe of curtain. Inside, everybody is sitting on benches around the walls. At one end hangs a tapestry of Christ with a flock of sheep. Beneath sit three drummers. This is the temple.

The place is brightly lit. Above the drummers there is a strip light, which makes everything clear and daylike. On the floor of the pen designs have been made in yellow chalk: a Star of David in front of the central drummer, obscure squiggles at each side of the square. In every corner a candle burns. Clouds of incense blow up from the ground beside one of the entrances to the space. In the middle of the David Star a large bronze dagger stands, the blade stuck in the ground. Several bottles and candles surround it.

The drums are West African – a small treble drum beaten fast with two spindly sticks, like a Nigerian talking drum, and two deeper played with one stick and one hand. All the drums sit between the players' legs. The two outer ones keep the rhythm going, helped along by shak shaks in the hands of many people in the congregation, while the central drum is the virtuoso. Its rhythm keeps changing, fighting away from the beat then suddenly coming back to it for an instant before hacking its way off the path again.

I recognize one of the three men drumming as a percussionist from Charlies Roots. The palais hire the drummers for the night. It is extremely hard work. There are six drummers here tonight playing in a rota. Every half hour one stops and gets up and walks out of the temple and another takes his place.

The congregation is mainly middle-aged women in voluminous

pink dresses and pink head ties. Shashu lets out a little cry. 'Pink,' she says. 'Who is pink?'

'That Oshun,' Baal replies.

Oshun is the lady of the ocean. Her colour is pink. Tonight is her night.

'Keep that bottle out the way,' Baal tells me. Oshun doesn't like strong liquor. She likes fine liquor, wine and milk, honey, oil.

I don't know what to do with it, so I just hold it down discreetly by my side. It would be hard to spot, in the loose crowd. It is wrapped in a ragged newspaper.

They are all still singing, 'Kalambek – too.' Then the drums speed up suddenly and no one sings for a while until a lone woman in a pink headshawl starts off again with a new chant: 'Sheme a moshe sheme.' After a while the crowd joins in with her, though they always allow her the first word. They sing only now and then: regularly but with long gaps between each line. In the gaps you hear the full complexion of the drumming, which is fast and intricate.

Opposite the central drummer a door stands open into a room hung with strips of cloth. On the door is an old Catholic print of Jesus bearing the legend: 'I am the door.' Over the door hangs a long banner saying, 'The great commandment brotherly love. Feed my lamb. Feed my sheep.' To either side of the lettering are yellow pentangles.

A man in pink pyjamas and with stiff grey hair and beard suddenly appears in front of me. He is tall. He is staring down at me with fiercely bright eyes.

'Put that rum away,' he says.

I am stunned, and struck through with guilt. The man saw not only through the crowd and through the newspaper, but through me too. He knew I was hiding something. This is the kind of ceremony where you would pay heavily for dishonesty. I feel like the man who scoffs at the seance and then drops down dead as he leaves the room. But I have nowhere to put it. My bag is locked in the boot of the car. So I take it outside and leave it among weeds by the gate.

Candles are burning in the little altars among the bamboo

flagpoles. A woman comes out with a bottle and pours a splash
on the ground in front of each one. They are little shelters, two
pieces of corrugated iron propped against each other, with the
nightlights beneath.

By the door two men are holding up another man. He is
slumped in their arms. He is completely limp, dangling towards
the ground. If they let him go he would fall like a rag doll. A
man comes out with a bottle of oil which he pours all over the
man's hair, smearing it around his scalp.

I go back inside in time to see a woman throw her arms open
and let out a great cry. Everyone in the corridor stands up. The
woman is in the inner temple and they all peer over one another's
shoulders to look. Oshun has arrived.

She stands stiff and erect with arms straight out in front. She
is wearing a long pink robe of a dress and a pink headshawl
wrapped like a turban round her head, and a pair of large glasses.
She could have been a suburban housewife in her bath robe about
to fix breakfast.

Before anything else happened two women were at her side.
First they took off her glasses. You could see her eyes in their
manic glory. They were wide open, her pupils ringed entirely
with white. And then they unwrapped her headshawl. She had
a mass of wiry hair that sprang out from her head in a great fan.
With that and the eyes she looked like she had just stepped off a
Hammer set.

Then the women tugged off her wedding ring. They each had
a go at it, pulling as hard as they could, before it came free. She
twitched a few times. The people drew back. Then suddenly she
was off stalking round the room with erratic steps. Her fingers
were splayed and she drew her hands up to her face one after
the other, again and again, while her enormous eyes scanned the
audience.

A man carried a wooden paddle out of the sanctuary behind
the door called 'I am the door'. He walked up to her, staring
straight at her, and held it against her head. After a while she
took it in both hands and started paddling around the room.
Then the same man took it from her again and she began to

swim, reaching her arms out in front alternately in jerky, brisk, wild strokes. She swam around and around, turning slowly and weaving her way through the crowd outside the temple and back again. She picked up one of the bottles that were standing by the dagger and made her round of the crowd again, this time stopping in front of each person and dosing them with the fluid, which was very runny honey. She did it in swift gestures, spilling plenty on our shirt fronts.

Meanwhile one of the women seated within the temple keeled over. She fell off her chair straight onto the floor. Several people picked her up and held her. She was slumped in their arms. They unwrapped her head scarf and applied various libations to her hair and waited. After a few minutes she suddenly leapt away from them, her eyes wide open and wild. She began her dance.

'When the god arrive you don't know what hit you,' Baal whispered to me. Then he chuckled like a drug addict talking about a high. 'They hit hard. You don't know where that come from.'

I was afraid. I knew I was gullible enough. I could already feel myself losing self-control. I was slowly getting hypnotized. I could already imagine suddenly being knocked out by a great blow to the head, but not a physical blow.

I wandered down the corridor in search of a little peace. There was a yard at the end. In the middle of it, tethered to a stake, were two goats. They were big strong goats. They looked at me with their necks stretched out inquisitively. I stared back. I wondered what they were doing here and then suddenly realized. A pang of dread went through me. The goats didn't seem to notice. They kept on staring me out and reaching for me as if I might be edible.

For a while more women got mounted and ridden around, all with the same Hollywood voodoo manners, until a problem arose. Oshun only mounted women, and it was her night, but suddenly a man in the temple went rigid on his feet, his arms by his side, his eyes bursting out of his skull. He was tall and thin, a young man. Slowly, little by little, he began to turn, and then spin. He bounced on his feet, his body still completely stiff, and span himself round. He went faster and faster and the drumming unmistakably altered tone, a new note of frenzy came in.

Ogun had arrived. Ogun wasn't wanted tonight. He was the god of iron. His night was tomorrow. Something had attracted him. Baal, who was standing next to me, said, 'What did you do with that rum?'

I told him.

'You should put it outside the gate,' Baal said.

It was too late. The man Ogun had mounted span his way all around the palais for the next hour and a half. There were two lulls in his dance when he hoisted a big clay water-jar onto his shoulder and went around giving everyone a drink.

The jar was like an amphora. It had a thin neck and broad shoulder. When he stood in front of me and I presented my lips to the spout he tipped it up and only a little dribble made it into the neck. He seemed to find some significance in this, because he drew the jar away and stared at me with his wide eyes. I didn't know where to look. Then held it out for me again. I moved my lips close and he tipped it right up, sending a great wave over the shoulder of the jar and splashing down my front.

After his water-carrying sequence Ogun went to the middle of the temple again where he span faster and faster, the drums getting more and more intense. Then the man suddenly went immobile, rigid as a corpse. At the precise onset of his rigor mortis, as if it had been rehearsed, the drumming ceased unanimously. In the moment of stillness that followed, in the sudden silence, the man tipped slowly then toppled like a felled tree. He fell stiff as a board and landed on the back of his head. Several of the wide-robed women picked him up and carried him to a bench where they laid him, his arms folded on his chest ready for the coffin. Immediately the whole place emptied, all the congregation flowed outside into the street. Ogun had finished, and it was time for a break.

Women came out with trays piled high with paper plates of rice and mutton stew. It was last night's sacrifice. Everyone munched on the food, plate in one hand, spoon in the other. It was like some bizarre lunch party. A few people talked. There was exactly the atmosphere of a break in a long late-night rehearsal on the eve of a big show. A glow of relief, of accomplishment, and also concern at what is still to come.

The man whom Ogun had ridden wandered outside after a while and took a plate of food. He was apparently unhurt.

The moment for one of the goats came much later, after another two hours of visiting from Oshun. A man led the animal up the corridor, the crowd parting for them, and then tethered it to a leg of the drummers' bench beside the Star of David and the big dagger. A crowd of robed women and men gathered around it. The drums played louder. A man emerged from the small throng with the dagger in his hand. It had a great bronze handle and a wide blade. He was wild-eyed and bouncing on his feet. He re-entered the little crowd.

Nothing happened. Everything went on as before, the drums playing hard and furious. After a few minutes the little cluster broke up. Two men were holding the goat off the ground by its legs. They carried it through to the room opposite. Then I noticed that there, where the dagger had stood, in the middle of the Star of David, the goat's head was sitting in a patch of brown dampness.

The drums were still going when we left, but they didn't have long to go. Dawn was less than half an hour away. The night had never thrown off its spongy warmth, and already cocks were crowing.

PART III

Mainland

THIRTY-THREE

It was raining at the Quito airport, Ecuador. A fine smoky rain that made everything tender and intimate. The jets on the ramp, the fuel trucks, the control tower of green glass, even the runway that banked up at the end like a ski jump, seemed small and unintimidating, even friendly. The raindrops were large but sparse. None of the passengers was in a hurry to get under cover.

Immediately my heart rose and my head turned light. I have seen this all before, I said to myself without believing it. These buildings, that door, that long bank of hills. This is where it happened, this is where I embarked on that fatal journey. And now I was back. To undo it? To retrieve an earlier life?

Along the main road into the city centre all the workshops and showrooms were closed up. Some restaurants were open, El Asadero, Pollo Dorado, El Tipico Bar, small places in need of paint and customers. At a junction the sound of a woman singing in a clear voice made me turn. It was an Indian woman draped in a sheet of plastic with a bucket in hand. She walked among the waiting cars selling pastries, and her call was a two-note song. Why did everything seem diminutive and welcoming, the shut-up garages, this dismal dual carriageway, the blocks of flats and offices built with a seemingly determined disregard for any congruence of style, the old buses with their big bonnets and tinsel-fringed windscreens, colourful like mobile shrines? Was it the mountains, that tumble together all life into the valleys? Or the place's poverty? Or the memory's trick of enlarging things?

And the old town, undulating streets of mildewed whitewash, squares with white colonnades and dark tile roofs, and no building more than three storeys high, and the towers of the churches nodding to one another over the rooftops, and the streets busy and here and there clusters of vendors, and long lines of them in the arcades, selling everything from curly full-length banana chips to self-expanding umbrellas, and Indian women sitting silently against the walls doing nothing – even though the city spreads up the surrounding hills it is built on a scale that, far from daunting, appeals to you, attracts you. It makes you want to go out, to be in it, to feel it, to stay longer than you planned.

An accumulation of images had an unexpected effect on me. A government building surrounded by a high wall covered in angry graffiti, a man carrying a sack at least twice his size, a tiny shoe shop called Creaciones Estrellana (that charming 'creations'), the mountains at the end of every street steep but mild, deep soft khaki in the blue smoke of the rainy atmosphere – they too seeming close and small – a woman roasting corn on a griddle, wisps of smoke drifting out from under the polythene canopies of brochette sellers. A feeling had been stealing up on me. It was a kind of sorrowful joy, a voluptuous melancholy that enveloped me for the rest of the day. I didn't know whether it was the tragedy of the indigenous civilization, a catastrophe whose ruins are still so evident today, or the stirred memories of my happy time here eight years ago, that fuelled it. The one thing I was sure of right away was that I had come to the only place where this journey could find its end.

The smallest unlikeliest things can trigger the sensation of a hollow, tingling confidence inside me in a new town. The particular roar a yellow bus makes as it climbs up onto a side street, and suddenly there it is, love of the exotic leaping up. For some reason the sound, throaty like a power-boat, reminds me of where I am on the globe, and of how free I must be.

At night you look up and see two pairs of lights high in the sky: aeroplanes coming in to land . . . until you realize they are houses, perched far up each on its own invisible spur. Or as you round a corner the two sides of a street draw apart to reveal a sky thickly splattered with heavy gold stars: so big, so rich. And then suddenly all the richer and bigger for not being stars but the lights of a quarter swarming up a mountainside. Or the blanket on a hotel bed, coarse-woven, beige with stripes of bloody brown. A rugged, simple blanket, something Clint Eastwood might wear as a poncho. It bespeaks a whole culture, tough and wise.

Strands of music weave through the city: a coach full of soldiers creaks over the brow of the square to topple off down a street. When it rolls by and tips up, there, on the back shelf, a silver euphonium and a stack of cases: a military band.

The fragrant smoke of a brochette grill on the other side of the square carries all the way across, and with it, from the cassette vendor next door, the thump and blare of a tropical tape. Ecuador, the southern boundary of salsa. And in every shop, in every bar, a radio or a tape playing: a cumbia from Colombian Joe Arroyo, a track by Kassav of Martinique, some Puerto Rican salsa, an Andean flute. Here and there, on a bench down the hotel corridor, leaning against the wall of a side street, walking through a busy throng, men blowing on pan pipes, practising to themselves. Outside the cinema three guitars, one of them the tiny charanga, two pipe-players and a big simple bass thump. The pipe players play in octaves between verses of the song, their notes loud and hoarse, and then sing in unison, their mouths open wide as if they are trying to suppress a smile. A thick ring of people stands around them. A girl on her father's shoulders is swinging from side to side and tapping his head. He is grinning at the band. He either knows them or the music. And the little record shops, scarcely more than doorways hung with faded album sleeves and a plastic-covered speaker turned too loud, to keep the vendors of a whole block happy. Most of the music is Andean cumbia, a weird hybrid, a tropical beat steeped in the melancholy of the mountains.

I have forgotten what it's like to be in a remote backwater of the world economy. After a night of impatiently waking again and again too early I am out to greet day's swift arrival. The vendors are already there. After yesterday's holiday old Quito is once again a market: every street full of people buying and selling. The narrow roads that climb up the hill contain the food market: huge pineapples stacked on the pavement, purple avocados, their thin skin bursting in little cracks where the soft green flesh escapes, tomatoes, spring onions black with soil and flooding the air with their sweet smart, pigs gutted, barbecued and sewn up along the back with stitches of thick black cord. They lie on long thin baking trays in congealed pools of coffee-coloured fat. Women cut them up into slices which they hand over on squares of paper to breakfasters. The flesh tears in pale strings like overcooked chicken. And the high cobbled streets that run across the hill are devoted to clothes, all kinds laid out on the ground, hung on doorways, stacked in chest-high piles. There is hardly room for two single files to pass between the heaps and displays and throng. The emotions, expressed in the same repressed tones, of a London traffic jam emerge in the pedestrians. People push, tut, exhort under their breath, and have shouts that they use like car horns.

Everywhere small-scale moneymaking. Splash, splash, on a street corner: an old man in a derby hat baling out the dregs, glassful by glassful, of his mobile juice-maker, a wooden box on a bicycle frame with a glass cabinet full of oranges. The liquid, a pale muddy orange, falls in a soothing cooling rhythm. An iced-drinks seller wheels an extraordinary Heath Robinson conversion of an old Singer sewing machine past the lavish and grotesque façade of a baroque church. His contraption has wrought-iron wheels of various sizes and perpendicularity finally interlocking with a set of spikes that claws a chunk of ice poised over a pair of blades. Beneath stands a bucketful of the shavings. In the middle of the street is a boy with a cardboard box containing a solid block of ice. On it rest six ice-cream cones, laid head to toe like sardines and smoking faintly.

Miles and miles of street are given up to marketing. And there are also indoor markets. I enter one, a great iron and wooden hall dominated by a huge altar on a scaffold. A Virgin floats on top of the altar, overlooking an enormous mound of fruits laid at her feet like an offering. Under her eyes, deep among the maze of alleys that thread between the vast mounds of produce, pork, fish, fruits, vegetables and money change hands. At one end sit the caterers, each in her tiled cubicle behind two or three aluminium cauldrons. Fish stew, pork stew, heaps of fried eggs and rice and yellow potatoes, sweet caramel-coloured coffee with cinnamon. Right beside them, in one corner, is the market lavatory: an open-doored room with a floor that at first appears muddy, until the penetrating, almost alcoholic, smell of sewage hits the adenoids.

And the music of the marketing: all around, from every corner, clear, strong voices raise their simple songs. They sing, they don't shout. Singing carries better. 'Para negocio, para negocio,' intoned on a falling minor third like a response. And a whole medley of calls that become intelligible only when you can actually see what they are describing. Small women shuffling along through the crowd with a baby on their backs and a basket in either hand and singing in thin plaintive voices endlessly, repetitively: 'Chilena, chilena.' In the basket red apples from Chile.

On a plaza in front of a church people have gathered around some spectacle. A man's voice is screeching from a loudspeaker. He is opening a wooden chest, microphone in hand, to reveal a snake – two snakes, or three. He seizes one by the throat and lifts it under his arm where it curls up trustingly like a lamb. He is screaming about people who have the eye and about how when a man is drunk he is not really drunk but no longer has light in his body. In front of him is a sheet of blue plastic covered with all manner of arcane supplies, from innocuous bags of dried nuts and beans and pods, and unusual twisted root spices, to a deer's head and a whole array of toucan beaks, mostly headless but some tufted with lank down. There are rolled up snake skins, jaguar skins, bears' paws, hoofs of many domestic beasts, wizened and dried, bones, lengths of bamboo stuffed with something black, and carefully stacked lengths of wood like kindling.

'What is all this for?' I ask a woman sitting at the edge of the spread. 'Cooking?'

She laughs. Some people who overheard laugh too. For a moment she seems unsure what to say, and then declares, 'Esto es remedios.' Remedies. This is a witch's apothecary laid out for the public.

And then I notice more and more superstition. I see a woman

blowing on a wad of notes she has just been paid and crossing herself with it before stowing it in a fold of her dress. She is either giving it the blessing that will make it attract more money or else cleansing it of any curse it may be carrying. A common one that can be laid on any bank note turns it into an insurrectionist who persuades any other notes it meets to desert their owner. If a shopkeeper has the misfortune to slip one of these into his till by morning the till will be empty.

At another stall, a tray propped on legs, a boy is selling magic soap: soap for love, for money, for health, for success. Wash your hands with it and they will magnetically attract what you want. Another magnetism on offer is coins that have been soaking in the beneficence of iron filings for a while: a bowl of filings and coins and little red beans (for some kind of leavening) all mixed up. Buy a coin and you have a money magnet in your possession. Money here behaves like a cartoon character, in a crazy world of slap-stick economics. To make sense of what the Andes have endured the hero, dinero, has to be as fickle, amoral, unpredictable as Bugs Bunny.

All day thin clouds came spilling over the hills that surround the city. They reach over in long white arms, reaching, reaching, through the gullies in the hills, and brimming over the brows. From the pedestal of the vast angel that overlooks the old town on the hill of Panecillo, Little Loaf, you see them slip down the slopes and then string out across the dark red roof tops – roofs like a rug, a fine weave of tiles. From up there it seems a small, sad city, a decayed, hopeless place lost up in the mountains. The white towers of the churches rise out from the brown crust, reminding you of gilt magnificence, of huge, rich congregations of the Spanish Golden Age. They are relics, mausolea of vanished wealth.

High on a saddle between the old and new towns rides a new Basilica, a structure of French Gothic begun in 1926, with see-through towers of intricate stone-work and rose windows. It is all but finished now, although the building site around it, with wheelbarrows and yellow scaffolds and shacks propped against the buttresses, doesn't suggest it. It was all but finished five years ago when Pope John Paul II blessed it. People say that the day they complete it will be the end of Quito.

On Sunday the streets are calm, quiet. There is silence like you find up in high market streets where no cars can go: a sibilant quiet of little plosive sounds, footfalls, speech somewhere, the rustle of dresses. It is the day of the Quito half-marathon. Here and there at a street corner is a little line of spectators, and every few minutes a jogger appears, or a group of joggers, progressively more and more exhausted, as if you were seeing the same runners further and further round the course when in fact you are seeing totally new competitors further and further down the order.

The plaza outside my hotel is loosely filled with people waiting for buses. At the pond beneath the statue of General Sucre a pair of old musicians, big-bellied men in hats and large dark glasses, are playing cumbias on saxophone and accordion. Cumbias have a simple regular offbeat step, heavy but infectious. Over the chords the melodies flow up and down the pentatonic scale like the pan pipes of the high mountains. The tunes rise and fall like sighs.

The accordionist sits on his case between numbers. They take long breaks. When the saxophonist plays he holds his head back and his belly out, motionless, as if stuck rigid in a seizure of musical ecstasy. A small listless crowd who might otherwise be waiting for buses watches.

As Sunday draws on more and more people come out. You notice the vendors especially, many of them selling the Sunday edition of *El Commercio*, and Indian women in their long dresses and trilby hats and woollen shawls, the shawl always wrapping either a box or a bundle or a baby to the back.

Above the plaza the hills rise from the rooftops, green, dark, moulded. The cumbia melodies flow over their curves like a wind.

THIRTY-FOUR

'Mandarinas.' Long, thin plastic tubes filled with mandarins in single file swing by their knots from the fingers of plump, young women, who sing the word with the plaintive cadence of a disappointed child. 'Mandarinas, mandarinas.' They come on the bus whenever we stop. Wherever people are waiting for a bus there also are fruit sellers, who come on board and walk the aisle slowly, exhausted, swinging their long catkins of fruit in no fear of the bus driving away with them.

We are climbing up, slowly up, out of the suburbs of Quito onto the moorland of the mountains. The city clings to the road, an undulating asphalt strip from Ecuador's oil decade, endlessly: districts of sandy-walled houses, small, laid out in grids, retail businesses, workshops, and then finally a bend around the shoulder of a hill closes it off. Ahead is a huge empty valley, one of those Andean valleys that takes a day to drive across and is a complete geographical and cultural region – fields, eucalyptus trees, villages, towns, smooth hills rising into cloud. We skirt it, and then rise out onto a paramo, a treeless highland.

I feel good. On the road again. Moving north into salsa country. The border is only a couple of days away. And from there we soon leave the mountains and pass down into the Cauca Valley and Cali, capital of Colombian salsa. At last I am on my way again, continuing my long-interrupted journey.

We wind down into the Province of Imbabura, a land of lakes and green volcanoes where the Otavalo Indians live. The Otavalos are a success story. You see them in New York and Europe and all over Latin America selling ponchos and sweaters, or playing Andean music on the street. The men have a distinctive dress of white bell-bottom trousers several inches too short and wide navy ponchos, while the women wrap up in long, thick, blue skirts of velvet, embroidered blouses and wear thick headshawls of starched wool and spirals of gold beads round the neck.

For three days of the week the town of Otavalo is draped in

woollens for sale to tourists. It is a small town of concrete houses with a pair of grand churches. I have been here before, this was as far north as I came last time. I stay only one night.

Soon after dawn the town is bustling, men and women going to work, children to school. I jump on a crowded bus that growls uphill at a pace I could outrun, up to a brow and then over the crest towards the lake of San Pablo, just the other side of a low hill. San Pablo is a circular lake. Islands of reeds drift around it, ferrying dragonflies and little yellow birds. Three mountains overlook it, but much the biggest is the huge pyramidal volcano of Imbabura, named after a giant Otavalo warrior. The lake was his undoing. He sank while trying to run across it. You can still see a great scoop of flesh clawed out of the mountain where he tried to save himself from drowning.

Eucalyptus trees shimmer along the shore. Above them is a patchwork of fields, and a torn net of hedgerows. Here and there a plume, and a little cloud, of smoke. And then up and up rising and sweeping up for thousands of feet are the great flanks of the volcano, lifting up to smooth shoulders and a craggy head. All day cloud shadows dapple the beast, stealing over the curves and carrying along pools of sunlight, making the distances seem greater still.

Women are washing clothes in the water, splashing and beating them on rocks. Sometimes a totora reed boat comes slowly past, an old man or a child paddling gently. Here, by the lake, beneath a volcano, is the kind of peace I have come for.

Then two bangs sound from somewhere round the shore. During the lulls in the sounds of the laundry I can hear music coming across the water: arpeggio tunes, Andean tunes, carrying the unmistakable blare of Latin trumpets. I am sitting on a terrace out over the lake, built of ill-fitting planks and uneven stilts at the back of a disused café. A wind gets up, shaking a washing line above me, making the prop heave back and forth. The music comes louder, until drowned by the gurgle of a bus making the round of the villages.

I set off in search of the music. Women are harvesting big, red heads of quinoa from a patch of cultivation. Next door is a waterlogged meadow where pigs and sheep and cows graze, sometimes plunging through deep puddles. A man in a blue poncho and derby hat greets me. 'Why don't you go to the fiesta?' he says. The skin around his eyes is deeply creased, as if he had spent decades staring at the sun. 'You could take photographs.'

'Where is it?'

He tells me, points to it across the lake, and then takes me.

At first it looks like a party: everybody sitting in a large open yard. But there are women selling cigarettes and sweets and snails steeped in herbs and green liquor. Beside them, a little apart from the main throng, and half of its members leaning against the wall of a small house, is the band: two drums, a sousaphone, several trumpets, a saxophone, euphonium and valve trombone. All the players are middle-aged and dressed in suits and hats. They are blasting away through a sanjuanito, a dance rhythm dedicated to San Juan.

At the heart of the fiesta is a long table covered in a white cloth. Along either side sit men in enormous colourful pantaloons. At the head is the captain of the fiesta, the coraza, the village headman. He looks like a cross between a clown, a transvestite and a conquistador. His face is painted white, except for the lips, which are red. He wears a costume of white adorned with beads and gold discs and a hat of multicoloured plumes like a Spanish helmet. Beside him stand two guards, each in furry leather riding breeches with a whip in hand. The table is a party of conquistadors.

They are feasting on big plastic bowls of chicha, maize beer, and yamor, a corn soup reboiled until it becomes a brown mud. All around sit their guests, among whom weave men and women distributing food and drink from buckets. In a yard at the back a washing line is hung with live chickens. Later on the men and women will begin eating their way along them.

The fiesta is in honour of the new coraza. He will hold his office for one year. This is the first of the many parties he will have to throw during his year of leadership. It is the usual story of Andean leadership: it carries a high price. When the man honoured with the post has finished his year he will be broke.

The fiesta is a satire on the Spaniards, passed down for four hundred years. The Otavalos still rent their land from absentee landlords. Along the walls of the villages again and again you see the graffiti against the tierratenientes and the foreigners: 'The foreigners took our land five hundred years ago. We have to organize to reclaim our patrimony.' Afuera los Extranjeros. It had made me a little nervous.

The band want pictures taken. While I am photographing them suddenly a hand grabs my shoulder and pulls me back. It is one of the men in breeches, with a knotted whip. Somebody is asking for me, he tells me, wheezing his maize-scented breath over me. The band, half of whom are playing a number, call out that I'm in the middle of something and an argument develops between the two sides. Suddenly several of the pantalooned host have risen and are backing up the chief assistant. 'Es el capitan,' they are saying. It's the captain who wants me.

I don't know whether this is an honour or something to dread, a summons from the headmaster. Several of the hosts escort me to him. He is holding a sceptre festooned in ribbons. Amid all the noise I have to squat to hear him. He leans his white face close. He is eerie, with his thick, red lips and small eyes and a great pasty moon of a face. 'Dos,' he is saying, holding up two fingers of a white-gloved hand. 'Dos fotos.' And then he says something which I conveniently don't understand. Some of the host pat their palms, explaining for me. Everybody is thronging around me. I reach into my trouser pocket hoping not to bring out too large a note. I hand one over to him. Not enough. The same again. Then he rises, a ghostly white figure, and calls over his son, a boy of around six in trilby and a few plumes. They stand beside one another unsmiling. The crowd draws back, making space for the photographs. On my request we move over to the yard at the back where the chickens are hanging. The men there laugh and move back against the wall. Somebody lifts a chicken the right way up so it flaps its wings around his face and squawks. The captain returns to his place at the table, where he resumes his sombre expression.

Then one of the conquistadors with a wispy beard and gruff voice asks me if I have any foreign money to leave as a souvenir. As it happens I do, in the back pocket of my jeans, a few Trinidadian coins that have been there since I left the island. I pull them all out in one handful and suddenly a mass of hands, palms open, comes thrusting towards me. For a moment I don't know what to do. Pop one coin in each? Then among the shifting mass of palms I catch sight of a white glove, the captain's. I reach out and deposit it all in his hand, hoping he will handle the distribution. It closes into so tight a fist that I can't pull my own fingers out. A dozen or two dozen faces staring up at me and calling out for foreign money: the captain, he has it, I reply. It doesn't make any difference. They know they won't get any out of him.

I retreat to the band. The pleas drop off one by one as I go. A boy with a bucket hands me a mug of chicha: sweet, grainy, speckled with dirt and flecks of husk.

The trombonist wants to hear me play. The instrument looks like it has been crumpled up and then unrolled again. The valves have lost their buttons, so you have to press on their sharp tops. There is something wrong with one of them which makes it impossible to use. Suddenly the band is starting up into a number. A trumpet player with a moustache, who appears to be the leader – he takes solos and nods the trumpets in – waves at me and shouts out to play. I turn to the trombonist, a small old man with a permanent smile, and he too tells me to play. So I quietly find the tonic and thump along for a while. The euphonium-player and the saxophonist come and stand either side of me, blasting away and throwing their bodies into the music. They are losing a lot of notes to laughter.

They both play with the police band in Otavalo. This is a reunion, they tell me afterwards, of an old band. The players come from villages all around the lake. They point out the white church of San Rafael on the far side, the roofs of Compania glittering among the trees, the scattered white houses of Camuendo scaling the lower slopes of Imbabura, among the netting of the field plots. Later they would move on to the next village for its coraza celebration.

More chicha, a bowl of sickly sticky yamor, and I leave to get back to Otavalo before dark. Already the clouds are rolling round either side of the volcano. Soon they will meet in the middle, like a cape, but closing off the mountain's head. As I walk away the music starts up again, and I hear more bangs to draw the villagers, and a firework crackling, invisible in the daylight. The lake is ruffled. On a wide mountain beside Imbabura, like a low monster with its two arms resting wide, puffy lead-bellied clouds have come to brood. Shadow is filling up the height of Imbabura like a drink in a glass. Dusk has not yet arrived. When it does there will be only a few minutes before nightfall.

From far away you can still hear the music, rising from among the trees like smoke, and drifting across the lake, up into the great bowl between the mountains.

The fiesta wasn't over till the end of the next day, when they had an electric band from Otavalo, trumpets and keyboards and bass, who sat inside the hut where the brass band had played. They had two speakers outside that blasted their music across the lake, and the echoing amplified voice of their singer. It sounded like he was performing to a huge outdoor crowd. In fact there were only a few couples, stepping heavily to the beat, where the conquistadors had sat the day before. Most of the people were inside the hut, crammed in so tight that when they danced they had to bob as a single unit. Between songs a long stream of men filed out of the hut to pee against the wall. Nobody was in costume. It was a day of dancing and heavy drinking, the ritual accomplished.

THIRTY-FIVE

The clouds that herald night blow up from the sea and the jungle. They wreath themselves about the peaks and turn luminous, from milk to neon, the last flicker before the ghost of day departs. Soon the sombre hills settle down into blackness.

Far below, from a pass, a city prickles the night: a little galaxy, a nest of sparks dashed open on the plain. Beneath the lights, in the darkness beneath, shopkeepers are selling groceries to children, women are walking down church steps, men are conversing in doorways. A city is settling down for the night.

Then the thrill of arriving in a small city at night – within walls still breathing out the absorbed warmth of the day, shops open till late, bars, and restaurants selling grilled chicken, Chinese noodles, avocado salads, and men and children and women out on the pavement, talking, strolling, buying, and a plethora of hotels, and newspapers for sale at every corner, and a cathedral on a plaza before which stands a row of kiosks each with a little bench in front selling grilled meat, soup, fried potatoes, and bottles of blackberry syrup, a speciality of northern Ecuador, and everything glowing with the particular warm glow of a mountain city reached by night, and sudden conversations with strangers that quickly get out of their depth – but after the night-time orgy of the senses, enhanced by a few days' rural deprivation, you wake to a morning of low cloud, now and then a hint of drizzle, grey glistening streets and huddled pedestrians and wisps of mist drooping out of the clouds.

All of a sudden I am remembering how dismal mountains can be. The little city now is high and cold, stranded among the hills, and dull, unbearably dull. You consider the possibilities, looking across the rooftops you can point to them: the cathedral; the tin-roofed market crammed with crammed stalls selling everything just like in the other cities; and somewhere up in the fog above, a hill with a view. But not today.

Fatigue overcomes you. There is nothing to do. You could resume an exhausting and disturbing conversation with a Colombian staying in the hotel, an itinerant clothes salesman who writes poetry. He is really as colourful as they come. His poems are highly romantic. His name is Wilson Arturo, and he is in his late twenties. He wears nylon slacks and cardigans from his stock and has light-brown, blow-dried hair. A long scar runs across his right cheek, and he has full, thick lips. He moved to Ecuador after some 'difficulties' he had had in the underworld of the city of Pasto.

'It was a matter of drink and a girl,' he explained. 'A man died.

But I didn't fall into the error of regretting this mistake. No, I decided to look forward, and so I came here to Ecuador. I left all that behind, drugs and motorbikes and *aguardiente*. Now I live well, and healthily. La vida sana.'

Conversation with him makes me uneasy. He is the first self-confessed murderer I have ever met.

The alternatives are equally appealing. More breakfast. A walk. A rest. A book. The best thing would clearly be to move on, but I'm waiting for my washing to dry. Rain at dawn set it back a few hours. And in fact I'm not sure that even if it were ready I would have the energy to go.

Wilson Arturo had made friends with two buxom teenage girls. He brought them to my room and we all sat on the beds talking about how far away London was and how much the air fare there was. Then he took one of them by the hand and got up and left. He gave me a wink from the doorway.

I panicked. Were they prostitutes? I didn't know what to do. The girl wasn't troubled by finding herself suddenly alone with me. She came and sat next to me on the edge of the bed, and turned to look at me with her wide, black eyes. I coughed to break an uncomfortable silence. Dread was rolling over and over in my belly, until I glanced at her chest. It threw a blast of lust at me like a flame-thrower. She put her hand on my thigh, and showed me how the young stay sane in a remote mountain city.

Now it is raining again. This morning I moved on. I am in a village on the Colombian frontier. The only place to eat is the market, all but deserted. One woman has a food stall. A farmer in poncho and Panama with a rugged, pockmarked face is feeding himself her chicken soup with one hand and with the other bites of her huge crumbly boiled potatoes. He breaks pieces off and drips aji, the hot sauce, onto them from a spoon. Two men are standing under the eaves opposite.

She serves me hot, sweet coffee in a wide enamel cup, and stiff rolls to dip. The rain water falling off the eaves makes a curtain of

droplets that closes off our stall. The farmer and I sit at either end
of her small, green table slurping and she stands looking out at
the silvered mud and the drenched, dark eucalyptus trees beyond
a wall. Less than a mile away is the huge volcano Chiles, but the
only clue to its existence is a steaming stream that runs down the
street. The clouds are just above us.

I am on my way to the city of Pasto in Colombia, waiting for
the rain to stop. At least I hope I am on my way. Wilson Arturo
recommended an obscure route over the frontier into Colombia.
It is also immensely complicated. I had to get my official exit and
entry stamps at the main border crossing and then return back
into Ecuador to the nearby town of Tulcan. From there to the
village of Tufiño, which is where I am now. From here, Wilson
assured me, you enter Colombia by walking under a pole in the
street. This simple barrier marks the frontier leaving locals free to
cross either way, but foreigners are not supposed to use it. From
the other side you can then surreptitiously take a ride on the daily
milk lorry to the village of Cumbal two hours away, from where
it is easy to reach the city of Pasto.

The journey began this morning with an early bus for the
border. It was a dreary morning. Despite its height, the landscape
was reminiscent of Berkshire, with hedgerows, intermittent trees
and drizzle. I found myself paying great attention to the retreating
row of passengers' heads that I could see in the driver's oversized
mirror: a series of black mops and nervous eyes bobbing up and
down above the seat backs. Then we were climbing gently into
the clouds, and I looked out to find that we were all of a sudden
skirting an immense canyon. I could tell this only because far
below there was a small hazy glow of golden grass. Otherwise
all was mist.

Soon we were over a brow, coming down a hill out of the
clouds and into a desert. Ahead stretched a huge valley of sandy
rock reaching down to the spate-bed of a fast river. A warm haze
was all that was left of the clouds.

Here in the northern Andes the hegemony of the mountains
that divide so decisively the jungle from the Pacific desert
collapses. The mountains come tumbling down, and over them,

like moss over the stones of a ruin, scramble both the desert and jungle. The cordilleras, the highest ridges, are narrower than ever, and great gaps allow the different climates through.

Our road curved along beside the river. Now and then we passed an oasis village: a few brilliant green fields in the valley bottom, all the more startling for the bare rock surrounding them, a few clumps of papaya trees, a cluster of brown mud houses, sometimes two or three traditional Indian huts of circular thatch, maybe twenty houses in all including a roadside restaurant.

We were following the River Chota, and descending sharply. Then for an hour we climbed, out of the canyon and onto the rolling hills again. Light snow had fallen up here. Everyone was discussing whether it fell yesterday or this morning. The woman beside me said she had never seen snow here before, and she was certainly in her fifties. But it was only a small patch. We were soon back in the autumn Chilterns and nearing the frontier town of Tulcan.

I got my stamps at the frontier and then went to a bank in Colombia where they wouldn't let me cash a traveller's cheque because of the disparity between its signature and the one in my passport, ten years younger. Suddenly I foresaw unimaginable problems waiting for me in Colombia, not merely financial. I decided that Colombia scared me and set about verifying the prophecy. The first step was to follow Wilson Arturo's advice and enter the country illegally by the obscure frontier post in Tufiño, which meant returning to Ecuador.

I made my way to Tufiño in the back of a truck under cover of a lunchtime thunderstorm, and now in the Tufiño market café I am still waiting for the rain to pass. I ran here as soon as the truck came to a stop in the plaza.

The woman has refilled my cup three times, and keeps handing me rolls I don't want. The farmer in the Panama has gone. Two Otavalo Indians have taken his place. They came in from the rain with enormous bundles on their backs. They are selling clothes to the villagers, which they carry wrapped up in sheets tied across the forehead. Their baggage takes up so much space they had to leave it in the next stall.

In the end I have to wait for more than the storm to pass. When the rain stops I walk down the track into Colombia, with a nod to a ponchoed policeman, and to the other half of the village, La Calera. Here a woman standing in a doorway tells me that because it is pay-day the Cumbal milk truck is running late. If I hang around it will probably give me a ride.

It doesn't entirely fill me with joy. I still have grave doubts about the wisdom of entering Colombia by this back door. I foresee police checkpoints at every bend of the road. 'But your passport says you crossed from Tulcan. What are you doing on this road? Foreigners cannot enter this way. You will have to come with me.' And then me nervously asking, 'Is there not some other way?' and hoping I don't hit on too large a denomination when I fumble in my money belt. But even the thought that the problem might add up to no more than a little slimming of the wallet does not console me.

I decided, thereupon, that what I needed was a good soak in a hot bath, and as there happened to be one only a mile away I eagerly set off up a track with a change of clothes and a towel.

The hot water came courtesy of the Chiles volcano, just then a brooding mass of slate-grey cloud, and was green and faintly foul-smelling. It was sulphurous. Two gurgling and steaming ditches flanked the track. At the top of the hill, which was a mere corner of the volcano's base, five swimming pools had been sunk into the ground, stepping down the slope. Only two were filled. I made for the higher, hotter one.

The water was totally opaque. The heads of several Indian families basking in the warmth had grins spread across them, and some laughed hysterically at the sight of me clambering down over the muddy ground to the pool in my shorts. Everyone smiled expectantly at me as soon as I was submerged.

'Te gusta?' a man asked, beaming.

'Sí, sí.' It did please me. This is a real bath, this is the only kind of bath, I was thinking. Hot and big enough to swim several strokes. There was also something satisfying about being invisible. You could lie back, floating just under the surface, and only if you allowed your toes to appear a couple of yards away

from your head did anyone know you weren't sitting on one of
the stone steps built into the sides.

'Up there it's more scalding,' the same man told me, pointing
to one end where the water splashed in from a pipe. A woman
was rinsing her hair under the stream.

I wallowed at the hotter end and then began working out
different plans for getting dry and dressed. I had to accept the
humour that was inherent in myself as far as the audience were
concerned. The problem was the mud: how to dress with muddy
feet without getting my pants, socks and towel muddy. It was
similar to the problem of dressing on a beach, but much worse. In
the end I didn't follow any of my plans and my clothes got dirty.
But at least I was clean, even if faintly scented with sulphur.

The price of the bath, however, was missing the milk truck.

I trudged back across the border and spent a nervous night in
Ecuador. The woman with the one telephone in Tufiño rented
out her sitting room whenever someone happened to need it. She
gave me supper then a hot cup of *agua aromática*. I wondered
what petal or bark it had been infused from. She ran to the
kitchen to fetch the packet to show me. 'Del supermercado,' she
explained. 'En Tulcan.'

I shivered on a camp bed under four thick, folded blankets.
It was very high and cold. Lightning flickered silently every few
minutes illuminating the flimsy furniture and religious pictures
in the room. Finally I was so exhausted by worry that I stumbled
into sleep.

After fried bananas and eggs for breakfast, I set off into
Colombia eager and hopeful. I'll hike until I meet the milk
truck, I thought to myself, but having clumsily negotiated the
obstacle of three drunken men on horseback who wanted me
to share their *aguardiente* – they had been drinking at least all
night, their eyes puffed and sore and glinting – the first vehicle
I came upon was a jeep carrying four travelling salesmen.

They had come out all this way from Pasto not to sell farm
machinery or fertilizer but lottery tickets. Cars and such things
are very expensive in Colombia, explained one of them, drawing
out of his briefcase a set of pictures like a concertina string of

postcards. It was one of the raffle brochures, and had pictures
of a car, three taxis, a fishing boat, a bus and a house. Because
such things were so costly, he said, they were helping people out
by offering them in a lottery.

They offered to make room for me and took me on a tour
lasting several hours of the region's farms, at each of which one
of the salesmen would climb out and the rest of us would wait
for as long as it took to make a sale.

Conversation was exclusively financial, these being men of
finance.

'In Chile it's the chileno.'

'The chileno? No.'

'Yes. Pesos chilenos.'

'No, no. Escudos. Escudos of the Bank of Chile.'

'And in Brazil?'

'Cruzados.'

'No. Cruzeiros.'

'No. Cruzados nuevos.'

'Cruzados novos. It's Portuguese.'

'And the sol of Peru?'

'No. The inti.'

'And the Bolivar?'

'Yes. In Venezuela.'

We rocked along the track while they continued to investigate
the economics of the continent. Finally I was in Cumbal, and at
once, before I had a chance to gain an impression of the town,
I was speeding along in the back of another jeep that served as a
bus to the small town of Guachucal. Thence, in another crowded
jeep – one that took vehicular decor to the extent of having two
little glass-doored cabinets above either corner of the windscreen
in each of which were three liqueur miniatures – to the next town,
Tuquerres, a town that had an impressive collection of working
horse carts and early Cadillacs.

THIRTY-SIX

As soon as I saw my first Colombian town, a bustling blend of a Western movie and southern Spain, with its roads furnished with chrome-plated monsters from the American fifties, Ecuador became a small, dull country in my mind, the Belgium of the Andes. Colombia was everything a tropical country should be, and more. It had every kind of climate. The towns and cities were like fossils of the Spanish era, and were crowded with friendly people. Everywhere there were blacks from the coast, Indians from the mountains and jungle, whites from the valleys, and people of every possible racial mix. And to complete the picture, every hundred miles or so you got stopped at military checkpoints with three or four tanks, their barrels draped with washing, and several polite soldiers of either sex in floppy sun hats.

I reach Pasto, having driven for two hours along a vast gorge that gradually widened and deepened, and right away I find the hotel of my dreams: two cloister-like courtyards, rooms with ceilings twenty feet high and floorboards smoothed by centuries of feet, tropical plants everywhere, and all for a dollar fifty a night. The street outside is lined with bars and restaurants, from which emerges a collective roar of salsa that smothers the sound of the traffic.

No sooner have I dumped my bag and started wandering the streets than I come across first a *grupo folklorico*, an Andean band, playing within a dense circle of people in the plaza, and second a salsa band. I can hear a voice booming over a PA system, and ahead a crowd is packed into a shopping mall. I fight my way through and there they are, just counting in to the first number – El Grupo Bemtu (Ven Tu – C'mon) from Cali.

Four horns hidden at the back, three male vocalists with big infectious smiles who dance in step, some rhythm and a lot of percussion. They are tight and 'very tasty', as the MC who runs up onto the stage to shoot his rap between numbers keeps saying. *Sabrosisimo*.

It's a free concert. At the end I get talking with the lead singer. He has a dense, short, black beard and sparkling eyes. He is still on adrenaline from the show. He tells me that the one thing the band badly needs is a trombonist. They have all the music – he shows me the book of trombone parts – but no one to play them. Would I come and rehearse as soon as I reach Cali?

Everything comes at once: pleasure in sensations, new ideas, a sense of moving on, of leaving things behind like exhaust smoke, and the desire to be happy. I seem to have fallen into a travelling rhythm. A day travelling, a late afternoon and evening in a town, a decision in the morning: to travel again or to spend the day in the town catching up on my diary and looking around.

The very act of travelling, of passing through changing scenery – like now, saddles and curves and long, leaning crests and wisps of cloud, and banana trees, then conifers, and green fields, bald slopes among the foliage, the steepest shaken into steps by earthquakes, and farms and villages with children and chickens in the streets, and streams the colour of black coffee as it pours – the very act of travelling keeps thoughts rolling by with the landscape. The land is always there, innocent, impassive, logical. It doesn't guarantee to turn thoughts to the positive, it makes no appeal, but there it is, rolling by, always changing: sooner or later the mind comes up for air, the eye opens.

San Agustín, a small town in southern Colombia, is a world so crowded that there is no empty space left. The street full of people, and noise, music, laughter, and talking, people walking by along the street in the newly fallen night talking, an endless stream of voices. And on approaching the town, above the people, the houses, white and crumbling, and with roofs of greying tiles, and above them the sky full of many-coloured clouds rising and falling and overflowing one another. And from the back, over family courtyards where pigs and hens grunt and peck, the hills, the steep, close, big hills, some covered thickly in trees, others bare for cattle. The world here is a naive painting.

This is the Colombia I have come for, a country full to bursting. I travelled north-east, from one side of the mountains to the other, from Pasto to the grim strait-laced city of Popayan, all two-storey, rococo Spanish whitewash and grills, and then to this warm, verdant town. All the way, until here, it was raining on the hills. They brooded grey under a dripping sky. Then flashes of sunlight broke through here, brilliant green leaves sparkled across on valley sides, and the whole town is still seized by a fiesta spirit, although it is only a normal Monday night.

In the hotel courtyard parrots, huge brilliant ones, pigs, chickens, dogs and two small homuncular monkeys are kept in a tall, thatched pen. The monkeys chase round and round on the chicken wire and over one another. They keep cuddling and then leaping apart and screeching in their high, sweet whistle, and then running over each other again. They look like two little people, a couple, coming together for warmth then scampering apart. And when they run on the wire they move so smoothly, they glide, they glide around their pen alive to every corner of their world, like fish gliding and sensing every tremor in the water.

The hills of southern Colombia, where the tumbled mountain range is first cut into three parts pursuing their separate ways to the Caribbean, are where the ancient peoples of San Agustín and Tierradentro lived. They are known today by nothing other than their monuments to death, the liths and chambers that they left at the gateway from life. The land is a close jumble of folded mountains covered in every kind of vegetation – moorland, forest, scrub, thick jungle – and cut up deeply by a network of bloated rivers which pour finally into one of two great rivers, the Cauca and the Magdalena, both of which flow all the way north to the Caribbean.

San Agustín and Tierradentro, the two clusters of monuments some fifty miles apart, which is ten hours by road, are the chief relics of ancient Colombia. The Incas never reached this far north, and the Chibcha, the civilization that the Conquistadors found on the highlands around Bogotá, built only in wood. Not necropoles but villages of the dead are what the two cultures left behind. On flat shoulders of the hills around San Agustín they erected fanged statues to guard their tombs. The jungle has been cleared back from them now and they stand overlooking deep valleys.

The fearsome statues all represent either animals or men and are mostly the height of a man. The biggest and best preserved have little iron roofs hanging over them for protection. The figures are block-shaped – square heads on square bodies – but are easily identifiable. A bird guards one tomb. It has two wide, saucer eyes, ringed and insane, and a long, pointed beak flattened over its neck, like a rat's snout, from which hangs a snake that curls down the side of the bird with its tail resting on the talons. It is a fat, squat hawk, simple and efficient. Many have faces that seem human – a triangular nose and a bridge between the eyes – except for an immensely wide mouth with two sets of interlocking fangs. They hold a variety of sceptres and cups and other ritual objects. They are manifestly related to the monolithic sculpture of Chavin in Peru and Tiahuanaco in Bolivia and, although the mechanics of that relationship remain unknown, they all tell of primitive hierarchy – the priest-chief ordered the building of this monument.

At Tierradentro the magnificence went underground. Again the tombs lie in clusters of ten or twenty on spurs commanding a view, but no deities use the vantage. Instead holes in the ground lead some twenty feet down in a series of steps to vaults.

The design of the vaults reached its peak around the eighth century, developing from bare caves to oval wombs ten yards in length with two thick columns of rock supporting the roof in the middle. The walls are ringed by ledges a couple of feet above each other, rising like the hoops of a barrel up to a small hoop on the roof encircling the pillars. Every few feet stands a buttress, between them the niches where the burial urns were interred. They buried only bones: the nobility and their retinue were moved here after a year or two in a primary grave, a simple

small stone-slabbed hole for putrefaction. They came as an urnful
of jumbled bones and ash, after a cremation rite.

The beauty of the tombs is not only in their shape but also
their decoration. They are covered in blood-brown squares and
diamonds and double lines and the pillars around the walls are
carved into deity figures with strong triangular brows that lead
down into the nose and mouth, mirrored by arms crossed with
the hands on either shoulder, in the posture of effigies. Together
the facial features and arms form an X. On the most eroded all
that remains is the cross itself, without trace of the anatomy it
represents. The whole impression is of a cosy wall-papered room,
perfectly balanced. Something about the play of all the curves and
hoops and sloping round roof with the geometrical decor makes
them places you don't want to leave.

A few are lit by a bulb lying on the floor. As more and more
detail appears out of the rusty glow the eye becomes more and
more satisfied. The silence rings, down in the cool earth. You
hear the hiss of your own ears.

A bumble bee had found its way into one tomb. It droned
round and round in the dark, its buzz amplified to a metallic
resonance. In the silence of another chamber I suddenly heard a
bird from above, whistling in the daylight. It had alighted near
the tomb mouth and was singing loud and hard, its voice instinct
with daylight. The contrast was perfect: the rhythmic silence in
the eye, the clear light in the ear, the voice of day, of life. It was
just enough, after letting myself fall into the loving embrace of
the tomb, to call me back to the upper ground. It came as a voice
of promise.

When I came out the guard of the site was walking by with
a saucepan full of water. He was a small, wiry man in a green
uniform and cap. Apart from him the only other people there
were two travellers I had met the night before. They were busy
taking photographs of the deep valley below. It was a beautiful
landscape, falling from black cliffs to bushy slopes and in the
valley bottom were clumps of giant bamboo, curved and downy
like feathers. They were like quills crowded into jars.

The guard stopped and asked me where I was from. We got

chatting and I went over to watch while he prepared his lunch. Every day he built a campfire by the fence. First he swiftly cut himself a heap of shavings from a stick of red wood with skilful, fine blows of a machete. When he had enough he lit them. Then he leapt over the fence into the brush and pulled at a branch of a young tree. With two strokes he had lopped it off, and then stripped it and brought it back to use as a support from which to hang his pot, leaning it on the bottom strand of the wire fence. He gently fed the fire under the pot. Into the heating water he threw a piece of pork, a handful of corn kernels, a peeled yucca root and a banana. It was only mid-morning. By lunchtime his meal would be ready. He would sit around waiting. His job was only to unlock the grates over the tombs and then lock them up again in the afternoon.

The two travellers I had met were an Australian restaurateur called Stavros and an Englishman, Phil, on his way home round the world after a decade of working abroad. Stavros was a successful young man. He was somewhat overfed, with a large chest and belly. He wore a very short beard and had buggy eyes that glinted coldly. He told me about his restaurant, one of several his family had run since they reached Melbourne from Greece after the war. It was doing a superb trade.

'We are Mickey Mouse,' he said. And then to explain this expression, he added, 'We're high quality. We run a tight business but we don't cut corners. We're chock-a-block these days.' But he had been getting stale over the last year, he said. His elder brother had suggested a big holiday, a year away.

Stavros had calculated his annual expenses at home and decided that since his year abroad was to be a holiday he would spend twice as much. He was travelling on a weekly budget that would keep many a traveller going for months. He had kicked off with a luxury apartment in Rio for two months. After that came three months' hopping around the continent, which were nearly over when I met him, after which he was off north to the States and Europe for another few months with a last stop at the folks in Greece.

He travelled with an enormous rucksack stuffed with unessential items: several changes of shoe, a large dictaphone, a heavy coin collection gathered along the way, several folders of business papers and a big machete. He also had extra bags. The rucksack was too heavy to be worn on the back. He zipped away the straps and carried it on a shoulder. Which restricted his choice of hotel: unless a taxi was to hand he had to take the closest room to the bus station. Since meeting up with Phil his budget had suffered. He was planning some Caribbean flights to make up for it.

Phil was a thin but strong man. When he wore a tee-shirt you could see his arms were hard and muscle-bound. He was balding on top of his head and his pate was rounded like an egg. Stavros used to call him Phil Collins, whom he resembled except in size. His eyes always had a vacant look in them, as if he were permanently perplexed and had given up caring.

For the past eight years he had lived in Australia, first as a geologist, then as taxi-driver, seismic surveyor and computer programmer. He was giving himself a year's holiday, on Stavros's monthly budget, before facing the music back home. He kept planning more and more excursions off the end of his journey, putting off the moment of truth when he would finally settle at home and start looking for a girlfriend. He had climbed mountains, taken boats where planes were cheaper, scrupulously covered every land mile by bus, no matter how much time it cost – in fact the more the better. His style and Stavros's were in evident conflict.

Stavros had decided to take a few weeks' stoop into the world of the conventional backpacker, out of curiosity. One of the rewards was a butt for his humour, which beamed regularly out of his magnificent confidence onto a weaker but nimble Phil, who dodged and defended himself with surprising success. His main tactic was to laugh helplessly and then give a very plain explanation of whatever was being held up to ridicule. He swung back and forth between a kind of feebleness of abandoned laughter and paper-thin seriousness. There was a hint of Laurel and Hardy in their relationship – Phil had the bewildered expression and Stavros was some way to the build.

192 TRAVELS WITH MY TROMBONE

'What are you doing with that old picnic bag?' I once heard Stavros say to Phil out of the blue as he was packing his canvas rucksack. 'Looks like the kind of thing my granny had.'

Phil fell back on his bed laughing uncontrollably. Then suddenly he sat up considering his reply. All trace of humour was banished from his face as he said, 'This pack has been round Asia three times. It's lasted me twelve years. And it had done a good few miles before my dad gave it to me.'

'Looks like it too. Why don't you get yourself a decent one with proper straps? Here, look at this. I've got padded straps, a nice, big belt, loads of compartments. And that piece of shit gets soaked the moment it starts to piss, I bet.'

Again, Phil collapsed in a heap of giggles. He apparently had never got over Aussie humour, despite having lived there for years. But he quickly recovered, and countered, 'But I bet yours cost you at least two hundred dollars. It'll fall apart within a year. They don't build them like they used to.'

'Nah,' said Stav. 'Bullshit.'

I met them on a bus, or rather, off a bus. The journey from San Agustín to Tierradentro was a matter of millimetres on my map. But on the ground it was a six-hour grind along one track, a short night in a flea-ridden shack of a hotel, and then a four-hour grind starting before dawn along another track. My departure on the first leg was delayed seven hours, and night fell soon after the bus set off. We hadn't been gone long when we were held up by what appeared to be a traffic jam: a line of lorries resolutely parked on the track. There were lights ahead. Something was going on but I couldn't make out what. I assumed it was a busy army checkpoint.

Someone shouted up from the ground to the driver: 'Slippery as hell.' The driver edged the bus forward, sweeping out from behind the lorries. Several passengers who had already figured out what the problem was cried out, 'Stop! Let me out! I don't want to die with you.' Others crossed themselves. The driver stopped. Everyone took the opportunity to spill out of the bus into the drizzly night.

The problem was now clear: a short, steep hill ahead had turned into a mud slide. There were several vehicles parked at top and bottom waiting whilst their drivers decided whether to try it. We were at the top. All the passengers stood around waiting and wondering what would happen. Would we have to spend the night here, on the bus? Or go back to San Agustin and try again in the morning?

A pick-up truck was whining its way slowly uphill, wheels spinning furiously. Every few feet it would stop moving, though the engine noise didn't drop in pitch, and then it would slide a little to one side, or even backwards, and then climb a little further. It was hard to make out exactly how it was doing, in the rain and the glare of its lights. Eventually it made it to the top only to find our bus blocking the track.

It took them twenty minutes to manoeuvre out of each other's way and then all of a sudden our driver seemed to have made up his mind. He was edging the bus towards the brow of the slope and was at the very brink when he appeared to have a change of heart, putting on the brakes, which sighed and let off a squeal of compressed air. But it was too late. The bus scarcely needed any momentum at all to continue its progress, and away it went, the back end gliding slowly and gracefully round until the rear wheels were abreast of the front. It was clearly the end of the bus. If it didn't roll into the ditch at the side there were plenty of trucks waiting to meet it at the bottom.

But then it started spinning the other way. By a miracle, just as it was swinging straight again the bus found a footing on the gentler incline near the bottom and swept straight on, through the channel between the parked vehicles. The driver switched on his flashing light on the roof, in a victory salute. All the passengers cheered and began their own descent in long lines with arms interlocked, which was not necessarily any safer than going singly.

'Watch out,' I heard somebody call. It took a moment before I realized I had just heard English. I looked round in time to see a big, burly man with a close-clipped beard slide into the back of a small, balding man, who threw his arms up for balance. They both fell over, onto their backsides, and slid a few yards down the hill.

'Jesus, Stav,' the small one shouted.

'I told you I was coming,' was the reply, delivered with the unmistakable Aussie lift at the end of the sentence. 'Fuck, I knew I should have worn my hiking boots.'

THIRTY-SEVEN

Among the detritus around a city's edge, where roads become tracks and heaps of rubble indicate an intention to improve them, there is a kind of peace. Between the city and the landscape lies a world, glimpsed through the tatters, of limitless possibility, of chaos, welcoming and heartening for the rootless. From up here on a suburban hill the city is nothing more than a distant throbbing hum, and a meaningless mosaic on the valley floor.

I have come to a rambling fantasy hotel attached to a nightclub. It is morning. It takes quarter of an hour for someone to come and unlock the gate. The hotel, the whole complex, is the kind of place that only comes to life at midnight. There are Turkish baths ('Mixto' conspicuously advertised), a swimming pool, several bars and restaurants, all on terraces stepping down the hillside and connected by staircases weaving through potted foliage. At night there would always be the view over the city lights, seen again and again from different vantages.

A thunderstorm has been passing over all morning. A stream of bright clay-red water flowed along the road for miles on the way up. The only dry place to sit is a little cement-roofed niche beside a discotheque. A window gives into a thick-carpeted room furnished only with cushions. A plaque outside says: 'Here the spirit yields, conquered by the irresistible sweetness of the most beautiful place on earth.' It is a quotation from somewhere, ready to boost a flagging courtship in the small hours. Every hackneyed love prop has been installed, to support loveless desire.

I have come up here for a morning of reflection. For the last week I have been exploring the music of Cali. From Tierradentro a bus and then a taxi brought me to the city. I rode on the roof rack of the first, a glorious morning's weaving along a valley, marred only by the sets of foghorns the driver had installed also on the roof, only a few feet from my ears. At every bend, at every junction, at every house, sometimes it seemed at every telegraph pole, he would tug on the chain by the steering-wheel, Casey Jones-style, and let the valley have it. We later climbed into a heavy rainstorm, just as the driver had predicted and, because I had not heeded his warning, he felt no obligation to stop for my sake. Not until we reached a roadside restaurant.

I leapt down and ran for cover. The wooden building, a single large room, was full of sweet wood smoke from the cooking fire. There was a long counter with stools that quickly filled with the passengers, and behind it several women were milling around a great platform of embers covered with huge pots. The rain was hammering on the tin roof. The women ladled out cups of coffee and cheese buns with great efficiency. In a moment the length of the counter was served. Some people, including myself, had chicken soup, a warming nourishing broth richly flavoured by the inclusion of unusual parts of the bird's anatomy – not only the two feet but underneath them, lurking among the dregs and grotesquely bleached by the boiling, the head.

The rest of the journey I made indoors. Then a change of transport in Popayan: a shared taxi, a popular form of travel in Colombia. Six people, including the driver, pile onto the bench seats of an old American car and race – for twice the price of a bus ticket and in half the time – to the destination. In this case Cali, a city of two and a half million, Colombia's third.

Cali's reputation is as a city of beautiful women and excellent salsa. It is the capital of the Colombian Latin music scene. Although I was planning to waste no time in contacting that tromboneless band I had met in Pasto a week earlier, fate wanted things to happen even faster. The very first night, I went out thoroughly preened and ready for any pleasure an urban night could put my way, to have a drink in the top-floor bar of the Torre de Cali, a new skyscraper. It was an extremely subdued place, and empty except for a few tables of solemn diners. It wasn't at all what I had been hoping for. There was an organ over in one corner, a Hammond with a lot of vibrato and as smarmy a cymbal beat as you could devise. Seated at it, and playing with one, sometimes two, fingers, and also with flagrant boredom, was a young man in dicky bow and tidy, black hair. I sat drearily sipping my beer a few hundred feet above the city's action.

The organist kept looking my way and smiling and nodding at me. After the second time I made a point of not catching his eye. As soon as he took a break he came straight over to me.

'Trombonista,' he said. 'We met in Pasto.'

I made as if a sudden flood of recollection had overwhelmed me, smiling and nodding enough to match all the smiles and nods he had given me. He was the keyboard player of the band Bemtu.

'We have a rehearsal tomorrow morning,' he told me happily. 'It's lucky we met. Come and play. The show is in the afternoon, in a plaza.'

He wrote down the band's address for me.

The rest of the night was an unmitigated flop. I traipsed from one bar to the next until two in the morning, ogling shamelessly at all the beautiful Caleñas I would never get to meet, and then had a meal of half-frozen dishes that arrived already smothered in tomato ketchup in a bar that probably only had a menu for the sake of its licence.

Bemtu was a young band. Most of the members were under thirty. Their success so far was limited to southern Colombia. They had had a few hit singles over the eight years since they formed. Five members owned the band.

They rehearsed in a garage outside the city centre. They had made some gestures towards soundproofing it, egg cartons had been taped to the walls here and there, but they played with the garage door wide open anyway. There were twelve of them, all crammed in along with speakers, drums, keyboard and music stands for the brass, and then me too. They wanted to work up three new numbers that morning, a merengue and two salsa songs, one of them written specially for the band.

I was pleased to find myself having no more trouble than anyone else in reading the music. On paper the rhythms looked bewilderingly complicated, endless dotted, tied semi-quavers and minimal rests, but as soon as you heard them they made sense. Mastering the difficult passages also contained its own solution, because every phrase, every passage, would be repeated several times before the end. To play through a number was to rehearse it.

Everyone else seemed pleased too. They liked hearing the extra sound. A new instrument, especially brass, can make a big difference in a band that has had the same line-up a long time.

Afterwards Carlos, the tres player and one of the band's owners, approached me while everyone was hanging around in the front garden. A small crowd of passers-by had gathered during the practice and several members of the band were chatting to a group of teenage girls. Carlos smiled and said quietly that I would be fine for the afternoon show and if I wanted to I could check out some more songs from the book of trombone parts. He would bring a band shirt along for me.

Carlos had short, dark-brown hair and an angular face with a pointed nose and chin, but incongruously mild and docile eyes. By the end of my first day with the band, after the outdoor concert in a big, concrete plaza where we shared the bill with three other salsa bands, Carlos had become my friend.

He had played guitars of all kinds – mandolin, cuatro, classical, tres – since childhood. He was now in his late twenties, and bored. His real vocation was poetry. Three years ago he had produced a volume of early work. He had written much of it spontaneously, he said. It was mostly love poetry. Since then he had written nothing. 'Soy inerte,' he lamented. He liked Cavafy, and by way of illustration he showed me Cavafy's poem 'The City', a monumentally depressing piece of work: just as you have ruined your life in this city so you have ruined it all over the world. You will always live in these same suburbs, wherever you go. I knew it already. I also knew Lawrence Durrell's positive interpretation: you can't get away, but you can go inwards. I explained that Cavafy's poem may also be seen as an exhortation to the inner voyage, a journey not for the feet. Carlos drew a little comfort.

He lived in a two-room apartment, one for living in, the other the band office: a desk, a phone, a notice board with press cuttings, dates, fees, two album covers. It was in a residential area of concrete homes with small gardens. It took me a while to find because I hadn't yet figured out Colombian addresses: every street has a number, every block has a number, and every house has a number. The number of the house is how many paces it takes to walk from the start of the block to the front door. 148 and 159 could be next-door neighbours.

Despite the load of misery and crushing frustration he was carrying Carlos was scrupulously attentive to me. He took me to a little bar called the Taverna Latina, run by a great expert on salsa. It was a meeting place for Cali's aficionados. Every night the owner, Gary Dominguez, a man with a bushy beard ('He looks like a Cuban. A real Cuban,' Carlos told me and laughed) would play selections from his huge record collection chosen around a theme – one night Cuban son; another, Colombian cumbia; another, great New York percussionists. You could only buy beer in jugs, or bottles of *aguardiente*. There was always a gang around the turn-tables, reading album covers and discussing the music, from which Carlos's modesty excluded him. He gave me his own private commentary on what we were hearing, pointing out the little differences between the various rhythms. 'This is guaguanco. You hear the cadence, rich, tasty, a lot of rhythm . . . A charanga. Very well marked, defined . . . Salsa. Smooth, a bit slower . . . A merengue. Really quick. You have to dance . . . '

I already knew that salsa was only a particular style, the blend of regional forms that had emerged in New York in the early sixties, based mainly on the Cuban son. Son was the oldest Latin form of music still alive. It had its origins in the remote eastern mountains of Cuba, the region of the Guantanamera,

the girl from Guantanamo. Son had been brought to Havana
in the teens of this century, where it gave birth to mambo and
cha-cha-cha. Then in the sixties the émigré Cubans of New York
revived it and propelled it onto the world market. But there were
many other forms too, changüi, guaracha, guaguanco, rumba,
charanga, pachanga. They all had their own particular beats and
origins. Most salsa bands would play songs in several genres.

In his flat Carlos had a comprehensive collection of Colombian
music. Outside Colombian salsa there was vallenato from the
north, musica llanera from the plains in the east, papayera brass
band music from the north, marimba music from the Choco,
the Pacific coast, and many folk styles for guitars of various
sizes from the centre of the country, derived from Spanish
folk music. Each had its distinctive rhythms and instruments.
In vallenato the accordion did the work of brass and guitars;
the harp was the emblem of plains music, chords plucked from
it in infectious, driving rhythms; papayera were something like
tropical Dixieland bands, with saxophones, clarinets and every
kind of brass playing over drums and shakers; the Choco music
was virtually uncontaminated West African, with huge bamboo
xylophones (marimbas) played by two musicians, as well as
call and response singing. Broadly, the tropical coastal music
reflected the larger African proportion in the population, while
the highland and plains music of the centre and east were more
European. Latin music was the meeting of the two.

Carlos took me to meet his brother-in-law, José. José was a
sculptor of fantastic prolificity who lived in a lavish apartment
attached to his roof-top studio, a terrace where he not only
worked on his grotesque erotic creations in clay, but also
kept the enormous collection of cacti that inspired him. He
had over two thousand different specimens, many of them
scarcely recognizable as living matter: rocklike chunks of grey
flesh, rippled like brain, or folded and fanned like coral, or
simply round like pebbles. There was also the usual range of
furs, downs, bristles and spikes.

When we called José was suffering from flu. He was wrapped
in a scarf and sweaters sitting at a table and drinking shots of

aguardiente to cure himself. He was unshaven and had dishevelled black hair. His moustache glistened, and his eyes had a warm sparkle, kindled in part by the alcohol, but also by the singing that he had been doing to console himself in his illness. He had a guitar in his lap, and soon after we joined him he launched into a song about freedom and spiritual growth.

José was not only an accomplished singer but had also recently written sixty-nine poems in nine days, which were about to be published. Carlos confided this last to me with eyebrows raised, as if to say: 'You see? What can you do? Life is not fair.' The list went on. He had a degree in marine biology, a diploma in psychology, he sold his art work regularly, he had travelled, had had all kinds of adventures. Carlos had his work cut out.

I played two concerts with Bemtu. The second was on a Friday night at the Estudio Bar, a night club in the Torre de Cali. We played three sets there, alternating with solo singers who sang national melodies that drove the local crowd wild. They were all drinking shots of *aguardiente* and were in just the mood to hear songs that roused their patriotism. Our salsa, on the other hand, left them surprisingly cold. There would be whoops of delight when we first came in on a familiar tune, but then only a few couples would step out onto the dance floor.

All the brass had music stands and fat albums of music parts to play from, but I was the only one who actually used them. The others knew their lines backwards, except in the odd new song. The parts were written out clearly, although there wasn't much light to read them by at the back of the stage. But the real problem for me was knowing what song to play next.

'Noches de fantasía,' the saxophonist would say into my ear. Or, 'Amor para ti'.

I then had to fumble through the pages looking for the right one, while the band ploughed on into it. I usually managed to join in for the second or third verse.

During the breaks between sets I met two women who spoke fluent English and drank *aguardiente* in rapid shots. They talked to me enthusiastically while one of the crooners sang romantic songs. They were happy to meet a Westerner. One of them had

her own shop on San Andrés island, I soon discovered, and
was also manageress of a credit card company. Her name was
Helena Maria. She had large eyes and curly black hair and a fine
face which became finer as the night wore on. She had been
divorced three times, in quick succession. She was still under
thirty. Her problem, she explained, was that few Colombian
men could tolerate a woman being independent. In fact very
few Colombian women could handle it either. Western men were
different, she smiled at me.

 # THIRTY-EIGHT

Cali sits in the Cauca valley, the western of the two
great valleys that reach north the length of Colombia.
The western cordillera forms one side of the valley. It is
the lowest of the three Colombian cordilleras, the peaks
rising to some ten thousand feet. Beyond it lies a strip of jungle
laced with rivers that wind back and forth on what without the
bends would be a short way to the Pacific. This Pacific area, the
Choco, is one of the country's least developed. It is inhabited
along the coast itself mainly by blacks, inland along the rivers
by Indians who still live in their traditional longhouses, and by
a few gold miners who operate with portable dredgers and small
boats. One of the most remote towns is Guapi. You reach it either
by boat or small plane. I wanted to make an excursion from Cali,
and this was where Carlos recommended. In Guapi the tradition
of Choco music was as strong and pure as anywhere.

The town was a short plane ride over the mountains and into
the clouds that shrouded the coastal lowlands. The one lorry
in town, a small truck with a cab built out of wood, met the
aeroplane and two boys on bicycles clung on at the back as it
bumped into town. I had one name in Guapi, a man who had
moved there from Popayan and knew the area backwards. Guapi

was easily small enough, with a population of 15,000 people, for the driver to know where to drop me off. It turned out that my host also ran one of the three hotels in town.

He was called Pedro. He had a pale, anaemic face and a jet black beard. His eyes were sunken and his cheeks, from a certain angle, looked hollow. Pedro couldn't stand the jungle. He couldn't stand Guapi. He had a wife and family up in Popayan whom he allowed himself to see once every few months. His marriage was as good as annulled. He devoted himself to the hotel, he explained. There was little business, and what little there was there were already people to take care of, but that made no difference to him. He had determined to put himself through a lifetime of dutiful misery. All day he sat on the hotel landing watching the wire doorway, looking down at the street, exchanging the occasional remark with someone walking by. His face had a vacant look, but his body was always rigid. He stood erect and very still. When you addressed a remark to him his brow would fall into a frown, his top lip would quiver and his eyes would dart back and forth from the wall to some part of your face other than your eyes. If you asked him a question he would answer very gravely, weighing every word, and ensnare his reply in a network of hedgings. He took everything gravely. When I had sunstroke he diagnosed typhoid.

He had a brother who also lived in the hotel, whose name was Camillo. Camillo was an extrovert. He had a thin beard, a pot belly and worked as a part-time gold miner. His hair was bushy and grey and his eyes shone out of his tanned face. His great passions were hunting and fishing, and he had arranged his life so he could be in the jungle as much as possible doing them. He had a small dredger set up somewhere in the maze of rivers. Most days he would speed off in a diminutive speed boat, switch on the machine, leave a man to watch over it, and vanish into the jungle with either rod or gun to return in the late afternoon with his bag and collect the day's takings from the filter, and speed downriver again. He had friends everywhere. In whatever bar he sat children would come sheepishly up to his table and he would put his arms round them before they could say anything.

Camillo loved children, and he loved living in the heat and the jungle. He had filled the hotel with motherless children and homeless mothers. There were only three rooms available for guests. The rest were permanently occupied. When customers showed up, which was rarely, the mothers cleaned and made the beds. The building had open terraces on every floor. Only the rooms themselves had four walls. The place was like a block of flats where everyone hangs out on the landings and staircase, chatting, eating, sitting, watching the life in the street below.

Camillo was also from Popayan, which was the capital of Guapi's department. Several times he had made the journey between the two by boat and on foot. But he was happy to have moved, not only for the sport. He liked the culture of the Choco, the coastal music, the dances and songs and marimba tunes – and the festive atmosphere. All day and most of the night, until the electricity supply was cut, salsa blared from every doorway. Every other house was a bar. 'Dicen que donde no hay negro no hay guaguanco,' he told me: where there are no blacks there is no guaguanco. He also knew several Indian villages upriver. He was friends with the most powerful shaman of the area.

He told me the story of the time he had been in this shaman's village when another shaman came to visit. It was a big feast. 'I saw this with my own eyes,' he assured me staring deeply into mine. The two shamans had apparently sat facing each other in silence. A long time passed. Then Camillo's friend blew down his arm. Camillo imitated the gesture, throwing out his hand and blowing towards it at the same time. A moment later the other shaman blew back the same way. And then backwards and forwards, harder and louder each time. Finally he blew once more, and the visiting shaman fell back to the ground. Camillo had walked over to him.

'Dead. He was dead. Dead from a man blowing at him. I said to my friend, what happened? How do you kill a man by blowing at him?'

The shaman had replied, 'Who was blowing? You mean you didn't see?'

'See what?' Camillo had asked.

'The spears we were hurling at each other.'

Camillo was still staring straight at me. He shrugged. 'I was actually there. It happened right in front of my eyes.'

Guapi was a ramshackle town spilling into the river of its name. The houses were built of flimsy wood. Many were collapsing. They and the weather were such that everything, every domestic quarrel, every meal, every friendship, every embrace short of the act of love, took place on the street. Every few hours you might hear a shriek from somewhere up the road. Everyone would go running to see what it was, who was having a row with whom.

There was little marriage in the place. Couples did what they do in the Caribbean: they went 'keeping' until the woman had had enough and kicked the man out. It wasn't unusual for a woman to have several children each one by a different man. The evictions were one of the regular spectacles. Drunks also offered entertainment. I was suddenly caught once in a stampede of people running up the street to watch a man who had just staggered out of a bar with a machete in his hand. He was swinging it at the air. A crowd quickly ringed him, and as quickly shrank back from him while he swung, and then closed again during one of the man's lulls. Back and forth, opening and closing like a ripple in a well, until he went shambling down the street and fell unconscious in the dirt. The absence of vehicles also helped the street life. There were some motorbikes, but they were few and far between. The main hazard was the hand-pushed carts of bottle crates and vegetables and fruit that came charging down the street with men running behind them and screaming at pedestrians. Once they had got their momentum up they would stop for no one.

One of the most vulnerable inhabitants was an eleven-year-old, deaf mute boy. Camillo introduced him to me as El Sordo. El Sordo had a face of disarming beauty. He stared at you for long minutes. His eyes were clear: no red, no yellow, just pure white, with shining black irises. His face was smooth and perfectly formed.

One day we were eating lunch in a simple restaurant with just one table on a veranda. The owner was a woman who cooked young shark over charcoal, a local dish. I bought a meal for El Sordo. He smiled, picked up the plate, and ran away.

'To his house,' Camillo said. 'He wants to share it with his brother and sister.' I could hardly believe it, not until I had seen that whenever he was given anything to eat or drink he always shared it. Everybody in the town loved him. Hands would pat him as he walked down the street.

'El pobre Sordo,' one woman said to me. 'He can't dance.'

Despite that he seemed to like music. He figured out that I wanted to hear music, and on my first morning he took me on a tour of the town's back streets, lanes lined with houses on stilts for when it flooded, and finally to a small home built of uneven planks nailed up vertically. Between the top of the wall and the tin roof was a big jagged gap, and the house itself was half hidden by banana trees. He knocked quietly. A young woman opened up and smiled at him. He mimed playing bongos. The woman nodded and led us through a kitchen, a space with stacks of bowls and saucepans and a fireplace, and through a storeroom full of hollow wooden cylinders evidently destined to be drums, and then into a sitting room where an old man was sitting with a drum between his legs. He was tying up the string to tighten the skin. It was a conga.

He was a drum-maker and a player. He showed me drums of various sizes drying on his balcony and then started playing. 'Eso es el currulao,' he announced and leapt into a rolling beat on a single conga. The drum had a high, echoing note. El Sordo smiled at me, his face bright. 'Un pasillo . . . ' and the boy grinned, overjoyed that I was hearing what I wanted.

Being with El Sordo made me think about what people say to each other. Maybe the words of a society collectively carry more hurt than love and he was living in an enchanted world, one in which we were all mutes.

It was Camillo who arranged for me to hear a marimba group. He took me to a house built on stilts down a side street. The whole group, all ten musicians, were crammed into the house's front room, as well as several neighbours who had dropped in to listen. The room was bursting at the seams.

The leader was an old man with few teeth and cropped, silver hair sprouting from his head. He played the two-man xylophone with the help of a young pupil. Both players had two short sticks wrapped up with a resin-coated rubber at the end for beating the keys, which were strips of the hard wood of a certain fruit tree. The pupil hit rhythm parts at the lower end while the older man took the tunes higher up, beating furiously in thirds, always two notes at a time.

There were also four percussionists who played on drums of various sizes and timbres, and four large middle-aged ladies who sang the songs and shook shakers. When they launched into their first song, after a rambling introduction on the marimba, the whole house shook. The floor, already sagging, bounced with the beat.

While the old man led the rhythm section one old woman, with a mottled face and white hair tugged back into a pigtail, led the singers. At the end of each number she would scowl at her colleagues and throw up her hands in despair and then sing out the line emphatically that someone had been perverting. She was exactly the kind of stern disciplinarian that such a tradition requires in order to survive, a direct descendant of the Africans brought here as slaves in the seventeenth century and still singing tunes that predated the middle passage.

The women sang in high, loud voices, boldly and rhythmically. Everyone performed loudly. It was thoroughly percussive music. Many songs used call and response, when one of the women would sing out a series of varied phrases answered each time by a short standard chorus from the other three, the same procedure that you hear in cult drumming ceremonies like Shango.

Although there are no West African cults on the Pacific coast, there are African adaptations of Christianity. When rains threaten a flood the people carry a local saint's effigy from the church to the river bank and plant it in the mud. They instruct him not to allow the water to wet his boots. If he lets them down he gets a sound whipping. Despite such humiliation the effigies are vessels of great power. Anyone reckless enough to tap one on the forehead is likely to be struck by lightning. Which is not such an unlikely event. During the first week I spent in Colombia eight people were struck in one province alone, and not a night passed when I did not see distant flickerings in the sky.

Camillo offered to take me upriver to an Indian village. In the end he could not go himself, because a gold miner from Florida had arrived, an unhappy man called Skip Casey, a Country and Western singer by trade who was looking for adventure, for distraction. He had been living all around Latin America on and off for years, in one frontier business after another. He would search your eyes nervously when you spoke to him. Camillo had to take care of him. They were planning to go into a joint mining venture.

Camillo sent me off with a young man called Isaiah who had grown up in the hotel and knew the rivers. Isaiah was a quiet, placid man. He hardly said a word all day. He would sit staring up the river with one hand on the tiller and a far-away look in his eyes. We shared the boat, a small fibre-glass dinghy with an outboard, with a salesman who was travelling to a town on the way, up the next river.

It took us three hours to get there, twice as long as it should have done. Firstly, the engine was not putting out sufficient power. To get it to drop into its high gear someone had to sit up on the prow – only when the blades of the propeller were in a few inches of water would it generate the required number of revs to change gears. Stuck in the first gear, the engine whined and we crawled along watching motorized dugouts speed past us. Secondly, the tide was low, and again and again we would get up speed only to come to a grinding standstill on a hidden sandbank. Whereupon Isaiah would jump out, in the middle of the river, and be standing in ankle-deep water. He would swing the boat into a deeper stream. And thirdly, we lost our way. The salesman was the worst kind of passenger. Two years before he had made the same trip a few times and thought he knew every bend of the rivers. He kept telling Isaiah where to go, and kept being proved wrong. The area was a giant maze. The only constant landmark was the cordillera glittering in the distance, when the trees allowed you to see it.

The Indian village was little more than a large tin-roofed hall on stilts, with a floor of opened-out bamboo. Several topless women had cooking hearths in the corners, and several men who were busy building a small new house that was to be a health centre put down their hammers when we arrived and came to sit in the hall. One of them talked at length about travel in the region, the various boats that called and where they went, and then they all went back to their work. I took some photographs of a child with a toy chainsaw, bought a hat from a basket weaver who normally sold to traders from Guapi, and left.

It was after we collected the salesman, who had completed his business in the town, that the real trouble began. We took some wrong turnings, but eventually found our way to the sea, as desired. We had to follow the coast for a few miles and then enter an arm of the Guapi river. The sun was setting. An evening wind was up, and the boat was bouncing on every wave. Whoever sat on the prow to get our speed up not only got soaked but was likely to be tossed off, so no one did and we crawled along. Then as we drew across the mouth of the Guapi river, when we were out in the middle in the full force of the current, the engine gave up.

Isaiah did some hasty repairs and made several attempts to get it started again, with no luck. Then I tried a few times, pulling hard on the cord and nearly capsizing the boat. The salesman tried. The current had already swept us at least a mile out, it was getting dark and I was starting to get worried. Isaiah shrugged his shoulders and kept trying.

Suddenly it worked. But then, while we were labouring back in, the engine cut again. And again. Then we ran out of petrol, and had to fill the tank from the spare can without a funnel and with the boat pitching up and down. Night fell. The salesman said he had never known such a dangerous trip. We had no paddle, no radio, nothing to help us except the engine, and it kept stalling. We were moving steadily out to sea.

There was an island that I knew of several miles offshore, the Isla Gorgona. It had been in the news recently because a large school of whales had been spotted frolicking in its waters. I kept wondering if we would make it to the island, and if we did make it that far whether we would land on it or drift past it, or suddenly find huge beasts rising out of the waves all around us and knocking the boat over.

The engine ran long enough for us to make it to the inside of the river mouth, though with only a few drops of petrol left. Not far away a light shone. It was a freezer plant. Isaiah knew the men who worked there. We moored at the wooden ladder that led up to their warehouse. A generator was humming, and you could hear music over it. They sold us petrol and wished us luck, although from there we were home and dry.

Only I still had a problem. I was shivering uncontrollably in the warm night air. I curled up with my arms under my legs hugging myself for warmth. I was freezing. Whenever I looked back at our wake glowing in the diffused light of the moon and thin low cloud I had poignant visions of eroticism inspired by the shape of the wake. I longed for past loves. Violent emotions surged through me.

Back in Guapi I had planned to eat, for the first time in the day. But when we arrived it was all I could do to clamber upstairs and into bed. I covered myself with Skip Casey's sleeping bag and fell into a sleep of delirious dreams, convinced that I was dying of cold. I awoke suddenly sweating and hot and infinitely relieved that I wasn't cold any more.

Pedro was in the room. 'You're not well,' he observed.

I told him my symptoms.

'It sounds like typhoid,' he said. 'It's common here.'

Just then Camillo walked in. 'Diarrhoea and fever?'

'Yes,' I said.

'Insolación,' he assured me, nodding.

I would be all right in a day or two, I was told. I had hoped to take a cargo boat the next day up the coast to the port of Buenaventura. The prospect of a cabin the size of a closet and a bunk the width of a bookshelf was more than I could bear. Nauseous and still shaking I took the plane back to Cali in the morning. I never again spent more than a few minutes under the Colombian sun without a hat.

THIRTY-NINE

I have just, all of a sudden, prized myself free of Cali – I had to leave, the need came abruptly – and dumped myself on Bogotá. Again the Andes, the gloomy weather I had first rediscovered in Quito and the lonely greyness everywhere. Parts of the city remind me of Germany, large wide streets, impressive turn-of-the-century municipal buildings. You expect to see a tram go by. Maybe it is the lamp posts, short and standing in the middle of the pavement. Other parts, however, are pure urban Andes: narrow dirty-white houses with tiled roofs, crumbling Andalusian architecture.

Many buildings in the centre are art deco. It is a good clean city in the centre, central European, and then very Spanish too on the main plaza, a huge terrace of paving amid the grandeur. On one side a massive banner depicting García Márquez now hangs, masking where the Palace of Justice once stood, until five years ago when it burned down in the battle following its seizure by a subversive group.

And suddenly I have understood what has been wrong: I don't want to travel any more. I have been on the road for five months and already it has become too long. It happens like this. Suddenly you realize your journey is over. Some part of you is replete.

Even the Bogotá gold museum makes no difference. The workmanship of the gold statuettes and the craziness of the faces provide some amusement, but the mythologies the pieces represent – it is a dead world to me. Once they would have taken the lid off a well of exciting speculation on the nature of human life for me, and on the possible significance of their belief in another reality in which men and beasts were not distinguished. Now there is no excitement for me, no significance. All I see is proof that they didn't know as much as we do.

Grinning, leering, sneering faces, faces with eyes literally on stalks, little Martian figures with bugles for ears and rings for noses, legs one tenth of their total height (with a note beneath mysteriously claiming, 'Human figures of great realism'), men or women with froglike legs, masks with great curved bird beaks and expressions of immeasurable stupidity, all manner of weird animals – a rat with a quasi-human head, strange creeping things, three-legged lizards, snakes both coiled and undulating two feet long – swizzle sticks adorned with primitivist rainbows and animals and men.

The museum could hardly have been designed to greater effect. Everywhere dim lighting, the pieces glowing in dark cabinets. The famous raft of gold from Lake Guatavita, a little model of the Chibcha ceremony when several priests accompanied a prince dressed from head to toe in gold to the centre of the lake to make offerings, turns slowly on a black mirror. A door slides open on a pitch-dark strong room once every five minutes. Inside only the exhibits themselves are lighted. All of them are huge pieces: complete head dresses and handbags of solid gold. Even a basket woven out of gold strips, and a set of golden pan pipes.

In the city, I notice that one part of the Colombian capital, where the mountains suddenly rise up steep behind the streets, is distinctly Swiss in character. A highway winding among fir trees into a canyon, a dainty set of artificial waterfalls, a cable car.

Viewed from the church at the top of the cable-car ride, Bogotá lies spread out in a perfect, soft milkiness of misty drizzle ignited here and there to molten silver – a cluster of rooftops, a street, a plaza – by a veiled sun finding here and there a tear to peep through. Then from beneath, from beyond the trees that fall away down a cliff, a uniform fog comes racing up, like smoke rising from a factory chimney, fast. In a minute this low cloud has drawn a screen over the city. It appears there is nothing to do but go down again. These observation posts exist only for their views. But then suddenly behind us, away from the city, the other side clears to reveal that we are up on the high plain, with hills, a mountain terrain, reaching away. A forest of eucalyptus, croaking and throbbing and singing with animal life, drops down and between the trunks a hillside of dense alpine cover appears softly glowing in sunlight, blue green. No doubt you could walk off from here along a trail, off into the mountains

away from the city to village after village so you would never need
to come back.

That, it spontaneously comes to me, is what I will do. I won't
stay in the city. Tomorrow I'll head off into the hills by bus,
travelling always now only as a conclusion to a journey – a last
leg, merely to bring me home.

I realize that years before when I was here I never understood
the similarities between the Andean cities. Each was its own
exotic experience. Now I see only how they are alike, how the
mountains confer their paradoxical atmosphere of clarity and
intimacy. At dusk, when for five minutes the roofs of the city
sparkle softly and the sky turns orange then green, you hear
domestic voices, children, men and women talking quietly in
nearby homes, their voices sounding clear like running water.
And the coldness flows in quickly, with the dark. It too bestows
an intimacy. You need a sweater. You close the window, check
there are enough blankets on the bed.

I don't delay in Bogotá. Starting out onto the mountains, my
journey is all but over. I am just finishing off the last crumbs,
because from here the mountains last only a little further before
they fall to the Caribbean lowlands. Soon I will have finished my
journey up the Andes. But there is one last place I want to visit
in the highlands: Lake Guatavita.

FORTY

A bus took me an hour north of Bogotá to the village
of Guatavita Nueva, a new village built in mock local
style, with white houses and red roofs. The government
erected it ten years ago when they flooded the valley to
make a reservoir. The old village of Guatavita is now two hundred
feet under water.

Lake Guatavita was two hours' walk away. It was already late afternoon, so I spent the night in the village. An old woman in jam-jar spectacles and a thick coat put me up in her house above a restaurant. I ate *sancocho* downstairs, a thick chicken and caper soup, and then went up to bed. I slept under a weighty counterpane.

In the morning I paid the woman, who was still lying in bed, drank coffee and set out with my bag on my back.

It was a rough walk along a stony track. Either side lay fields where cattle and sheep grazed. The landscape was green and damp rolling hills. The sky was overcast. I walked through a wood, and finally up towards a hill where the track widened. Ahead I could see a gully in the hillside. The track ended and a path led on, up into the gully. It was slippery and steep. I clambered up it, clinging to rocks and bushes, and came over the rise, and there it was: Lake Guatavita.

It is a small, circular lake, not more than quarter of a mile across. It lies in a deep bowl, the crater of an extinct volcano. It is surrounded by a ring of steep forest. The gully through which I had climbed is the only chink in the bowl.

It is an enchanted place. The woods all around it, the rim of mountainside, the circle of rock that encloses it, make it remote, peaceful. This very lake is what the world's bravest dreamers spent two centuries searching for. Because of this lake men underwent ordeals by heat, disease, hunger, solitude, and many died for it.

Lake Guatavita was the seed from which grew the greatest myth since the Middle Ages. The Chibcha controlled the highlands of Colombia at the time of the Spanish Conquest. It was here that the Chibcha priests would smear their prince from head to toe in resin, and then blow gold dust all over him, until he was thickly coated in gold, and had become the golden man, El Dorado. They would then drift slowly out to the middle of the lake on a wide balsa raft, and one by one drop offerings of gold, fine gold artifacts, down into the deep dark waters. The final and greatest offering was the golden prince himself, who would dive in and swim around the lake until all the gold dust had washed off him, had become a golden rain falling gently towards the lake bottom. From this ceremony in this lake grew the legend of the city where people dressed in gold, and lived in houses of gold and walked on streets of gold. While the prince was transmuted into a whole city, little Lake Guatavita became a vast open lake, Lake Parima, into which many rivers flowed. The city stood on the lake shore. The natives called it Manoa. It was the capital of a whole kingdom, the Kingdom of Guiana.

The myth was created by the Europeans. The treasures of the Incas and Aztecs and the alchemical theory of the equatorial gold sources together implied that there must be an even richer better conquest waiting to be made. When the explorers interrogated Indians about it they always got the answers they wanted. El Dorado was a fairy tale that its hunters themselves created.

Throughout the sixteenth century the rumours grew larger and larger. By 1590 the population of the kingdom was two million. The people were either Incas who had fled from the Andes across the jungle when the Spaniards arrived in Cuzco, or they were at least harbouring many Inca refugees, including the ruler Huayna Capac's son, along with all the greatest Inca treasure. The men wore their hair in pigtails.

Nothing inhibited the growth of the myth. A Spaniard named Juan Martin was lost on an expedition, like many others, but he was found again still alive seven years later. He declared that he had spent all that time living with Indians right in the area where El Dorado was supposed to be. He neither saw nor heard anything of it. Within weeks the grapevine had adjusted his story: Juan Martin was the only European alive who had actually been to El Dorado. The Indians had blindfolded him, taken him there and kept him a whole year in the city. He had been walked along all its streets. Then the Indians had led him away again, only taking off his blindfold when they were several days away from the city.

It was finally decided that El Dorado was a province of New Grenada. Antonio de Berrio, whose lieutenant, Domingo de Vera y Ibargoen, founded St Joseph on Trinidad, spent more than twenty years searching for the province when he inherited its governorship. His son took over the search after him, in the early seventeenth century.

In 1596 an Englishman wrote a book about El Dorado which he called *The Discovery of Guiana*. He had recently sailed up the Orinoco collecting stories about the kingdom from the local Indians. His book was a best-seller all over Europe. He worked into it every detail he had ever heard. The city was not only magnificent and paved in gold, but vast. The refugee Inca heir had his palace in the centre: to walk from there to the edge of the city took one and a half days. In the surrounding countryside every stone you picked up 'promised either gold or silver by his complexion'. In the provinces lived the Tivitivas, 'goodly valiant people' who spent the summer in houses on the ground and the winter living 'like rooks' in the trees, some thirty feet up, 'where they build very artificial towns and villages', and also the Ewaipanomas, headless people, people whose heads were in their chests. The Amazons were their neighbours, the tribe of female warriors who secured progeny according to some by capturing baby girls from the surrounding tribes, and to others with the help of captive studs. All agreed that they had only one breast, on the left. A right breast would have got in the way of their archery.

The Englishman laid down his plans for the union of Guiana and England. He had heard of a prophecy that had been found in the chief Inca temple at the time of the Conquest which stated: 'From Inglatierra should those Incas be again in time to come restored, and delivered from servitude of the said Conquerors.' England would not only protect the Guianans from the Spaniards but help restore Huayna Capac's heir to his throne in Cuzco. There would be free cultural exchange. Young men of either nation would study in one another's universities. The Queen of England and the King of Guiana would form the most powerful alliance in the world.

The author of *The Discovery of Guiana* was Sir Walter Raleigh. Until 1591 he had been a favourite of the Queen, but then he had married and fallen from grace. It was to win back his place in court that he had sailed out west in 1595 and written his book. His Queen could hardly reject him if he won her the greatest prize on earth. Spain might have conquered the Aztecs and Incas, but he would bring her the richest colony in the New World, in the world.

His first act on his voyage had been to sack the town of San José de Oruna on Trinidad and capture Berrio. He then spent three months sailing on the Orinoco and Caroni rivers. He gathered all the stories he could, as well as a collection of ore-laden rocks. He saw, or came close to seeing, a mountain of solid crystal, and three waterfalls 'every one as high over the other as a Church tower, which fell with that fury, that the rebound of waters made it seem, as if it had been all covered over with a great shower of rain: and in some places we took it at the first for a smoke that had risen over some great town.' But he did not find the great town.

When he returned home, after sacking Caracas and Santa Marta to finance the voyage, the Queen had not been impressed. His rocks had proved worthless. In desperation he had written his book. Its success, and its implied flattery of her as the sovereign most worthy to be allied to El Dorado, restored him to her court. But only temporarily. She died six years later, whereupon his enemies in court engineered his downfall. The new king, King James, who had a policy of appeasement towards Spain, imprisoned him in the Tower of London for illegally encroaching on Spanish possessions in the New World.

For twelve years Sir Walter Raleigh appealed to the king from the Tower to be allowed one last chance, one more voyage to the New World. Finally King James secured him permission from the Spanish crown to resume his search for Guiana.

In 1617 he once again saw the mouth of the Orinoco river. By then he was an old man, too old and sick to venture up it himself. Instead he sent his lieutenant, Keymis, and his own son. A few months later Keymis returned alone to report the utter failure of the expedition, and promptly committed suicide. Raleigh's son had been killed in a skirmish with some Indians.

The following year Raleigh sailed home defeated. The welcome that awaited him, schemed by his enemies, was his own execution.

For twenty-five years Raleigh had pinned all his hopes on El

Dorado, on a mythical place. It was not only the most valuable thing in the world, it would also solve all his problems in one fell swoop. It was a fantastic elsewhere that would give him everything he lacked in England.

I walked back down to the road and caught a bus to Villa de Leiva, a hundred or so miles northwards – the last stretch on the roof rack through a bare rocky land with the lights of villages glinting below. It was a small land stranded up on top of the huge mountains, a spread of farms and villages among the bareness. Villa de Leiva appeared like a carcass – a beautiful white town of bone, a Spanish skeleton of the sixteenth century bleached by the high sun and invaded by visitors, overrun with wealthy Bogotános and the tourist trade.

I watched builders in the hotel, a colonial house, sifting sand. One shovelled, the other shook the sieve. They strained it through the sieve into a clean, fine heap.

And then on to the next big city, Bucaramanga, a large modern city already lower and warmer than any settlement I had been to in months. From there, down off the mountains and that was it, the Andes were finished, were now only two small spines of hills, a mere thousand feet of green-blue hill shimmering in the distance, little crenellations along either horizon. I had dropped into the valley, really a plain, of the River Magdalena. Now it was a new land, the low Magdalena, the coastal lowlands.

FORTY-ONE

It was in the town of Aguachica, a few miles in from the river, that the heat of the lowlands first hit me. I had made my way to the front of the bus. As I stepped down through the doorway a wave of hot air leapt up at me. I took it to be some fan-driven current streaming from the engine. It was like those blasts of hot air that greet you in the open doorways of Oxford Street shops around Christmas time. I hopped down onto the dust at the edge of the road, walked along the side of the bus to where the man was pulling out my bag from a locker. No change. I was still in the hot air.

It was in something like panic that I made for the first café I saw. I downed two Cokes and a bottle of purified water. I wasn't thirsty, I was automatically obeying a kind of logic. If I soused my insides that ought to cool things down. The second reflex was to get away. This was an environment best escaped as quickly as possible. I bought a ticket for the first bus to La Gloria, a nearby town on the river, which didn't leave for a suffocating pair of hours.

Meanwhile I bought a meal at a stall in the tin-roofed market, and played host to a swarm of lively flies. I ate a lump of fish and great stringy chunks of yucca. The only condiment was a large bottle that stood in the middle of the table. It was stuffed full of chilli pepper seeds infusing in a mixture of lime juice and water.

An old man at the other end of the table had brought his own cutlery, a single machete which he used with impressive dexterity. He had a coarse, white stubble on his chin, damp with juice. He urged me to try the gunpowder solution.

'All the flies will go away,' he claimed. 'The mosquitoes won't enter your room.'

I assumed he was referring to whatever hotel room I found myself in that night, which he could safely predict would be infested, and so I decided to apply the magic. My senses were anyway so enervated by the climate that a little burning here or there would scarcely be noticed. In fact it turned out to be just enough to wake up at least my tongue.

From there on I lived by night, or rather by evening. I would spend the day in a trance, and become aware of the exterior world only from five until seven, like a goldfish opening its eyes for a brief look beyond its globe. The liquid through which I peered was of course sweat. By about eight o'clock weariness would overcome me again, and I would stumble around from then until whenever I found myself in bed.

I managed to set up this daily routine right away. That first day my period of wakefulness coincided with the bus journey to La Gloria. La Gloria was a sleepy town on the sleepy low reaches of the Magdalena. It is the kind of place you could get drunk in without even noticing, the heat and the humidity make you so slothfully lightheaded.

I arrived at night. I had just booked in to the one hotel in town, a place doing a roaring trade in stranded salesmen, and was planning a sleepy evening of *farniente* when two bangs stirred me from my settling torpor. Something was happening up the street. I stepped out in time to hear a peal of drums skip into a marching beat. It was a military band starting up. They made their slow way up the street: a xylophone band, the kind of Catholic troupe you see in Ireland, with girls and boys in tartan and two mace-wielders. After them came a procession of men and women in white holding paper lanterns. They were nurses and workers from the hospital. Their glowing globes of colour floated above their heads brushing the leaves of the trees that lined the road. In every doorway men and women sat in rocking chairs with children sprawled in their laps. The procession itself was surrounded by a shifting mass of people loosely keeping pace with it.

La Gloria was a town of only two thousand but it had its own hospital, which had been opened eighteen years ago to the day. The whole population was out in the street to celebrate this coming of age.

I then heard a different beat coming from down the street, something that cut right across the march. I moved through the crowd. Whoops and cheers and screams became audible as the sound of the other music grew. And there it was: a papayera band.

They too wore white, and they smiled wide and white in the darkness. Papayera is one of the most popular forms of music in northern Colombia. They take a few brass instruments – trumpet, valve trombone, French horn, euphonium, anything they can lay their hands on – and blast out a rhythm of arpeggios. With them, four percussionists were laying down the beat to which the brass added their notes. The leader was the man with the shaker. The brass playing seemed to be completely random, notes and little scales and arpeggios played *ad lib* without any consensus. The crowd loved it. They whooped at the beginning of every number and roared at the end, and danced through the duration.

It wasn't long before my screen of lethargy rattled down again. I found myself wandering down a side street to the river, which was only fifty yards away. The river was high and swollen and black with not a light glinting on it except now and then when a boat either swept by with the current or crept by against it.

The next day there was more: in the morning the papayera played outside the hospital. They were a new band, young and under-rehearsed, despite daily practice. They invited me to play with them. The event was very informal.

I strolled back to the hotel to fetch my trombone. By the time I had unlocked the door of my room I had forgotten what I had come for. I sat in the dimness, on the edge of the bed, wondering what I had to do. I looked over my belongings hoping my memory might be stirred. I even opened up my trombone case to check the accessories pouch, in which I sometimes kept small important things like keys and earplugs. Nothing. My mind was dead. I clearly needed a sleep.

My head touched the pillow. I stretched out, began to relax, and suddenly I remembered.

On the one hand, it was difficult music to play along with. There seemed to be no pattern at all to what the other two trombonists played. They filled their lungs and exhaled heavily through their instruments, in and out, in and out, jumping harmonics as they did so, bellowing like angry cows. Their rhythm seemed to be set by their breathing. There was nothing for me to follow. But on the other hand, it was easy to play along with, because anything went. I later discovered that not all papayera is so permissive.

In the evening there was a party at the school. The billed folkloric dances were rained off. Instead there was a disco and three barrels full of beer bottles. The man in charge of the beer was a clothes salesman with a stall on the main plaza. He had a pot belly and laughed loudly and often. His face shone with sweat.

'I'm Coca-Colo,' he laughed. 'Coca-Cola es la embra (the female), y Coca-Colo es el macho.'

He was a brilliant dancer and challenged me to a dancing duel, even though I knew none of the steps. We faced each other a few paces apart. He would shake himself and edge closer to me with bewilderingly fast and intricate steps and conclude each approach with some *pièce de résistance* – an ankle hooked behind a knee, or a scissor leap, or a shivering belly – then wait for my comic attempt to mirror what he had just performed. A small crowd gathered to watch. It was like the Generation Game. Everybody was enjoying it, so he kept on fuelling me with beer. In one brief rest he introduced himself.

He tried to pair me off with one of his plump girlfriends, but I had already met someone else, who led me away with a group of her friends to a small hidden discotheque by the river. It was called the Mini-Teca, and its dance-floor was veiled by a curtain behind which couples danced vallenato.

You hear vallenato everywhere in northern Colombia. It is a music with a long history, as I was later to learn. Its two essential instruments are the accordion and a very high male voice, a plangent crying tenor. From every bar and every shop vallenato blares out. It is music that the aficionados take very seriously. Many books have been written about it. Its most celebrated lover is Gabriel García Márquez.

The night ended with a session of guitar-playing on the plaza. I swapped songs with two vallenato singers for longer than I wanted and than my memory served, urged on by a teenage

schoolboy with a loud hoarse voice who was determined to see
that the fiesta went on till the not-so-small hours.

I had lost all sense of purpose and direction. But I was still
aware somewhere deep down that my travels were edging me
northwards, to the Caribbean. The prospect of an open sea shore
was a comfort, and in a way it relieved some of the pressure to
move: I was going, I was on my way, so it didn't matter if I
wasted a day or two, or even a week or two, in rest or nullity.
Three days slipped by unnoticed in La Gloria.

Then one morning I found myself stepping into a *chalupa*, a
small launch with four rows of benches and a canvas roof, bound
for El Banco, the next town downriver. Within I was experiencing
a mixture of excitement and regret – a mixture heavily diluted
with semi-consciousness. I kept finding it hard to leave places.
Each time I wondered whether if I had only stayed a bit longer
I would have made some significant friendship, or found love.
And I was nearing the end of my journey. I had only to reach
Cartagena, a city on the Caribbean coast, and it would be over.

Chalupas are the bus service of the river. Just as with the buses,
you buy a ticket at a counter near the departure point, where there
are always wandering fruit and cake vendors, and then wait for
the scramble aboard when the vehicle arrives.

The boat had an enormous V6 outboard motor. The hull sat
very low in the water as we gurgled out into the flotsam of the
main stream. The river was like a milkshake, swollen and puffed
up and thick and brown. It was exactly the colour of coffee with
milk. The helmsman, who sat at a small steering wheel on the
front bench, pushed the throttle forwards. The boat reared a
little, the engine roared smoothly, and in a minute the bow
dipped again and we were racing along with most of the hull
clear of the surface. It was a flat-bottomed boat, and it scudded
over the ripples with little jolts. Now and then the captain would
steer abruptly one way then the other to avoid a floating log, and
the boat would pitch alarmingly either way. For two hours we

weaved between islands of tall reeds and around huge meanders, stopping at villages that were sometimes no more that a single bamboo and mud house, until El Banco appeared.

El Banco is named after the bank of huge long steps that climb from the river to its church. You see them from a long way off, a white scar on the river bank. On the bottom steps fishermen fish for small fry. They stand thigh-deep in the brown body of the water. They fish with nets slung between two long canes tied together in a fork. They dip the poles under and sweep them round hard, overtaking the current. Then they lever the prongs clear of the water, with the crux resting on their thighs. As the net rises little silver flashes leap out into the brown. Some of them don't make it, and go rolling down into the pit of the net. The men swing the haul ashore and tip it onto the third or fourth step of the great bank, where the fish lie fluttering in the sun.

El Banco is a busy town full of busy shops and market stalls and jeeps from the surrounding cattle country. I ate a late breakfast of fried fish and banana and caught another *chalupa* to Mompós.

Mompós has almost no traffic. Two or three jeeps parked in the market square by the river wait for passengers to the outlying villages and ranches. Its population travels by bicycle and by boat. In the first centuries of colonialism it was a wealthy river port full of goldsmiths. It was the town where in 1811 Simon Bolívar first announced his intention to secure for the New World total, unconditional independence from Spain. He later declared that if he owed his life to Caracas (where he was born) he owed his glory to Mompós (also spelt Mompóx). Since then Mompós's glory has faded, leaving it a perfectly preserved eighteenth-century colonial town, as if stored in formaldehyde. The most conspicuous print of the march of time is the bicycle.

More remarkable than the architecture is the culture it houses, which is equally old and intact. Mompós is a miniature, complete society. It is a town not yet touched by the modern world. The culture is entirely distinctive. It is not Spanish, nor does it have any longer the pioneer spirit of the New World. It is what García Márquez writes about. Slow, methodical people, scrupulous in corruption and honour, precise in etiquette yet open-minded, a backwater yet cosmopolitan – the Turkish shopkeeper, the foreign schoolmaster, the black restaurateur, the Indian canoe fishermen living on the edge of town, the petty nobility of Spanish descent – a place of clockwork routine and great upheavals.

Mompós is a ready-made film set. Many television programmes and films have used it. Their crews provide the livelihood of the best hotel in town, a beautiful old mansion with three spacious cloistered courtyards, two of them filled by the spreading branches and enormously fat trunks, folded like curtains, of two ceiba trees, the Laurel de India, and the third by a swimming pool, immaculate as if taken from a Hockney print. The pool is an unblemished sky blue, and full to the very brim. When someone dives in water laps over the surrounding paving stones and runs back in down little channels. For a few weeks or months of the year a film crew will fill the hotel. The rest of the time it is open but deserted.

I spent two afternoons in the pool. I would let myself sink to the bottom and blow out my air, watching it turn into golden bubbles in the refracted light of the declining sun.

I made three friends in Mompos, three brothers aged seven, nine and eleven, who conducted me all round the town every day. All three of them had lank mops of black hair that drooped into their eyes. At nine in the morning they would take me to the park by the river where an old man with a walking stick fed bananas to six monkeys. The monkeys slept among the highest twigs of the trees. Each morning at the same hour the old man stood fifty feet beneath them and let out a high-pitched cry: 'Veng!'

He would look up to watch them drop to the low branches, and then peel their bananas, which he left out for them on a table.

The boys showed me all the sights: the cemetery, the *casa de cultura* where a young man gave music lessons to a budding papayera band, the religious museum with a small and lavishly spaced out collection of ecclesiastical robes and gold, and the various houses where women made their own ice cream.

I was feeling uneasy and indecisive. A friend of mine was spending a few days on the island of San Andrés, two hundred miles north of Colombia in the Caribbean. We had made a loose arrangement to meet there. If I didn't rush to catch a plane I would miss them. If I did, I would miss the carnival that I knew was about to begin in Cartagena. Cartagena was only a few hours away now. I was unable to decide what to do, which way to go, and allowed the days to drag by so the decision would make itself for me. I was reluctant to reach the end.

But, in the event, the final trip north was good: a jeep's roof rack from Mompós to a tributary of the Magdalena, a fine ride through cattle fields marred only by the running over of an elderly Alsatian bitch that trotted directly into our path as we hurtled along the ruts of the track. The driver stood no chance of stopping or swerving. Miraculously the dog was only spun over by the collision. I saw it pick itself up and limp the rest of the way across the road yelping quietly. Then, by another *chalupa*, I made it to the town of Magangué, just in time to catch the last bus to Cartagena.

We were held up for an hour by a carnival cavalcade in the next town: a throng of men and women on horseback, and then a long file of carnival trucks and masqueraders. Mixed in with the salsa and vallenato that was blaring from the mobile music systems I heard now and then the distinctive beat of Antillean soca. It was irrefutable proof: I was back in the Caribbean.

FORTY-TWO

A mosquito the size of a dragonfly is in the basin of my hotel bathroom. Another, regulation size, above the cistern. I don't kill either. They fly off and I regret sparing them. At this hour, seven o'clock, with the hotel television booming through the hall, they are nothing. But on the midnight visit when only their whine disturbs the susurrus of the sleeping city they can bring on an acute loneliness: as if it weren't already enough to be alone with my bowels aching in this ceramic cell reminiscent of an abattoir.

And the sweating. You sweat continually here. You dry off after a shower and by the time you reach your room you're wet again, all over, not moist but wet, clean and wet, as if from a quick dip. You awake with damp sheets clamped to your thighs. All day long in the streets or on the balcony or in your room, wet, wet body and wet clothes.

The heat has blurred my impression of Cartagena, as if my own sweat had made its ink run. The image I have is of a watery haze, only here and there a little patch of clarity. For example, it is a thoroughly sensual city. Not only prostitutes everywhere, but open discussion of the sensual merits of the various grades of skin colour the city has to offer, between upright citizens. Strangers bed together as easily, as lightly, as two men at the urinal in an English pub exchange jokes. You catch an eye, a remark is cast, you bite on the hook, you talk, you walk off together without the slightest doubt or questioning. And amid the compliments afterwards agree a rendezvous for tomorrow. If you miss it, if you meet again by chance a week later, it will be as if you were both keeping the agreed rendezvous. No recrimination, no regret.

It began, my entry into the life of Cartagena, at once, as soon as I got there. The city was in the last days of its carnival. Exhausted characters in costume, with mud or flour or coloured paint smeared on their cheeks and foreheads, wandered around the streets waiting for their costumes to ignite a little explosion of enthusiasm among any of the groups at café tables or making their way from one party to another. A laugh, a cry of delight, and the character would go into its routine, a dance, or a series of gestures, or some ingenious use of a prop. One man, bearded but wearing a wig, had a life-size, rubber doll attached to his front. The doll was a woman wearing a long dress that fell to the ground, while her legs were raised and clamped around his hips. His act was a simple one, but extremely popular. More than once I approached a roaring crowd on a street corner or plaza and caught a glimpse of him at the centre of it. These masqueraders were the leftover pieces from the broken-up processions of a day or two ago.

Each year Cartagena celebrates the Miss Colombia contest with its July carnival. Eighteen girls, each from a different department of Colombia, parade along the boulevard of Bocagrande, the modern part of town built along the beach, and then for three or four days perform various stunts for the press – modelling bikinis on the beach, attending official functions, going out to dinner with naval officers – until the final contest. All the newspapers print special sections devoted to the competition.

There was a weariness already about the merrymaking. After five days the hangovers and the drunkenness had become intermingled. The drink no longer made you drunk, it just sustained you. It was like food. Inhibitions had long since melted. There was nothing left for the drink to work on. But there were only two days left to conclude the week so there was a kind of last-lap energy, a thrill of impending accomplishment.

Out on the beach of La Boquilla, a huge, wide beach of orange sand reaching out east for miles and miles, so big that even when most of the city has spilled onto it to cool in the surf it can never seem crowded, the beach-bars are thumping all day and all night with drum groups. Some have an accordion and a singer too, some only a clarinet, some only a singer. They play folk music of the north coast, vallenato and gaita and rumba, party music.

I take a bus out on my first morning. The road is the beach itself. I try a few different bars, a few different beats. Already, after only one night in the city, my sense of purpose, usually manifest as a continual low rumble of anxiety, as of a distant but approaching storm, has dwindled, dissolved by the customary solvent certainly, but also by the carnival and the kind of contact between people that it generates. As well as by the heat. The world, life, has been veiled by a heat-haze.

Somewhere along the beach I mentioned my interest in music to someone. Now, after a tour of several of the bars, which are nothing more than sun shelters built of thatch with a counter at one end, my three self-appointed escorts have brought me to a man of English descent. He is called Numa Bateman. He has a grey beard and wrinkles round his eyes. His cheeks are evenly and lightly tanned. He is in his fifties, and he plays accordion in a vallenato band. His great grandfather, Mr Bateman, came over as a railway engineer and married an Italian. Now there are Batemans scattered all over northern Colombia, he assures me.

He is very friendly, and concerned about my understanding of north coast music. He carries a small table in from the beach, and then two tree stumps, and he sits me down to give me a face-to-face lowdown on the history of vallenato.

I am already well into one of those chains of events that pick you up and carry you for a day or a week and then drop you, dazed and confused and wondering where you have been.

Vallenato comes from the town of Valledupar, in the valley where the Upar Indians used to live. The Indians used singers to carry news up and down the valley. The singers were the newspapers. They would sing with two or three percussionists. Then the Europeans arrived and brought with them their musical instruments. It was Nikolaus Federmann, according to Numa Bateman, who brought the accordion, although the discrepancy of three centuries between their respective origins cast some doubt over this: he was one of the earliest explorers, who came with half an eye on El Dorado and found the Chibcha instead; the accordion developed in the nineteenth century. Sooner or later, anyway, the Indian singers got hold of the instrument and added its technicolour to their print. Now vallenato was the biggest music scene of tropical Colombia. Vallenato bands were everywhere on the north coast. They were better paid even than salsa bands.

Towards the end of Numa's spiel the agent of a big Cartagena band, Anne Zwing, arrives. Anne Zwing play music from all over the Caribbean. They are doing well even internationally now. The agent joins in the conversation. Ten minutes later I am in a taxi with him heading for the band's lead singer, Viviano Torres, and heading also into a whole new cultural territory.

Then I am in a house deep within Cartagena's worst neighbourhood listening to Viviano Torres. He is telling me the story of his life and success, showing me press cuttings and photographs and album sleeves. He has short locks onto which he has threaded beads of many colours. They swing and clack against each other as he turns his head. His eyes are brown and wide open, he has a warm, calm face. He starts telling me about his home town, Palenque, a name that lies at the heart of black culture on the north coast. He talks about the founding of Palenque, Palenque culture and traditions, the Bantu language of Palenque, illustrious sons of Palenque (three world-title boxers), music and dance of Palenque. Palenque was founded as a maroon camp in the seventeenth century amid swamps an hour by car from Cartagena. The colonial authorities never discovered the tortuous path to the camp. The settlement remained a centre of fervent Africanism. Even today some of its inhabitants still speak Bantu. Viviano had taken the traditional music of Palenque, the terapia dance, and added it to his repertoire, dressing it up for a wider audience.

It is a relaxed household. Several children and three women are sitting with us. One girl of five clambered into my lap as soon as I sat down, where she has been squirming and giggling ever since, looking up at me with her eyes creased up by laughter.

Then we drive slowly along a track between the houses. It climbs up and down little slopes. People have set rocking chairs out in the road. There are groups of people outside every house. Several times we have to stop where ribbons have been hung across the road. Children come to the car window with bowls of water in hand. Either you pay them to drop the ribbon and let you by or they throw the water at you. A carnival trick.

The agent, Tano, is telling me all about the festival of Caribbean music hosted annually by Cartagena, and about his international plans for Anne Zwing, and his other life as a professional photographer. I notice he has a long, straight scar down his left cheek. Night is falling. We are back in the centre of the city, on the edge of the old town. We ditch the taxi, walk through a tunnel in the old wall, a wall thirty-feet thick right around the town, and then along several narrow streets beneath ornate wooden balconies. Then we are in a small bar covered with posters and graffiti and run by a salsa aficionado, a fat asthmatic man who plays Cuban records, the real McCoy of Latin music.

Then another taxi out to the Barrio Chino, another rough

neighbourhood. Tano makes the driver take us over a whole chain of pot-holes rather than dump us with a hundred-yard walk to where we are going, which is a tent, the Caseta del Club Bonny. A tent here is what it is in Trinidad: a place where bands play around carnival time, sometimes a real tent, sometimes not. This one was an outdoor bar come social club.

The place is empty. It's early. We start in on more beers. The bands arrive, Anne Zwing and the Vallenato Executives. There is a great crowd out in the street planning on a free concert. Now and then a couple or a party part with the entrance fee and slip through the iron gate. The place is about half full when two MCs start delivering their repetitive raps on a microphone with too much reverb. They alternate with the disco for at least an hour. Finally Anne Zwing are playing, heralded by two go-go girls in tasselled bikinis and high heels who come skipping onto the dance floor in front of the stage and start shaking themselves with bewitching flexibility.

The band's repertoire, composed by Viviano, is an ingenious synthesis of all Caribbean styles. In a single set they trot all round the sea, from Cuban salsa to Haitian compas, Dominican merengue, Antillean zouk and soca, Jamaican reggae, and terapia from Palenque. The dancing girls vary their steps accordingly, but the couples on the dance floor achieve an astonishing disregard for the different styles. At the end of every number they clear the floor, sit at their tables for five seconds, and return for the next. At first they dance apart with movements appropriate to the rhythm, but soon come together, arms tight around one another, and get into the usual vallenato dance step, close, tight, careful dancing with very small movements. If you couldn't see their feet moving nimbly in step you would take it for slow dancing in a discotheque.

Between the sets Viviano sits me at a table occupied exclusively by his many girlfriends. He ceremoniously introduces me to each one, then ministers the shots of *aguardiente*. Everyone at the table wrinkles their nose at the vallenato band: vallenato is boring. No matter how they dance, they like to hear his pan-Caribbean mix.

I wake up at noon trapped in a sweaty marsh. A hot wind is blowing. I struggle to free myself, but only get more securely ensnared. The situation needs to be assessed, but I can't face opening my eyes. Last night's, or this morning's, drink has turned sour, has pickled my belly into a hard onion of dread. I have woken up into a sudden attack of anxiety. What did I do last night? What have I got to do today? Where should I be? How can I get out of here? And then the realization: I am only in bed, beneath the ceiling fan of my windowless, hired cell. But even bed offers no sanctuary. Nowhere am I safe from this anxiety, only in sleep, which is no sweet gift, merely a brief annihilation.

Another day of music and drink and impassioned lecturing awaits me. I am the stump onto which Cartagena's musicians throw their hoops, the ground they trample with their hobby horses. I am nothing, at best their vessel, but really a sieve. No doubt they are a good cause, but I am no champion. I can bear no more. I can bear nothing at all.

Breakfast of fish, rice and beer. Lunch of vallenato on the beach, courtesy of Mr Bateman. It is afternoon. It is evening. It is night again. I am in the little plaza de la Trinidad in the old town. Beneath the lofty whitewash of the old church, adorned with giant carnival masks of gold and scarlet and blue, a magnificent display of folk dances from all along the north coast is playing to a small throng and two television cameras. Every kind of music can be heard, all of it percussive, every kind of dance, the dancers young and old, all gifted with an innate agility, an inner receptiveness to rhythm. They become the visual manifestation of the beat. Every snap of the congas, every shout of the bongos, finds an immediate echo in an elbow or knee or belly. Some tell stories, some overdo the theatrics, and some are a non-stop undulation of the human form.

Then it's over, the fiesta fulfilled.

But not for me. My mildly delirious daze endures for the rest of the week. It must be the heat and the alcohol, I conclude, that are still incapacitating some vital zone of my brain. Time to assess, to evaluate, to recover my consciousness. But I can't. I can't.

FORTY-THREE

Something woke me up. There was some kind of commotion in the room. Then the light was on and somebody was calling to me. I opened my eyes and saw a soldier standing by the door. He was wearing a green uniform and a cartridge belt slung over the shoulder, and pointing a machine-gun at me.

'Out,' he said, firmly but not aggressively.

So it was happening at last. The nameless, unaccountable dread that had been churning my insides had finally found its incarnation.

He repeated the command and stepped outside the door in consideration for my modesty, and perhaps also to allow me a moment of privacy in which to savour my despair.

I looked at the clock. Five in the morning. I got out of bed and dressed. I didn't know what else to do. It evidently wasn't a practical joke. There was no question about that at all. He was a real soldier with a real machine-gun.

He tapped on the door and looked in again. 'Leave everything,' he said. His hair was black but cut so short his pale scalp was showing through. He had a swarthy face. 'Just bring your passport.'

Why me? I thought and thought and the first answer that came to me was that I had originally declared my purpose in the country to be pleasure, when in fact I had come to grind my nerves on an attempt at exploring the music scene. No doubt you had to have special permission for that.

The fear came on in waves. I didn't even think about trying to control it. I walked out, locked my door and slipped the key into my money belt, with the obsessive concern for detail of a man going to his execution, and walked downstairs, where a surprise awaited me – not only eight more soldiers, but also, gathered in the lobby, all the other hotel guests. They were all standing in silence.

The silence was finally broken from upstairs. A man was talking loudly in bad Spanish. He kept repeating, 'Ma por qué? Ma por qué?' From which I deduced that he was Italian. He appeared on the stairs. He was a burly man with short, cropped hair and he scowled at everyone, and fell silent.

Then the soldiers opened the door, herded us out into the empty street and along it to the first corner, where they turned us to the left and then hemmed us all against a wall.

For a moment I thought: this is really it. This is a police state and if they want to shoot us all like this no power in the world can stop them. They are actually allowed to, by their own law. We can all be drug dealers.

But instead the soldiers just stood around with their hands on their guns.

We were on Calle Media Luna, Half Moon Street. It was a well-known street, busy, with a lot of shops and small hotels and prostitutes, ever since the seventeenth century, and now it was deserted. All the steel shutters were down. It could happen here, it could happen anywhere.

There were several other foreigners amongst us. We started talking quietly. The wife of the hotel-keeper, a small, friendly woman with big black eyes, looked up at me and told me it was nothing, nothing at all. They would check our ID and send us away. We should be out by the afternoon. But her eyes were looking deeply, nervously into mine.

Just then another posse of civilians came round the corner under guard. Their soldiers penned them up against the same wall, further down the street: the catch of another hotel. Two, three, four more groups arrived, until there were a good two hundred people clustered along Calle Media Luna, and at least fifty soldiers watching over us.

People spoke little. The soldiers didn't explain and no one asked. It might be better for us not to know.

With dawn it got light faintly, softly at first, and then richly. All the houses glowed in their pastel washes. Bells pealed somewhere in the distance. A car came down the road. It slowed right down. The soldiers waved it by.

Then the police trucks arrived. They were what we had been waiting for, it appeared. The soldiers crammed us into the trucks' corrugated metal cages and drove us out of town. No one asked where we were going. We passed an army barracks, its surrounding wall adorned with brief flights of baroque prose about Duty and Valour and Right. The sun broke free of a low hill, as we swung into a military compound with a big, plain building like an office block. Two soldiers opened a gate for us and closed it after the jeep that followed the last truck.

We were unloaded into a pen with a high wire fence, all of us, and left there. Soldiers stood by outside.

The sun got up. It started to get hot, and people began to talk. The wisdom was unanimous: they would check our ID and let us go. It was just some kind of check. Maybe they were looking for someone. The only unknown, apparently, was how long it would take. Some said we would be out by noon, others expected to spend a few nights here. There were cells in the big building: they wouldn't have brought us here if they weren't planning to keep us overnight. But still the pervading mood was numbness. Mostly people were silent.

There was a handful of foreigners. A New Zealander with a long pigtail and a glistening alcoholic's face got into a hearty conversation with a Scottish couple about Glasgow and a fight he had had in a pub there. But the heartiness was all on his side. He had been travelling three years now, he said. Right fuckers, these, he said of the soldiers every few minutes. Then he mellowed, Nah, they're not so bad. They're just kids. They mean well.

There was no room to sit. Sometimes fear gave way to outrage, a voice screaming in my head: They can't make me stand out here in the sun for no reason at all. And I didn't have my hat. Two hours went by.

Then they summoned all the foreigners and led us to a bleak

office. We stood in a line waiting to be called up by a police colonel with a thick moustache who sat at a desk far down the other end of the room.

By now I was sure my illegal entry into Colombia had somehow been discovered and had aroused suspicion. I was going over and over in my mind what I should tell him, but I couldn't decide on my safest story. The more I tried to convince myself of my own innocence the more I lost sight of any legitimate reason I could give for being in the country at all. Huge patches of sweat broke out on my shirt at the armpits and back. I was clearly guilty of something.

When he called me forward he spent a long time reading my passport and studying my face and apparel. He copied every detail down onto a form, and consulted several microfiches at his machine on the desk. With no hint of what he had found, he sent me outside, where I found myself once again cooped up in a pen with the other foreigners.

We stood under the late-morning sun for an hour. Five soldiers came and herded us into a lorry again. There was not a word about where they were taking us now, but I noticed that we seemed to be going back towards town. Sure enough, we drove into the centre, all the way back to Calle Media Luna. I was wondering if we were being delivered to the next police station when they stopped the truck and two soldiers opened up the tailgate. They waved us all out with their guns.

We spilled onto the street and lingered there. One of the soldiers shouted, 'Away! Away!' and shooed us off like cattle. It was over. But no one believed it at first. We all stood looking at the soldiers as they climbed aboard. None of us walked off, afraid of making a wrong move.

Then our group began to disperse. The Scottish couple immediately walked into a shop, the New Zealander ran down the street and the Italian glared back at the truck. I just stood there perplexed.

I heard the driver starting up the engine again. He was a fat man with long sideburns. Suddenly I felt the urge to go over to him.

'Why?' I called up to his window. But as I said the word, even through my confusion and anger, I realized that I didn't know if I was referring to our arrest or our release.

At first he waved me away, but I didn't move. After a moment he turned and grinned down at me knowingly from the cab. I thought he wasn't going to reply, but then, slipping the truck into gear, he shouted back to all of us, 'The fiesta. We have to have a little fiesta too.'

A sudden wave of elation lifted me up as I realized I had concluded my journey. I had hardly noticed until now. It was over, I had done it.

I walked across the plaza with its long avenue of busts of eminent Cartagenans. I strolled the gauntlet of the city's illustrious sons. Around the hot-dog stands at the far side old drunken men and young prostitutes argued with one another. I walked straight past them, under the arch in the great thick wall and into the old town. I was free now. Free.

I went straight to the Palace of the Inquisition, a plain eighteenth-century building with white courtyards full of bottle-green trees. Upstairs there was a map room. It was a large room with low recessed windows and a floor of smooth, pale, old wood that sagged under every step. The sunlight came in in wide bands, but softly, because the windows were low. If you stooped you could see the view over the thick defensive wall and into the Bay of Cartagena.

The maps, each in a black frame, covered the walls. Many were of Cartagena and its bay. But most were of South America. They dated from the sixteenth century to the nineteenth. From 1607 until 1811 El Dorado was as regular a feature as Cartagena itself. There in the middle of the Venezuelan hinterland, on every map, the little dot, the name, either Manoa or El Dorado, and beside it the wriggling outline of Lake Parima, erroneously labelled 'The Prime Lake' on an English map. It was an illusion, consistently sustained on the maps, in the fervent hope that wishful cartography would triumph over official realism. And then, from the early nineteenth century onwards, it had vanished, like perishable ink. Men had had enough of it and had buried it beneath the terrain of modern geography. And the cartographers were free and anyone who had to look at their maps was free forever onwards of that myth. El Dorado was no longer there. The burden was gone. There was no longer an unattainable waiting to be attained, no more golden grass.

I went straight to the airline office to buy a ticket out.

A NOTE ON CARIBBEAN MUSIC

Music is perhaps the finest fruit produced by the cross-pollination of cultures in the Caribbean. The region, often referred to as a 'basin' by geographers, is indeed a bowl in which peoples from four continents, Amerindians, Europeans, Africans and Asians, have been stirring themselves, mixing and blending together in every conceivable way, over half a millennium. Out of the multifold mixing of cultures emerged the region's different musical styles. Today they stand as monuments to its ethnic history.

The story of music in the Caribbean is the story, broadly, of how West African religious drumming and chanting blended with European dances and songs to emerge as the popular music of today. In North America the African rhythmic heritage acted on four-square northern beats to produce the Blues, which eventually spawned rock and roll, but further south there were the syncopations of Spanish folk music to blend with, and the many intricate rhythms of Latin music came into being. It is also the story of how the indigenous American Indian music either disappeared along with the Indians themselves or else survived to adopt features of the newcomers' music – the accordion, for example, or waltz time, or drums and shakers.

Popular Latin music, or salsa as it is sometimes wrongly called – salsa is a particular style of Latin music that emerged in New York in the sixties – was first heard in Cuba. The son, a rustic dance from the eastern mountains of Cuba, became popular in the dance halls of Havana during the twenties. The first son bands provided the basic structure of the Latin band, with its horns, guitars, bass, percussion and singers, and sometimes violins, as well as the basic beat, the 'clave', a particular two-bar rhythm played on the wood blocks. As the sound grew popular with audiences of Americans holidaying in Havana, then the nightlife capital of the world, they began putting out new dressings-up of other old rural dances, and invented new ones. Every so often, through the war years and after, a Latin craze would sweep up from Havana across the United States – mambo, cha cha cha, conga line, rumba.

After Castro came to power many Cuban musicians left for Miami and New York and formed new bands. They played a mix of several Latin styles, with son as the foundation, and brought modern salsa into being. The name itself came from the cry 'Salsa', which means sauce, particularly the hot sauce eaten throughout the Caribbean, that Latin DJs would use to rouse the crowds in dance halls before their favourite tracks.

Salsa enjoyed a boom in popularity in the seventies, owing largely to the hard work of the Fania record label. The company was run by a Latin lawyer and by Tito Puente, one of the giants of the New York scene who plays timbales in his own orchestra and is a high-priest in the Santeria cult, the Latin equivalent of voodoo. Although salsa hasn't quite achieved the mainstream popularity for which it once seemed destined, it is still going strong with such new voices as Ruben Blades, the Harvard-educated Panamanian lawyer who has brought contemporary urban issues into the music.

Meanwhile Cuban musicians who stayed in Havana, such as Elio Reve, with his hugely successful Orquesta Reve (one of the few bands to have a large horn section consisting exclusively of trombones, and a four-piece violin section) and Irakere, a Latin jazz band who play for a month at Ronnie Scott's each summer, have been faring well under Castro. He decided to foster his national folk music in the same way that the Eastern European regimes did, and many of the bands have revitalized older rural styles and created new dance rhythms for Latin lovers weary of New York salsa. Several Cuban bands regularly tour around the world, and Cuba still claims pride of place in Latin music.

The rise of merengue, from the nearby Dominican Republic, is a similar story: a rustic dance conveyed from the provinces to the capital, Santo Domingo, where it became fashionable in the twenties. Since then, like son and salsa, it has turned electric, and sometimes keyboards even replace its distinctive centre-piece, the accordion.

There are many different Latin rhythms, and a typical band will be able to play most of them. Each has its own beat and steps, which a good dancer will know. Charanga, guaguanco, pachanga, cumbia, changüi, montuno – they were all once rural dances that developed through the mixing of Spanish, African and Amerindian rhythms in different parts of the Caribbean. Cumbia, for example, found all over Central America and Colombia, was originally a simple Indian dance. But by the twentieth century the female dancers were wearing long, white ball gowns, a garb they borrowed from the Spanish aristocracy, and the musicians meanwhile had added to their original flutes and scraper drums, trombones and guitars, instruments also taken from the immigrants. But the basic rhythm never changed, only its dressing.

On the French islands, Guadeloupe, Dominica, Martinique and Haiti, the old folk styles like beguine and jing ping that emerged in the late nineteenth and early twentieth centuries and still survive here and there are the clearest reflection of the Caribbean's ethnic genealogy. They consist of ballroom dances like the polka, mazurka and waltz played over African drums and shakers that transform the dull European beats into brilliant jewels of rhythm. But since the seventies the French Caribbean has been known for its popular styles, like cadence, or cadass, compas and above all zouk, which means 'party' in Patois. Zouk is a slick high-tempo music for energetic, erotic dancing. It has become tremendously popular in Paris, where big zouk bands like Kassav, with their thirty or more performers on stage, attract enormous crowds.

In the English-speaking Caribbean the best-known styles are reggae and calypso. Reggae emerged, through its early incarnation as ska in the sixties, from mento, the traditional Jamaican folk song. The lilting beat, the idiomatic language and scansion, come from mento, although the inspiration is supplied mainly by Jah, by the cult of rastafari, which itself owes a great deal to India and the worship of the goddess Kali – the vegetarianism, the uncut locks, the marijuana.

Calypso has a long history. It has been going strong as a musical form for close on a hundred years. It originated in Trinidad, which is still its capital, but is popular up and down the Antilles. The first calypsos probably grew out of the chants of carnival stick-fighters, who take one another on in ritualistic duels with wooden truncheons, but they also owed much to the Trinidad folk songs that preceded them. By the turn of the century the form was established, and did service at first as a local news relay. Calypsonians sang about current events – whether a battle in the Boer War or a domestic quarrel resolved with a blow to a fleeing husband's head from a frying-pan – and were the chief social commentators of the day, as indeed they still are. The two most popular modes remain social commentary and lewd double entendre ('Mister, don't touch me tomatoes.')

Calypso's role in community affairs certainly grew out of the West African tradition of story-telling and of passing on news in oral anecdotes. It owes its language, of course, to Europe, and one of the skills of a fine calypsonian is to scan the longest polysyllabics he can find over the bouncing beat. The beat itself likewise emerged from West African percussion rhythms, which are still alive in Trinidad to this day. Shango, similar to Haitian voodoo, is a possession cult in which the gods are invoked with various drum beats, some of which find their way into calypso. The gods, the drums, the trances, all come directly from the Gold and Ivory Coasts.

It was from ritualistic drumming that the steel band, too, was born on Trinidad. The drums themselves developed between the wars from the old bamboo tubes that carnival bands used to beat, and were going strong by the end of the Second World War when the American airmen based on Trinidad had stocked the island with tens of thousands of oil drums. The steel band is arguably the most elaborate flowering of African drumming there has ever been. Today the best bands play arrangements of well-known classics, with complicated harmonies and chromatics, but always over a rolling African beat.

Voodoo, Santeria and Shango remain vibrant and highly influential forces on Caribbean popular music. Many percussionists in bands moonlight as drummers at the ceremonies. When a performer plays a solo break on stage often he skips into one of the divine invocations. Behind all the popular beats lurk the shadows of the gods.

GLOSSARY OF CARIBBEAN MUSICAL TERMS

Aguardiente Popular Colombian anis drink served in salsa bars.

Beater Player of any percussion instrument, but especially a steel drum, as in 'pan beater'.

Beguine Dance rhythm popular in the French Caribbean in the twenties.

Bongos Small double drums played with bare hands.

Boom boom Bamboo tube blown to produce a bass sound in Dominican jing ping music.

Cadass (cadence) Dance rhythm from the French Antilles that developed in the seventies as a precursor of modern zouk.

Calypso Song and dance form from Trinidad now found all over the Caribbean. The songs, sung in English, are typically either light-hearted and lewd, or pieces of social commentary.

Celia Cruz Perhaps the greatest female Latin (salsa) singer ever. She started in Cuba in the thirties and is still going strong.

Cha cha cha Latin dance rhythm that became popular all over the world in the forties.

Changüi A rustic dance form from eastern Cuba recently made popular by the Havana bandleader Elio Reve.

Charanga A Latin dance style featuring flutes and violins.

Clave Wood blocks played by a percussionist; also the basic two-bar beat that underpins the rhythm of son and of salsa.

Compas A popular modern Haitian dance beat.

Congas Two large upright drums played with bare hands.

Cumbia A popular Latin dance rhythm with a strong off-beat that originated from an Indian dance of the Colombian Andes.

Currulao A Colombian dance rhythm from the Pacific coast.

Engine Room The rhythm section of a steel band, usually on a raised platform. It consists of various percussionists, most numerous and important of whom are the 'ironmen', who beat old brake drums.

Fete Any big party in Trinidad with either live music or a DJ.

Gaita Northern Colombian dance music, usually played by percussion and clarinet.

Guaguanco A Latin dance rhythm renowned for being 'sabroso' (tasty).

Iron A percussion instrument found on Trinidad: an old brake drum beaten with two short metal sticks.

Jing Ping An old folk music and dance form on Dominica. The accordion is its centre-piece and plays ballroom dance tunes over an African rhythm section.

Jump-up A Trinidadian dance party.

Kassav The best-known zouk band in the world, and the largest. They have been known to have as many as forty performers on stage at their concerts.

MC The Master of Ceremonies who introduces the acts, particularly important in a calypso tent, where he is expected to tell jokes and work up the crowd into frenzied anticipation of the next singer.

Mambo A Latin dance rhythm popular in the forties.

Marimba A giant bamboo xylophone found in lowland tropical areas of Latin American, played by one or two people.

Matancera The Sonora Matancera, the Latin band who backed Celia Cruz for many years.

Mento Jamaican folk song, more or less equivalent to Trinidad's calypso.

Montuno A rural Cuban dance rhythm; also a bridge passage in a salsa song.

Pachanga A Latin dance beat with a strong two-two, march-like feel.

Pan A steel drum. A pan man is a steel-drum beater.

Panorama The big steel band festival and competition held bi-annually in Trinidad.

Papayera Brass bands from the north of Colombia. They feature large ensembles of eccentric brass instruments playing over drums and shakers.

Pasillo A Colombian dance rhythm.

Porro A Colombian dance rhythm particularly favoured by Papayera bands.

Ragamuffin A modern form of reggae in which the singer 'toasts', or raps, over a regular beat.

Reggae A modern popular dance and song form from Jamaica. The name may come from the term 'ragga boy', meaning a bad boy, or outlaw, which in turn may come from the word 'ragamuffin'.

Road March A prize awarded to the song played most on the streets during the two days of Trinidad carnival.

Rumba A Latin dance rhythm popular in the forties. Also a dance with religious origins still practised in Cuba, and a general term for a party, as in, 'Vamos a la rumba' (Let's go to the party).

Rum Shop A bar anywhere in the islands, typically small and ramshackle.

Salsa A Latin music and dance form that developed in New York in the late sixties based on the old Cuban son form. The name itself was first used by DJs to rouse their audiences and refers to the very hot sauce found all over the Caribbean.

Sanjuanito An Andean dance rhythm dedicated originally to San Juan.

Santeria A drumming cult similar to voodoo of West African origin found all over the Spanish Caribbean, and in New York and Miami.

Shango Trinidad's equivalent to voodoo.

Soca 'Soul-calypso', the modern form of high-tempo calypso popular at fetes and dances and during carnival on the islands.

Son A rustic dance form from the eastern mountains of Cuba that became popular in Havana dance halls in the twenties and formed the basis of later Latin music.

Steel band A band of steel drums, usually ranged around an engine room and fitted onto rolling frames that can be pushed along the streets while the beaters play. Now there are large 'steel orchestras' with as many as 150 beaters that can play complicated harmonies and chromatics and even perform classical works.

Steel drum A metal drum made out of an oil drum and capable of producing musical notes. It is played with two small sticks. Steel drums were developed in Trinidad during the last war and it is there that they are most cherished. There are many sizes of drum, all appropriately named for the pitch at which they play: bass, cello, tenor and guitar pans are the most common.

T and T The nation of Trinidad and Tobago.

Tent A calypso music hall.

Terapia A folk dance with strong Bantu origins performed by Afro-American communities on the Caribbean coast of Colombia.

Timbales A pair of side-drums played loudly with thick sticks, indispensable to any salsa band.

Vallenato A popular song and dance form of northern Colombia, featuring high tenor singing and virtuoso accordion-playing. It originated in the town of Valledupar from the singing of the Upar Indians, who used to relay their news in song to the rhythm of a wood scraper.

Voodoo The famous Haitian drumming cult involving possession by an eclectic host of gods.

Wine The erotic dance of calypso and soca, in which partners swing and thrust their hips to the beat.

Zouk A popular modern dance beat of the French Antilles, named after the Patois word for a party.